East Coast Pilot

Great Yarmouth to Ramsgate

Colin Jarman, Garth Cooper and
Dick Holness

Imray Laurie Norie & Wilson

Published by
Imray Laurie Norie & Wilson Ltd
Wych House St Ives
Cambridgeshire PE27 5BT England
☏ +44 (0)1480 462114 *Fax* +44 (0)1480 496109
Email ilnw@imray.com.
www.imray.com
2015

1st edition 2005
2nd edition 2008
3rd edition 2011
4th edition 2015

ISBN 978 184623 646 4

British Library Cataloguing in Publication Data.
A catalogue record for this book is available from the British
Library.

PLANS

The plans in this guide are not to be used for navigation. They
are designed to support the text and should at all times be used
with up to date navigational charts.

The plans and tidal information have been reproduced with the
permission of the Hydrographic Office of the United Kingdom
(Licence No. HO151/951101/01) and the Controller of Her
Britannic Majesty's Stationery Office.

CAUTION

Whilst every care has been taken to ensure accuracy, neither
the Publishers nor the Authors will hold themselves responsible
for errors, omissions or alterations in this publication. They
will at all times be grateful to receive information which tends
to the improvement of the work.

CORRECTIONAL SUPPLEMENTS

This pilot book will be amended as and when necessary by
publishing corrections and updates on
www.eastcoastpilot.com. These may be read and downloaded
free of charge. Printed copies are also available on request from
the publishers at the above address.

Printed in Malta by Gutenberg

East Coast Pilot

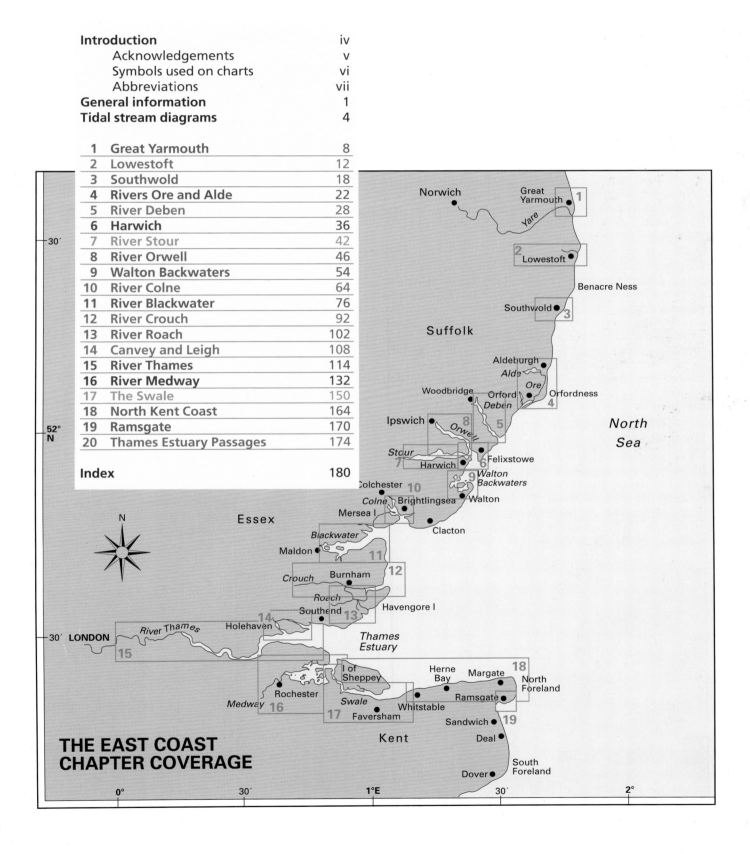

**THE EAST COAST
CHAPTER COVERAGE**

Introduction

FULLY REVISED FOURTH EDITION

Welcome to the fourth edition of *East Coast Pilot*. Once again, the East Coast has been a busy place over the last few years and the huge number of updates and changes has made this new edition essential.

Large numbers of *ECP* readers are regularly visiting our dedicated website at www.eastcoastpilot.com to download updates. By incorporating these into your copy of the book, you will keep it current and ensure that you get full benefit from it as you pilot your boat in and around the Thames Estuary. However, when we fully research the area afresh, as we did for this new edition, we always find even more changes and these are incorporated now, but may not have been published on the website.

Owners of earlier editions of *ECP* will find some significant changes in this new one. The most obvious is that we have, to satisfy popular demand, stretched the northern limit to include Great Yarmouth. We have also expanded the tidal stream diagrams to give more information on each one and have used larger photographs with more overlaid tracks and annotations to make it easier for the pilot approaching a strange port or harbour. You will also find some 'QR codes' in information boxes, which give quick links to the related website when scanned by your smartphone or tablet, enabling fast access to extra information if needed.

Shoal Draught

We occasionally use the description 'shoal draught' and it's as well to understand that we use this term to mean a draught (depth from waterline to foot of keel) of between 3ft 6in and 4ft or 1–1·2m. This is important, because boat sizes (and draughts) are commonly increasing, but many creeks and anchorages are becoming shallower. Beware!

Accuracy and updates

The East Coast and Thames Estuary is an area of huge and frequent change. We have done our best to ensure accuracy at the time of writing, but even by the time of publication there will have been changes, particularly with regard to the entrance channels in river mouths like the Ore and Deben. We must, therefore, caution you to watch for changes and alterations, particularly those shown on www.eastcoastpilot.com, and to exercise seamanlike common sense, always referring to the most up-to-date charts and published corrections.

The advice and guidance in *ECP* is given in good faith and is as accurate as we can make it, but neither the authors nor the publisher can accept responsibility for any errors or omissions in the published material.

Electronic chart plotter displays

As the use of chart plotters becomes widespread, so too does the temptation to rely upon them not only for position fixing but also for pilotage.

The authors all base their navigation on paper charts, but are finding that the use of a modern plotter positioned in clear view of the helmsman can be a valuable aid to pilotage. However, if you are running paper charts in parallel with either a chart plotter or the Imray Marine Charts software, it is quite possible for the two systems to be at odds if you have not been perfect in keeping track of all updates and Notices to Mariners (NtMs).

It is appealing to think that one can perhaps find the way up an unmarked creek by following the dotted line on the plotter display that indicates where the deepest water was when the survey was last done, but remember that gutways move and the majority of such creeks will have been surveyed in detail only many years ago.

Sailing upriver towards the spectacular Orwell Bridge

Before plotters, we might have approached such a shallow creek challenge by gently weaving from side to side and watching the echo sounder – and that is still a sensible method.

The plotter can be a valuable aid, but it is just that – an aid.

Honorary Port Pilots

With the second edition of *ECP* we introduced Honorary Port Pilots (HPPs) who helped us gather updates and offered local, on-the-spot advice to readers who contacted them. Some of these have now stepped down, having perhaps moved away or even given up boating, and we took this opportunity to review the concept. In some places we know that the harbour staff or their equivalent are helpful and friendly, making HPPs less needed than they once were, so we now have a shorter list – John Powell (Lowestoft), Phillip Attwood (Orford and Ore/Alde entrance), John White (Deben), Alec Moss (Walton Backwaters), Nigel Harmer (Blackwater), Jim Dew (Crouch and Roach), Rob Scriven (Canvey), and Simon Smedley (Conyer and Swale).

The contact details of these HPPs are listed in the relevant information boxes at the beginning of each chapter and are also listed on the *East Coast Pilot* website.

QR codes

In this fourth edition we are introducing QR codes – the black and white chequerboard patterns printed in some of the information boxes. If you use a smartphone or a tablet (with the appropriate free app on it), you can scan these QR codes and link directly to the website wherever you have internet access. It's easier and quicker than trying to type in the web addresses, particularly when butting into a Wallet chop!

ACKNOWLEDGEMENTS

Within Imray Laurie Norie & Wilson, we are indebted to Willie Wilson for his continued enthusiastic support for the *ECP* project. We are also grateful for the help

Burnham at dawn

Seal on the banks of the Butley River

provided by the editorial and production team at Imray, without whose patience the development of this fourth edition of *East Coast Pilot* would have been much more painful.

We would like to say a special thank you to Jim Dew, Roger Gaspar, Alec Moss, Adrian Munnings, John Ramuz, Rob Scriven, Roger Smith, Tim Thomas and Fred Trice, all of whom joined us in the research process.

We would also like to thank Patrick Keating and Gareth Stephens for providing particularly detailed help and advice, and to record our thanks and acknowledgement for photographs we have used from Duncan Abel, John Buckley (Harbour Marine Services), Fox's Marina, Roger Gaspar, John Neligan, David Parry, Gareth Stephens, Canary Wharf Group plc, Matt Stickels, and Port Flair Ltd/Commission Air.

Finally, we must not forget the many readers who have kept us sailing a good course with a clean wake and provided a steady flow of pilotage updates for our companion website www.eastcoastpilot.com.

Colin Jarman, Garth Cooper, Dick Holness
January 2015

DEDICATION

To our long-suffering wives – Mary, Liz and Angela – without whose unstinting support this fourth edition would not have made it down the ways.

Fal's Cappa on the Swale

East Coast Pilot authors (left to right): Colin Jarman, Dick Holness, Garth Cooper

SYMBOLS USED ON CHARTS

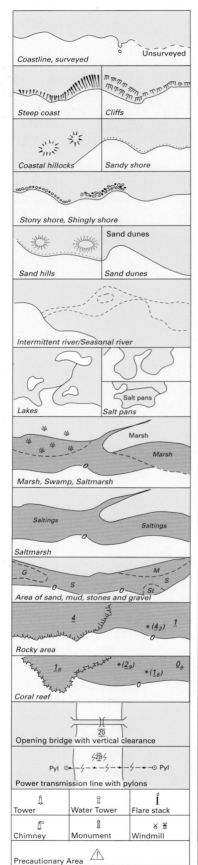

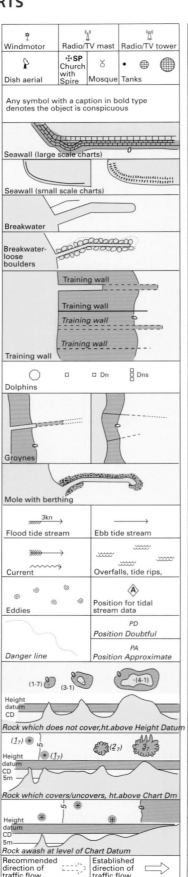

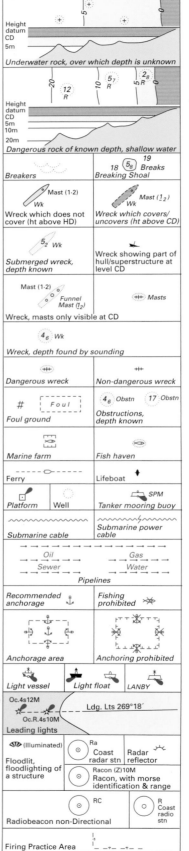

ABBREVIATIONS

Bn	Beacon
By	Buoy
CC	Cruising Club
CG	Coastguard
Ch	Channel
Conspic	Conspicuous
DSC	Digital Selective Calling
E	East, Eastwards, Easterly
ECB	East Cardinal Buoy
ECM	East Cardinal Mark (eg beacon)
F	Fixed light
Fl	Flashing light
ft	Foot, feet
G	Green
H	Hour, eg H+15 is 15 minutes past the hour
hr	Hour, hours
HW	High Water
HWN	High Water Neaps
HWS	High Water Springs
IDM	Isolated Danger Mark
IQ	Interrupted Quick flashing light
Iso	Isophase light
kn	Knot, knots
L.Fl	Long flash
LNG	Liquefied Natural Gas
LOA	Length Overall
LPG	Liquefied Petroleum Gas
LW	Low Water
LWN	Low Water Neaps
LWS	Low Water Springs
M	Mile (nautical mile)
m	metre
MHWS	Mean High Water Springs
min	Minute
mins	Minutes
MLWS	Mean Low Water Springs
MMSI	Maritime Mobile Service Identity
MSI	Maritime Safety Information including inshore waters forecast, gale warnings and navigational warnings
Mo	Morse
N	North, Northwards, Northerly
NCB	North Cardinal Buoy
NCM	North Cardinal Mark (eg beacon)
NE	Northeast or Northeastwards

NEly	Northeasterly
NW	Northwest, Northwestwards
NWly	Northwesterly
Oc	Occulting light
ODAS	Ocean Data Acquisition System
PAYG	Pay As You Go
PH	Port Hand
PHB	Port Hand Buoy
PHM	Port Hand Mark (eg beacon)
PLA	Port of London Authority
Pt	Point
PWC	Personal Water Craft (jet ski)
Q	Quick flashing light
R	Red
S	South, Southwards, Southerly
s	second(s)
SC	Sailing Club
SCB	South Cardinal Buoy
SCM	South Cardinal Mark (eg beacon)
SH	Starboard Hand
SHB	Starboard Hand Buoy
SHM	Starboard Hand Mark (eg beacon)
S'ly	Southerly
SW	Southwest, Southwestwards
SWB	Safe Water Buoy
SWly	Southwesterly
SWM	Safe Water Mark
TSS	Traffic Separation Scheme
UKHO	United Kingdom Hydrographic Office (the Admiralty)
UTC	Universal Time Corrected (same as GMT – Greenwich Mean Time)
vert	vertical
VQ	Very Quick flashing light
VTS	Vessel Traffic Service
W	West, Westwards, Westerly; White
WCB	West Cardinal Buoy
WCM	West Cardinal Mark (eg beacon)
Y	Yellow
YC	Yacht Club

VHF Channels

VHF Ch 37 is often listed in *ECP* as the calling channel for services such as harbour ferries. We have used this outdated designation, because VHF radios variously show the channel as 37A, M1, N1 or P1. Correctly it is now known as M1 but manufacturers have not yet standardised radio displays.

SMALL CRAFT SYMBOLS

The following symbols are used on larger scale charts and plans, and are shown in magenta

⚓	Visitors' moorings	⊠	Post office
Ⓥ	Visitors' berths	▮	Building
⚓	Yacht marina	✈	Airport
⤥	Public landing	⚑	Flagpole/flagstaff
⤙	Slipway for small craft	🏰	Castle/Fort
⚓	Water tap	⊕	Hospital
⛽	Fuel	⊤	Notice Board
⤸	Public telephone	🌲	Wooded
⊖	Customs	⊙♨	Beacon (with various topmarks)
🏠	Public house, inn, bar	⚓	Mooring buoy
✕	Restaurant	⊖	Crane
⚑	Yacht or sailing club		Chimney
WC	Toilets		Radio/TV Mast
P	Public car park		Water tower
⤓	Hard standing for boats		Tower
⊡	Launderette		Monument
🚐	Caravan site		Wind turbine
△	Camping site		
⚓	Nature reserve		
⚓	Harbourmaster		

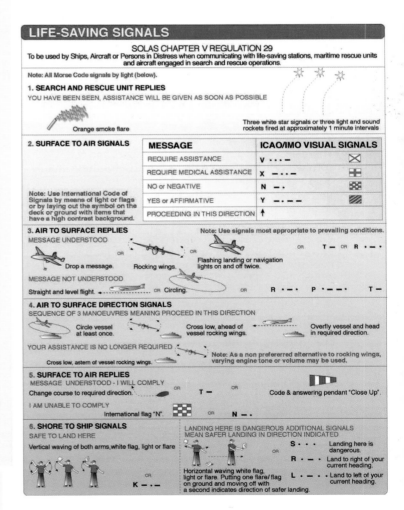

Keeping your East Coast Pilot up to date

We believe that *East Coast Pilot* remains unique amongst pilot books in having its own dedicated website, www.eastcoastpilot.com, created and maintained by the authors, as the primary vehicle for providing updates.

Generally we show changes on the website soon after learning of them, although we sometimes take a few days to verify the information if we are unsure of the source.

By using a website to provide this information, we can afford to be generous with words, chartlets and pictures – we can give full descriptions of the changes and provide visual evidence as well, for example a photo of a new approach buoy or changes to a marina entrance.

Apart from pilotage changes and updates, we also aim to keep you abreast of other information that may affect you as you cruise the area. This we do through a 'News' section where items are left available to read until they are no longer current. Everything else is left on the website until the next edition is published.

We also offer 'E-newsletters' – distributed by email, approximately monthly in summer, but less often in winter – designed to call your attention to Updates and News that we have put on the website. These are completely free, just part of the service, and you can easily sign up for them via the button on the website. There are many hundreds of subscribers and the considerable feedback tells us how useful these emails are to *ECP* readers.

You can also 'follow' us on Twitter, where we are @eastcoastpilot, and where we also broadcast news of changes.

We are delighted when readers get in touch and we do encourage you to tell us if you find that features we have described have changed. You can contact us by email through the website and you will usually get a quick response if we're not away sailing.

Incidentally, something we do not do on the website is provide Notices to Mariners or chart changes that are readily available from the UKHO or other publishers, although we will bring them to your attention if they are of particular importance. (Relevant NtMs can quickly be found at www.crossingthethamesestuary.com.)

For those without ready access to the internet, updates for this fourth edition are also available in paper form on request from the publisher. This is an abbreviated version of the fuller descriptions published on the website and without any photos, but will still be right up to date, because it will be printed from the website at the time of the request. Again, we believe this to be a unique feature of *ECP*.

We do urge you to use these facilities, via the internet or by requesting regular updates from Imray, to keep your *East Coast Pilot* up to date.

Through the website we can even supply you with an *ECP* 'community' burgee, so stand up and be counted – join the *ECP* Users' Community!

ECP 'Rolling Roads'

Most chapters in this book have at least one 'rolling road' diagram to assist pilotage.

Read each rolling road from the bottom upwards.

The long blue arrow through the middle of the diagram shows which buoys are to be left to port and which to starboard. Distances between buoys/waypoints are also given.

The angled short blue arrows are designed only to inform the helmsman of the general direction to turn when passing buoy X, to port or to starboard, until the navigator/pilot works out the exact new course to steer and compares it with the approximate required COG on the diagram.

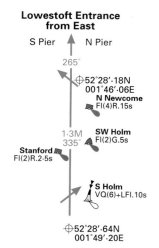

Lowestoft Entrance from East

S Pier   N Pier

265°

⊕52°28'·18N 001°46'·06E
N Newcome Fl(4)R.15s

1·3M   **SW Holm** Fl(2)G.5s
335°
Stanford Fl(2)R.2·5s

S Holm VQ(6)+LFl.10s

⊕52°28'·64N 001°49'·20E

General information

Chart datum

The charts are based on UK Hydrographic Office (Admiralty) data and, therefore, drawn to Lowest Astronomical Tide (LAT). This means, in essence, that they show a 'worst case scenario' and that there will normally be more water in an area than is shown.

The horizontal datum is WGS84, which complies with modern GPS equipment.

Courses and bearings

We have applied the general pilot book convention of providing courses and bearings in degrees True, but have used the qualifiers 'about' or 'approximately'. This is because it is the skipper/navigator's responsibility to confirm such courses and bearings with regard to tide, wind and sea conditions as well as applying corrections unique to the particular boat. We also believe that to steer a course in a seaway to within ±10° is acceptable; to steer within ±5° is good; to steer a precise course of (say) 241° is impossible. That impossibility makes it reasonable to quote a course of 'about 240°' and let the reader make the necessary corrections.

Distances

Readers have asked for a simple table of distances as an indication of the distances between landfalls. Agreeing that this might be useful, we turned for the information to that excellent passage planner *Crossing the Thames Estuary* by Roger Gaspar and published by Imray. Roger kindly gave his permission to use the data he'd developed and helped us with additional material not directly covered by his book. We highly recommend *Crossing the Thames Estuary* as a planning companion to *ECP*.

Tides

In previous editions we have based all tides on HW Dover, but this time we have instead referred to the nearest standard port, be that Dover, Sheerness, Walton or Lowestoft. Differences in time are given before (-) or after (+) in hours and minutes, e.g. HW Sheerness +0120 is 1hr 20mins after HW Sheerness.

Landfall waypoints

In order to provide a starting point for the pilotage notes, we have selected a point in the offing and called it the Landfall Waypoint. It is a point in clear water, which we feel can be approached safely and from which pilotage can reasonably begin. You are strongly advised to plot the waypoint and decide for yourself whether you actually wish to use it. You may well decide on another position nearby. Do not just put our chosen waypoint into your GPS and passage plan without checking it and agreeing with it.

Chart lists

We have given the numbers of paper charts covering a particular area published by Imray and the Admiralty

DISTANCES (IN MILES) USING INSIDE ROUTES

To and from Ramsgate:

Ramsgate (approach Ch) to River Blackwater (Sales Point)	
via Fisherman's Gat and Sunk Beacon	38·20
via N Edinburgh Channel	37·01
via Foulger's Gat	40·88
Ramsgate (approach Ch) to River Colne (Colne Bar)	
via Fisherman's Gat and Sunk Beacon	34·06
via N Edinburgh Channel	32·87
via Foulger's Gat	36·74
Ramsgate (approach Ch) to River Crouch (S Buxey)	
via Fisherman's Gat and Sunk Beacon	33·20
via N Edinburgh Channel	31·64
via Foulger's Gat	36·04
Ramsgate (approach Ch) to Harwich (adjacent to Cliff Foot PHM)	
via Black Deep	39·35
via Barrow No 2 and E Swin	38·71
Ramsgate (approach Ch) to River Deben (Woodbridge Haven Buoy)	
via Black Deep	40·84
via Barrow No 2 and E Swin	38·37
Ramsgate (approach Ch) to The Swale (Columbine SHB)	21·08
The Medway (entrance to Medway buoyed ch)	30·42

To and from the Kent Rivers:

Medway to Crouch (S Buxey)	23·20
Medway to Blackwater (Sales Pt)	29·07
Medway to Colne (Colne Bar)	24·93
Swale to Crouch (S Buxey)	24·06
Swale to Blackwater (Sales Pt)	29·93
Swale to Colne (Colne Bar)	25·79
Medway to Harwich:	
via Wallet	36·71
via Barrow and E Swin	40·85
Medway to Deben:	
via Wallet	39·82
via Barrow and E Swin	42·40
Swale to Harwich:	
via Wallet	37·57
via Barrow and E Swin	38·16
Swale to Deben:	
via Wallet	40·66
via Barrow and E Swin	39·69

Data reproduced from *Crossing the Thames Estuary*
by kind permission of Roger Gaspar.

(UKHO). We have not attempted to list electronic charts, because there are too many permutations of publisher, plotter and 'packages' and compiling the list would waste valuable sailing time.

Coastguard

At the time of writing, the Thames Estuary is covered by Humber and Thames Coastguard centres, with London CG specifically responsible for the River Thames, and an overlap into Dover CG around the North Foreland and Ramsgate.

However, Thames CG is currently scheduled to close in June 2015. After the closure, although a call to Thames by VHF or by phone will be re-routed and answered as now, the correct procedure will be for vessels N of latitude 51°43'·20N (just south of the River Blackwater estuary) to call Humber CG, while vessels S of that line should call Dover CG.

When calling the Coastguard, it is best to use their MMSI from a DSC VHF set, but with non-DSC sets they can all be contacted via Ch 16 using their name as the call sign, e.g. *Humber Coastguard*.

With the exception of London, which does not make MSI (Maritime Safety Information) broadcasts, all the CG stations announce these useful broadcasts on VHF Ch 16 and give the channels on which they will be made.

London Coastguard
DSC MMSI 002320063 ☎ 0208 312 7380. Covers area from Shell Haven Point (N bank) and Egypt Point (S bank) to Teddington.

Before the Thames CG closure in 2015:

Dover Coastguard
DSC MMSI 002320010 ☎ 01304 210008. Covers area including Ramsgate to Reculver Towers. MSI announcements on Ch 16 at 0110, 0410, 0710, 1010, 1310, 1610, 1910, 2210 Local Time.

Thames Coastguard
DSC MMSI 002320009 ☎ 01255 675518. Covers area from Reculver Towers to Southwold. MSI announcements on Ch 16 at 0110, 0410, 0710, 1010, 1310, 1610, 1910, 2210 Local Time.

Humber Coastguard
DSC MMSI 002320007 ☎ 01262 672317. Covers area from Southwold Northwards. MSI announcements on Ch 16 at 0150, 0450, 0750, 1050, 1350, 1650, 1950, 2250 Local Time.

After the Thames CG closure in 2015:

Dover Coastguard DSC MMSI 002320010 ☎ 01304 210008. Covers Dover Strait and southern Thames Estuary up to 51°43'·20N. MSI announcements on Ch 16 at 0110, 0410, 0710, 1010, 1310, 1610, 1910, 2210 Local Time.

Humber Coastguard DSC MMSI 002320007 ☎ 01262 672317. Covers area from 51°43'·20N Northwards. MSI announcements on Ch 16 at 0150, 0450, 0750, 1050, 1350, 1650, 1950, 2250 Local Time.

With this edition coverage has been extended to include Great Yarmouth, which this yacht is approaching from the north

National Coastwatch Institution (NCI)

www.nci.org.uk

NCI stations are now equipped to use VHF Ch 65, a channel for their dedicated use in communication with seafarers on a variety of non-emergency routine tasks. Skippers of leisure craft can use it for radio checks or to request local information, such as actual weather and sea state conditions. Note that NCI stations are open for daylight hours only and not all are open every day.

Any other communications, most especially those of an emergency nature, must still be made with the CG via DSC and/or Ch 16.

NCI stations on the coast covered by ECP are as follows, from north to south:

Gorleston	☎ 01493 440384
Felixstowe	☎ 01394 670808
Southend	☎ 07815 945210
Holehaven	☎ 01268 696971
Whitstable	☎ 07864 646209
Herne Bay	☎ 01227 744454

Danger – pot markers

There are many pot markers and fishing floats in the Thames Estuary and they are, generally, very poorly marked or not marked at all. It requires a very sharp lookout to spot small floats or empty drinks containers, which may be half submerged in a strong tide. At night it is all but impossible to see them until it's too late.

All of this makes motoring or motorsailing a time for extreme caution, especially at night. Indeed, such is the problem that it may sometimes be wise to take a longer route or remain further offshore so as to be sure of going round infested areas.

Areas to beware of are off the North Foreland, around the Naze and towards Harwich, off Felixstowe S of the Deben entrance, East Lane (S of Ore entrance), Aldeburgh and Sizewell – there are even scattered pots in Harwich Harbour and the approaches to Lowestoft.

Patriotic potmarker, but probably illegal. Sighted off Felixstowe

Medical help

For emergency medical help make a VHF call to the Coastguard when at sea or call 999 by phone when in harbour.

For non-emergency help and advice, when in harbour, call the NHS by dialling 111, available 24hr.

Riding lights

The International Regulations for Preventing Collisions at Sea, 1972 (ColRegs), require vessels of more than 7m length to display a black ball during the day and an all round white light at night when riding to an anchor.

In these days of crowded anchorages and heavy traffic, our advice would be for ALL vessels (including, in some areas such as the Orwell, those on moorings) to display these signals, particularly at night, when crew are on board.

Wind farms and commerce

Love 'em or hate 'em, wind farms are now a fact of life in the outer extremities of our waters. The nearest to shore are Scroby Sands off Great Yarmouth and the Gunfleet Sands off Clacton. The London Array is in the very middle of the Thames Estuary, while the Gabbards affect those of us who aim to venture across the North Sea. The Kentish Flats wind farm is being expanded and needs care to pass in the shallows off the E entrance to the Swale.

The Thames Estuary is the most crowded sailing area in the UK after the Solent. It has a charm and character that makes it unique, but the commercial traffic using the Thames is so continuously heavy that the Port of London Authority (PLA) is the largest port authority in the country. Felixstowe is the largest container port in the UK, one of the busiest in Europe, and accommodates the very largest cargo ships in the world. The Thames Estuary is the funnel through which much of this shipping travels to reach either Harwich in the N section or the Thames in the S.

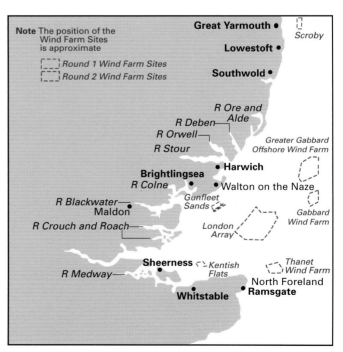

The Estuary is becoming even more crowded with expansion of the container port at Felixstowe and the Thames Gateway in the Thames itself. There is also a rising demand for yachting facilities and, on top of all this, the explosion in wind farm developments with increasing traffic in the form of large barges used to install and maintain them and fast craft that service them. The poor old yachtsman could be forgiven for throwing up his hands in disgust and going elsewhere.

As if that weren't bad enough, craft wishing to leave to the N of our area, say beyond Lowestoft or across to the North Dutch or Friesland coasts, will eventually run the gauntlet of a new massive multi-thousand tower wind farm stretching from just S of Lowestoft to as far N as the Dogger Bank with a width greater than half that of the southern North Sea.

To aid ship safety, the towers in all wind farms are painted yellow up to 12m above sea level and the corner towers, plus those at some key points down the sides of the farm, have yellow flashing lights, also at 12m. There is, however, doubt that, at this height, these lights will be visible to crews of recreational craft navigating in fog or dirty weather. The farms emit sound signals in fog.

It has been generally agreed that the rotor tip clearance will be 22m above MHWS and at this height 96 per cent of yachts will, if forced into the arrays, pass underneath without being struck by a rotor. Unfortunately, on the Gunfleet, just off Clacton, the clearance is only 20m, bringing the percentage of yachts able to go through without danger of being struck by the rotor tips down to 88 per cent.

General advice to yachtsmen is to avoid the farms as much as possible, but to be aware of their positions, marks and lights, which are shown on current charts.

Tidal streams

The figures against the arrows denote mean rates in tenths of a knot at neaps and springs.
Thus 06,11 indicates a mean neap rate of 0·6 knots and a mean spring rate of 1·1 knots.

TIDAL DIFFERENCES ON DOVER

Allington Lock	+0210
Broadstairs	+0037
Burnham-on-Crouch	+0115
Canvey	+0125
Chatham	+0140
Colne	+0050
Gravesend	+0200
Harty Ferry	+0120
Harwich Haven	+0040
Herne Bay	+0110
Ipswich	+0115
London Bridge	+0252
Lowestoft	-0133
Maldon	+0130
Margate	+0045
Mistley Quay	+0105
Orford Haven	+0010
Orford Quay	+0100
Paglesham	+0110
Pin Mill	+0100
Queenborough	+0130
Ramsgate	+0030
Sheerness	+0130
Slaughden	+0155
Snape	+0225
Southwold	-0105
Stone Point	+0040
Waldringfield	+0100
Woodbridge	+0105
Woodbridge Haven	+0025
Whitstable	+0135
Woolwich Ferry	+0225

Entering the Tollesbury North Channel

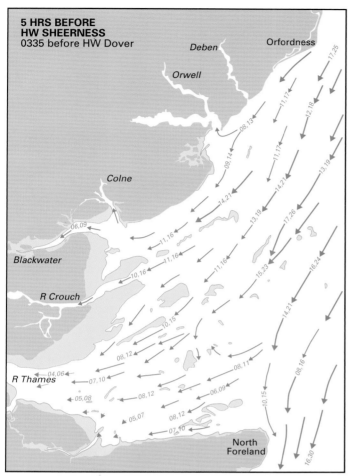

**5 HRS BEFORE
HW SHEERNESS**
0335 before HW Dover

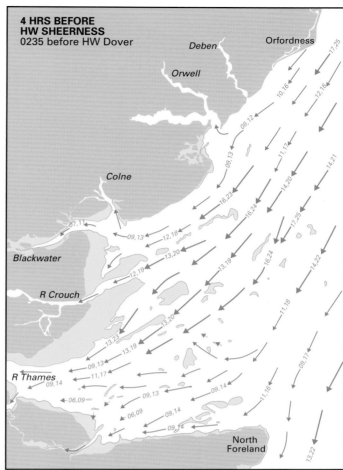

**4 HRS BEFORE
HW SHEERNESS**
0235 before HW Dover

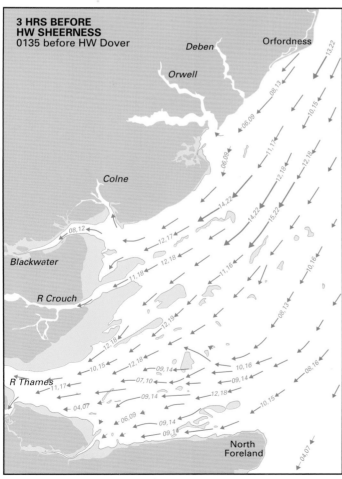

**3 HRS BEFORE
HW SHEERNESS**
0135 before HW Dover

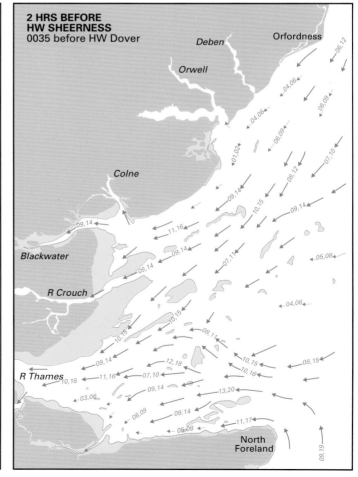

**2 HRS BEFORE
HW SHEERNESS**
0035 before HW Dover

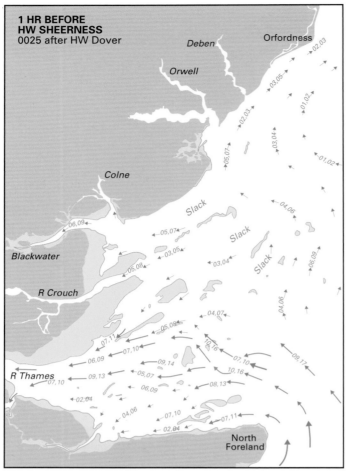

**1 HR BEFORE
HW SHEERNESS**
0025 after HW Dover

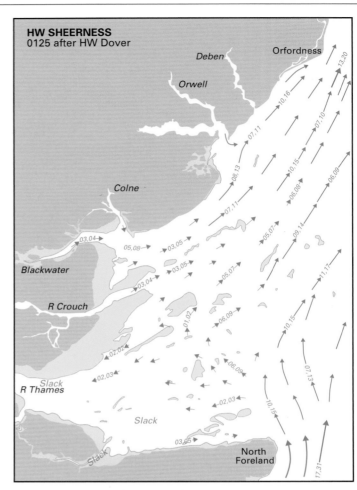

HW SHEERNESS
0125 after HW Dover

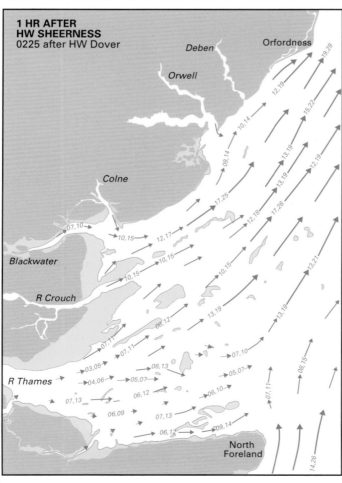

**1 HR AFTER
HW SHEERNESS**
0225 after HW Dover

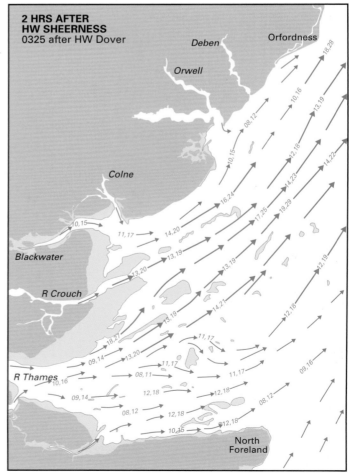

**2 HRS AFTER
HW SHEERNESS**
0325 after HW Dover

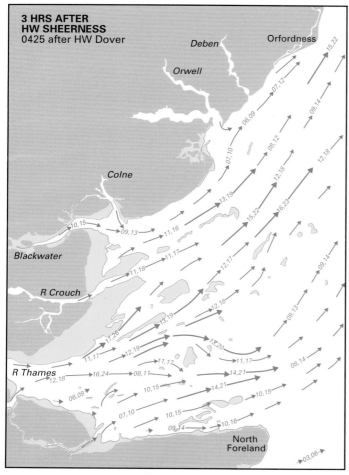

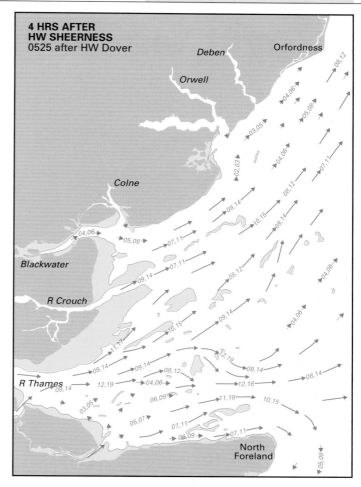

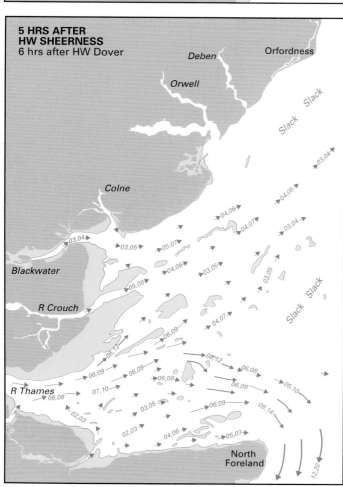

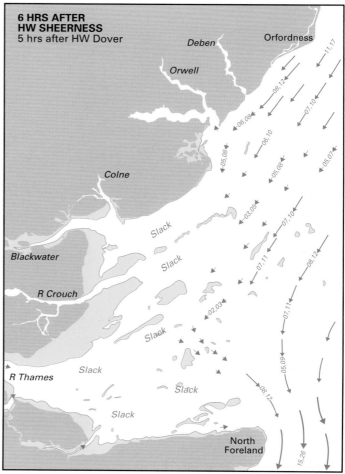

1. Great Yarmouth

⊕ Landfall waypoint
  52°34'·34N 001°45'·19E ½M E of entrance
Charts
Imray C28
Admiralty 1543 1534
Tides
HW Lowestoft -0035
Harbourmaster Pat McNamara
VHF Ch 12 Call sign *Yarmouth Radio*
☎ 01493 335502 *Email* portops@eastportuk.co.uk

Entry to the outer harbour (East Port) is strictly prohibited.

Great Yarmouth harbour is a long, narrow concrete channel running from the entrance at Gorleston to the Haven Bridge, the first of two bridges that give access to the northern Broads via Breydon Water. The harbour was built down either side of the river Yare, which runs through the harbour in a NNW to SSE direction with the man-made entrance flanked by Gorleston Pier to the S and the S retaining wall of the commercial East Port (shown as Outer Harbour on charts) on the N side. The entrance opens due E and is narrow.

Within a short distance from the pierheads the river turns through 90° to starboard, so visitors are at first faced by a high blank reinforced concrete wall. The bend

Great Yarmouth harbour

is blind to traffic in both directions, so it is vital to obey the port control lights mounted on a lattice tower on the N side of the entrance. Beware strong cross currents that can set you against the N pier.

Watch out too for wind farm and oil rig support and supply vessels, which use the space in the entrance to turn round and go astern into their berths further upstream.

Vessels approaching Great Yarmouth from the N should not enter the first entrance they come to as this is East Port, which is not open to leisure craft. Instead, they must pass this entrance and follow the S wall of East Port until the entrance to Yarmouth harbour itself opens up.

There is little to commend Yarmouth as a leisure port and we don't recommend it as a port of last resort, because a strong N-S tidal flow, coupled with anything up to 6kn of river ebb, gets piled up by strong winds with

Harbour entrance from outside, beware large vessels in narrows

RNLI

East Port

Traffic lights

any E in them. Indeed, it is not advisable to enter with a small yacht in anything over F4. Fortunately, there are no inshore sand banks to worry the careful sailor, although some shoaling can occur in the entrance during strong easterlies with depths reduced by as much as a metre.

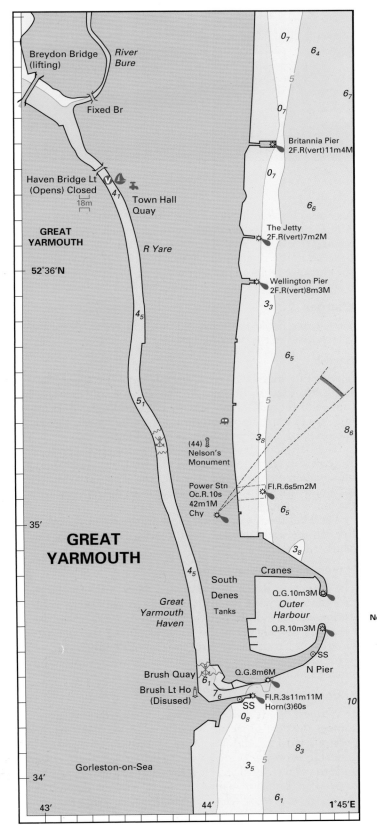

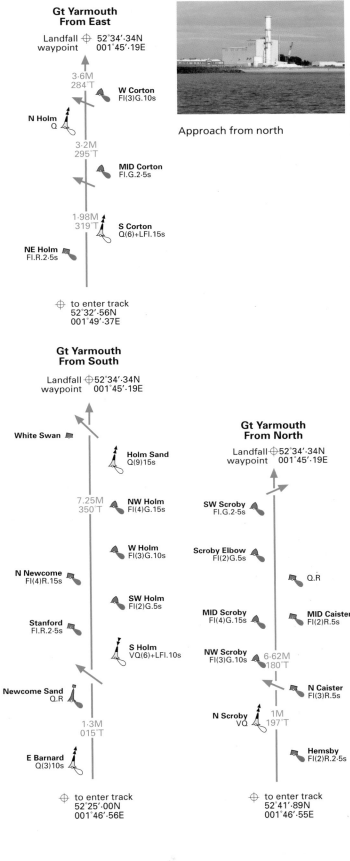

Gt Yarmouth From East

Landfall waypoint ⊕ 52°34'·34N 001°45'·19E

3·6M 284°T

W Corton Fl(3)G.10s

N Holm Q

3·2M 295°T

MID Corton Fl.G.2·5s

1·98M 319°T

S Corton Q(6)+LFl.15s

NE Holm Fl.R.2·5s

⊕ to enter track 52°32'·56N 001°49'·37E

Approach from north

Gt Yarmouth From South

Landfall waypoint ⊕ 52°34'·34N 001°45'·19E

White Swan

Holm Sand Q(9)15s

7.25M 350°T

NW Holm Fl(4)G.15s

W Holm Fl(3)G.10s

N Newcome Fl(4)R.15s

SW Holm Fl(2)G.5s

Stanford Fl.R.2·5s

S Holm VQ(6)+LFl.10s

Newcome Sand Q.R

1·3M 015°T

E Barnard Q(3)10s

⊕ to enter track 52°25'·00N 001°46'·56E

Gt Yarmouth From North

Landfall waypoint ⊕ 52°34'·34N 001°45'·19E

SW Scroby Fl.G.2·5s

Scroby Elbow Fl(2)G.5s

Q.R

MID Scroby Fl(4)G.15s

MID Caister Fl(2)R.5s

NW Scroby Fl(3)G.10s

6·62M 180°T

N Caister Fl(3)R.5s

N Scroby VQ

1M 197°T

Hemsby Fl(2)R.2·5s

⊕ to enter track 52°41'·89N 001°46'·55E

Breydon Bridge (lifting)

River Bure

Fixed Br

0_7

6_4

5

6_7

0_7

Britannia Pier 2F.R(vert)11m4M

0_7

Haven Bridge Lt (Opens) Closed
18m

4_1

Town Hall Quay

GREAT YARMOUTH

R Yare

52°36'N

6_6

The Jetty 2F.R(vert)7m2M

Wellington Pier 2F.R(vert)8m3M

3_3

4_5

6_5

5_1

5

3_8

8_6

(44) **Nelson's Monument**

3_8

Fl.R.6s5m2M

Power Stn Oc.R.10s 42m1M Chy

6_5

35'

GREAT YARMOUTH

3_8

Cranes

4_5

South Denes

Tanks

Outer Harbour

Q.G.10m3M

Great Yarmouth Haven

Q.R.10m3M

SS

Brush Quay

Q.G.8m6M

N Pier

6_1

Brush Lt Ho (Disused)

7_6

Fl.R.3s11m11M Horn(3)60s

SS

0_8

10

Gorleston-on-Sea

34'

8_3

5

3_5

6_1

43'

44'

1°45'E

Yacht entering Yarmouth harbour

The close approach to the harbour entrance is in clear, deep water with depths ranging from 7m to 17m. The entrance is somewhat sheltered by the southern extremity of the Scroby Sands with the deep water Holm Channel forming a NW–SE gap between the S tip of the Scroby and the N tip of the Holm Sand.

Anyone coming in from due E should aim for the S Corton (Q (6)+L.Fl.15s (bell)) SCB and turn NW up the Holm Channel until the entrance or the pierhead lights are abeam, then turn due W to pass between them.

Coming along the coast from N, enter Caister Roads by passing (in close order) the Hemsby (Fl.R.2·5s) PHB and the N Scroby NCB (VQ). The Scroby Sands wind farm opens to port. Opposite the Great Yarmouth entrance, turn to starboard and head due W to enter.

From S, pick up the E Barnard ECB (Q(3)10s) S of Lowestoft, follow the Stanford Channel and continue N past the entrance to Lowestoft Harbour. Ensure you keep to port of two cardinal buoys about ½M off the end of Lowestoft Ness (an SCB (Q(6)+L.Fl.15s (bell)) and an ECB (VQ(3)5s (bell)) marking a charted obstruction. Follow the coastline N until opposite the Yarmouth entrance.

The entrance to Yarmouth is marked by 2F.R (vert) on top of the harbour building on the end of Gorleston Pier, which forms the S arm of the entrance, followed closely by a Fl.R 3s on a red brick building at the shoreside base of the pier. Also at the base of the pier stands the disused Gorleston Lighthouse, a red brick distinct tower. The N side of the harbour entrance is marked with a Q.G. mounted on a green post on what used to be the N pier until it was extended to form part of the S wall of East Port, followed by a line of four 2F.G. lights leading to the bend into the main channel. Two corresponding 2F.R (vert) lights indicate the port hand side.

Marine Services controls the port operations on VHF Ch 12 with the call sign *Yarmouth Radio*. Contact should be made prior to entry or departure and, if outward bound from the Broads, when passing through Haven Bridge.

Small craft must comply with the Port Traffic Signals displayed at the harbour entrance on a lattice tower on the N side. These are IALA signals showing 3 Fl.R for

harbour closed and also do not proceed until instructed, 3 Fl.G proceed, G/W/G proceed only when told to. For leaving harbour, 3 R (vert) means no vessel should proceed down river of the RNLI station sited just above the entrance bend on the Gorleston or W side.

A good time to enter the river is at slack low water.

Charges

Vessels are liable for tolls, but waivers are in place for vessels visiting the Norfolk Broads.

Berths

Small craft moorings are available on Hall Quay, just south of Haven Bridge on the E side of the river (opposite the red brick Town Hall building). Mooring tails are in place to aid mooring from the vessel. Vessels should moor adjacent to the access ladders.

The berths on Hall Quay have an alongside depth of at least 3m at MLWS. When mooring at Hall Quay, make adequate allowance for the tide when arriving on the flood and ensure that you are not set upriver towards the Haven Bridge.

The Hall Quay berths are close to the town centre. A five-minute walk along Regent Road will take you to the Market Place.

Haven and Breydon bridges

The Haven Bridge is only manned when a lift is due to take place. Breydon Bridge is manned from 0800 to 1700 during winter months and from 0600 to 2200 or sunrise to sunset (whichever is the shorter) during the summer months, i.e. from Easter until the end of October.

Requests to lift the Haven Bridge between sunset and sunrise incur a charge of £200.

Bridge booking

To request a lift for the Haven or Breydon Bridges, contact the Port Operations Office prior to 1645 on the previous working day (Monday to Friday) on ☎ 01493 335503. Breydon Bridge will be lifted in conjunction with the Haven Bridge, but a Breydon Bridge lift can be booked in isolation using the same contact details. A vessel at sea may relay a message via Port Marine Services (Yarmouth Radio) on VHF Ch 12.

Top end of the harbour

Passing through the port

Both the Haven and Breydon Bridges have river traffic control lights on the bridge buttresses. These traffic signals are not exhibited constantly but are switched on approximately 10 minutes before a planned lift and are initially switched to red (stop) in both directions.

Vessels that can pass under Breydon Bridge without needing a lift should use the side spans, which have a greater air draught clearance. Vessels requiring a Breydon Bridge lift pass through the centre span. The bridge operators will advise if there is two-way traffic.

Mariners should be careful when approaching either of the bridges not to be set onto them, as tides can be strong and, at the Haven Bridge, the rates can exceed 3kn.

Inbound vessels must contact Yarmouth Radio on Ch 12 before approaching the entrance, to request clearance to enter. They should also obey the IALA port traffic signals displayed on the North Wall opposite the end of Gorleston Pier.

Vessels required to wait outside for an outbound vessel must stay clear of the port entrance, in order to give departing ships adequate room to manoeuvre.

Outbound vessels should initially contact Breydon Bridge (or Haven Bridge, if Breydon Bridge is not to be used) on Ch 12. When through the Haven Bridge vessels should contact Yarmouth Radio on Ch 12 to advise their intentions. They should obey the IALA traffic signals exhibited at Brush Bend, where the channel turns sharply E and, if a stop signal is exhibited, stop their vessel north of the stop sign that is displayed on the W bank to N of the RNLI lifeboat station.

Vessels navigating through the port should be aware of large vessels manoeuvring or swinging in the narrow channel.

Speed in the river

All vessels should maintain a slow speed in the river. There is a maximum speed limit of 7kn, although a slower speed may be appropriate. Take care with vessel wash and avoid causing a nuisance to other vessels either moored or underway.

Wind and tide

There is a tidal range of approximately 2m within the harbour and tidal flows can be very swift, particularly during spring tides when rates of 4kn can be encountered. Mariners should be aware that during certain wind and meteorological conditions, tidal flow rates can reach 5-6kn. Slack water at the harbour entrance is approximately 90 minutes after HW/LW, but this may vary with weather conditions.

At the entrance to the harbour sea conditions can become confused with wind over tide, particularly on the ebb or with wave reflection from the pier structures.

Inside the harbour, there is generally good shelter, however wind over tide with N or S winds can cause uncomfortable conditions on the berths at Hall Quay and fenders should be carefully adjusted.

Nelson's Monument stands N of the harbour

2. Lowestoft

⊕ Landfall waypoint
52°28'·18N 001°46'·06E ½M E of entrance

Charts
Imray C28, 2000 series
Admiralty 1536, 1543

Tides
HW Lowestoft

Harbourmaster
Lowestoft Port Control VHF Ch 14
Callsign *Lowestoft Port Control*
Harbourmaster ☏ 01502 572286

ECP Honorary Port Pilot John Powell ☏ 07774 822820
Email lowestoft@eastcoastpilot.com

Port Control Lights

Three vertical reds – Do not enter

Green, white, green vertical – Clear to enter (or depart) on specific orders from Port Control.

Before entering or leaving, request permission on Ch 14. Small craft and yachts without VHF may take the green, white, green signal as clearance to go ahead, but with extreme caution and navigational courtesy; those vessels in the Yacht Basin and Hamilton Dock must contact the Port Control before departure.

Mariners should note that both Port Control, which is located at the harbour bridge, as well as departing vessels within the Outer Harbour basin, have extremely limited vision to the N of the entrance piers and should navigate accordingly.

Main hazards

Shifting sand banks make it imperative for the first time or occasional visitor to stay in the marked channels. With wind against tide, heavy seas can build off the entrance, which is quite narrow and marked by two lighthouses on the pier ends.

Unless urgent, do not attempt entry during strong E or NE winds. It gets rough in anything over F4, especially with wind against the tide, which sets strongly across the entrance.

The whole Lowestoft Approaches area is under almost continuous survey, because of the formation of sand waves, which can give rise to rough waters in certain conditions, and continually moving sand banks.

Once inside the harbour watch out for low flying helicopters. There's a helipad on the buttress between the outer harbour and Waveney Dock. You may be asked to stand off if one is landing or taking off.

Landmarks

Half a mile N of the entrance stands Gulliver, the tallest and most E'ly wind generator on the English mainland, which makes a good landmark, being visible from well out to sea. From N or NE the white-painted Lowestoft Lighthouse on top of the cliffs N of the harbour is also conspicuous and a good mark to aim for. Inland from Gulliver stands a complex of pale coloured factories.

Lowestoft Outer Harbour entrance

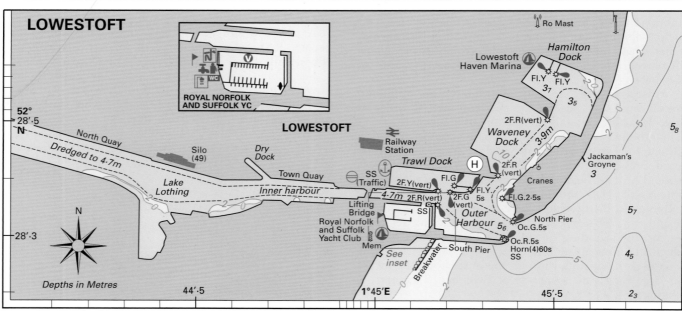

Looking west across the harbour and town of Lowestoft

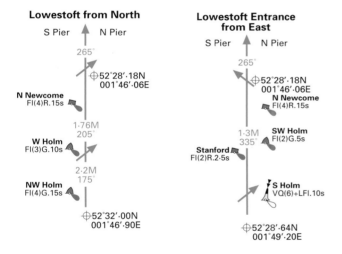

Lowestoft from North

S Pier   N Pier

265°

⊕52°28'·18N
001°46'·06E

N Newcome
Fl(4)R.15s

1·76M
205°

W Holm
Fl(3)G.10s

2·2M
175°

NW Holm
Fl(4)G.15s

⊕52°32'·00N
001°46'·90E

**Lowestoft Entrance
from East**

S Pier   N Pier

265°

⊕52°28'·18N
001°46'·06E
N Newcome
Fl(4)R.15s

1·3M
335°

SW Holm
Fl(2)G.5s

Stanford
Fl(2)R.2·5s

S Holm
VQ(6)+LFl.10s

⊕52°28'·64N
001°49'·20E

Lowestoft from South

S Pier   265°   N Pier

⊕52°28'·18N
001°46'·06E
N Newcome
Fl(4)R.15s

Stanford
Fl.R.2·5s

2·1M
350°

S Holm
VQ(6)+LFl.10s

**Newcome
Sand**
Q.R

1·3M
015°

E Barnard
Q(3)10s

⊕52°25'·00N
001°46'·56E

Two white pagoda-shaped lighthouses on the pierheads distinguish the harbour entrance itself. The S pier is canted to face NE so that the prevailing swell from SW doesn't drive into the harbour. Immediately N of the entrance can sometimes be seen a gas rig accommodation platform under construction or repair or at other times it is possible to see huge blades from wind turbines in for repair, jutting up against the skyline.

Most of the town is low lying, but a good reference point is the top of the grain silo N of, and behind, the harbour. Because of the offset of the entrance, this silo will appear at first to be S of the harbour.

Approaches

From E Make for the East Newcome PHB (Fl(2)R.5s). Although this buoy lies E of the entrance to Lowestoft, a direct course in is blocked by the shallows over the tail of the Holm Sand. With light enough draught and some local knowledge you can head straight in, however for the first timer we recommend the following route.

From the E Newcome steer roughly SSW to round South Holm SCB (VQ(6)+LFl.10s) before turning NW. Follow the Stanford Channel towards the harbour, passing between Stanford PHB (Fl.R.2·5s) and SW Holm SHB (Fl(2)G.5s). On reaching the N Newcome PHB (Fl(4)R.15s) turn due W towards the entrance piers with their twin white pagoda lighthouses.

In fair weather and calm conditions and with a sufficient rise of tide, many skippers will take the direct route W from E Newcome to N Newcome, crossing the

Labels: Entrance · Crane at rig depot · Goliath · E Barnard ECB

Lowestoft from S

Lowestoft lighthouse

Holm Sand tail in about 3·5-4m of water, and then on into the harbour, keeping clear of two wreck or foul ground buoys just N of the entrance.

From S Pick up the East Barnard ECB (Q(3)10s) on the 10m contour marking the edge of the Newcome Sand. To the N lies the Newcome Sand PHB (Q.R), which marks the N extremity of the sands and is the S gate to the Stanford Channel.

Follow the Stanford Channel, passing between Stanford PHB (Fl.R.2·5s) and SW Holm SHB (Fl(2)G.5s). On reaching the N Newcome PHB (Fl(4)R.15s) turn due W towards the entrance piers with their twin lighthouses. Do not be tempted to cut the corner from the S Holm direct to the S pier, because it shoals to 1·9m at LAT and any onshore wind cuts up a nasty, short, steep sea.

From N Keep within sight of the shore in the buoyed channel through Corton Roads and inside the Holm Sand until abreast the entrance piers.

Watch out for a pair of cardinal buoys about ½M off the end of Lowestoft Ness – ECB (VQ(3)5s Bell) and

SCB (Q(6)+L.Fl.15s Bell). They mark a charted obstruction, so do not try to pass between them.

The South Pier shows a set of international port control lights: G over W over G meaning clear to enter; 3 vert R meaning do not enter. Seek permission on Ch 14 from *Lowestoft Port Control* to enter. Both pierheads are lit: the North Pier (Oc.G.5s), the South Pier (Oc.R.5s). Beware an eddy in the entrance between the two piers.

Entry

The entrance is narrow (maximum commercial ship beam is 22m) and canted at an angle so that vessels leaving or entering cannot see each other. This makes it essential to call Lowestoft Port Control for permission to enter. The narrowness and angle of the entrance prevents very heavy S swells driving in, but it's open to NE winds and seas.

Strictly observe the Narrow Channels Rule 9(b) of the ColRegs. There is a minimum of 4·3m of water, although 6m is more generally found.

Once inside, the harbour opens out into a series of basins.

Just inside Lowestoft Outer Harbour

Labels: Silo conspic. · Bridge · HM · Entrance to Trawl Dock

LOWESTOFT HARBOUR

The harbour entrance widens into the main or outer harbour, from which a number of lesser basins branch off.

There is a shallow area in the SW corner of the outer harbour. Off to starboard is the entrance to the Waveney and Hamilton Docks, both having charted drying areas on the E or NE sides and are dredged to a minimum of 4m elsewhere. Up river to starboard is the entrance to the Trawl Dock where oil rig and wind farm support vessels moor.

If planning to stay in the Hamilton Dock marina, turn hard to starboard into the Waveney Fish Dock, but beware low flying helicopters taking off or landing on the port buttress helipad. Pass through the Fish Dock, go past the rig building and repair yard to starboard, and into the Hamilton Dock, where the 46 berth marina is on the far side.

The berths will accommodate boats between 10m and 17m length. The facility is run from Lowestoft Haven Marina on Lake Lothing. Call on VHF Ch 80 (call sign *Haven Marina*) for a berth. A CCTV camera ensures you go into the right berth; you'll get a call on the VHF if you

LOWESTOFT HAVEN MARINA / HAMILTON MARINA   NR33 9NB

Contact VHF Ch 80
Callsign *Lowestoft Haven Marina*
Contact ☎ 01502 580300 (0730–1930)
    www.lowestofthavenmarina.co.uk
    (also www.transeuropemarinas.com)
Facilities WC, Showers, Launderette, WiFi (PAYG)
Water On pontoons (use own hose)
Electricity On pontoons
Fuel Diesel (on hammerhead of pontoon A)
Gas Calor
Pub/Restaurant The Third Crossing ☎ 01502 583596
Boat hoist 70-T (out of hours by arrangement)
Workshop
Engineers, riggers, electronics and chandlers/support services Contact marina office
Boat Sales ☎ 01502 517711
Taxi ☎ 01502 515151, 511771 and 500000.

ROYAL NORFOLK & SUFFOLK YC   NR33 0AQ

Contact VHF Ch 80
Callsign *Royal Norfolk Harbourmaster*
Contact ☎ 01502 566726 (0730–1930)
    Email admin@rnsyc.org.uk
    www.rnsyc.net
Facilities WC, Showers, Launderette, WiFi
Fuel Diesel from berth below marina office at head of marina alongside the slip
Electricity On pontoons
Water On pontoons
Launching slip (trailers)
Launching crane (2½T)
Pump out Berth near slipway
Pressure wash Coin-operated at head of slipway
Provisions Shops nearby
Pubs/restaurants Nearby and in town
Local services Include chandler, electronics, engineer, rigger and sailmaker
Taxi ☎ 01502 515151, 511771 and 500000.

get it wrong! There is a direct line telephone mounted on the outside wall of the amenity block to call and book in and collect the security and block number. There's usually around 3·5m of water at low tide.

Some of the small Lowestoft inshore fishing fleet still use part of this dock although most of the bigger boats land their catch in the Waveney (or Fish) Dock.

Opposite the Trawl dock, to port, is the yacht basin at the head of which stands the Royal Norfolk and Suffolk YC (RN&SYC). The RN&SYC marina has visitors' berths on the N side of the first linear pontoon and on the W of the cross pontoon in front of the clubhouse. It is essential to call the club's harbourmaster on Ch 80 (call sign *Royal Norfolk Harbourmaster*) for directions before entering. Yachts over 12m LOA should lie against the large bumper tubes against the outer wall (to starboard inside the entrance) and guard against warps chafing on the rough stone quay. Enter with care, because boats may be manoeuvring inside. On leaving, obey the light signals on the E side of the marina entrance (green, white, green – go with caution; three reds – do not go). Port Control must approve departure (Ch 14).

Hamilton Marina, Lowestoft

The Royal Norfolk and Suffolk YC

Helicopter taking off from harbour centre heliport

The Lowestoft lifeboat is also moored in this basin alongside the pontoon serving the Lowestoft Historic Ships museum.

Just up river from the RN&SYC marina is the Lowestoft Harbour Bridge. Passage through is free, but opening times are strictly observed (see below.) Yachts waiting to go up river may get permission to wait in the Trawl Dock if they can't get into the marina. Do not approach the bridge unless the green light on the N wall is showing.

Lowestoft Harbour Bridge

The Lowestoft Harbour Bridge, between the outer and inner harbours, is only opened on demand to commercial shipping and then not between 0815 and 0900, 1230 and 1300, 1700 and 1730 to allow commuter traffic unimpeded access.

Small craft may pass through at the time of opening for commercial shipping, so long as Port Control has agreed beforehand. If yachts give at least 20 minutes notice of passage, the bridge can be opened for them at 0300, 0500, 0700, 0945, 1115, 1430, 1600, 1900, 2100 and midnight on weekdays and 0300, 0500, 0700, 0945, 1115, 1430, 1600, 1800, 1900, 2100 and midnight at weekends and Bank Holidays.

Call Port Control on Ch 14 or ② 01502 572286.

Approaching the bridge from the E there are traffic lights on the N quay.

There is a pontoon in the SE corner of the Trawl Dock (opposite RN&SYC) to use while waiting for the bridge.

The inner harbour and Lake Lothing

Above the road bridge is the Inner Harbour, which swells out into Lake Lothing. The channel is buoyed and dredged to 4·7m up to a point abreast the Lowestoft Cruising Club pontoons on the starboard hand. It shelves to 1·8m from there to the Carlton Road railway swing bridge.

Opposite Lowestoft CC is the Lowestoft Haven Marina. Although the general environment is that of an industrial area, visitors are welcome at all three of Lowestoft's yacht basins, which are in the forefront of the redevelopment of Lowestoft into a major yachting centre.

Lowestoft Harbour Bridge

LOWESTOFT CRUISING CLUB   NR32 3LY

Contact ☎ 07913 391950
www.lowestoftcruisingclub.co.uk
Facilities WC, Showers
Water On pontoons
Electricity At each berth
Slipway
Mast Crane on quayside
Berths To book, phone John Cooper, LCC moorings officer,
☎ 07913 391950

There are 70+ berths in finger boxes. Visitors should use the E end hammerhead or empty berths on the S side of the main pontoon with a green triangle indicating they are vacant then call the berthing officer.

Provisions, banks, pubs, trains 10 minutes walk
Taxi ☎ 01502 515151, 511771 and 500000.

Mutford Lock

Lowestoft is the main gateway to the S Broads. To make the final transition from Lake Lothing into Oulton Broad itself, boats have to go through (in order from the E) Carlton Railway Bridge, Mutford Road Bridge and Mutford Lock.

It is advisable to book transits in advance with the lockmaster. VHF Ch 73 or 14, ☎ 01502 531778 (Lock) or ☎ 01502 574946 (Yacht Station). The lock is operated by the Broads Authority and is 22m long and 6·5m wide with a minimum 2m depth (plus state of tide). There is a fee for each lock transit or day return.

The bridges and lock open on request during the following hours daily: April to October 0800–1800H. November to March 0800–1100. The lock is crowded at weekends and bank holidays.

Lowestoft Cruising Club berths

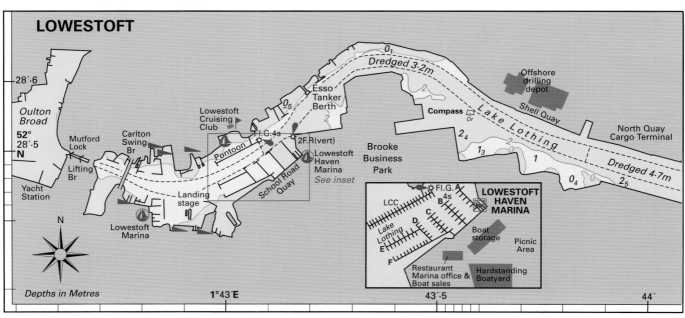

3. Southwold

⊕ **Landfall waypoint**
52°18'·75N 001°40'·70E About ½M SE of entrance

Charts
Imray C28
Admiralty 2695

Harbourmasters
Peter Simmons and Gerry Hilder ☎ 01502 724712
(0800-1700 in season)
VHF Ch 12

Call sign
Southwold Port Radio

Tides
HW Lowestoft +0105

Main hazards

There are shifting sand banks close to and within the entrance. There is a sand bar across the entrance that extends NE of the N pier. With wind against tide heavy seas can build up off the entrance and the depth over the bar can alter drastically after E gales.

Do not attempt an entrance during strong E or NE winds, especially if they are blowing against the tide.

Strong tides run athwart the entrance and in some conditions a 'bore' or standing wave runs in between the piers. There's between 0·9m and 1·3m of water on the yacht track at chart datum.

Visiting vessels must contact the Harbourmaster (Ch 12) for entry and berthing instructions before approaching the entrance and again before leaving their berth for departure.

There are 16 visitor berths alongside stagings opposite the Harbour Inn pub, where boats can form rafts up to four deep. Shorelines are obligatory to cope with the 6kn ebb tide and, because departure should always be on the flood, the suggestion is to moor with the boat heading down the harbour so that she can be eased out ahead into the stream and motored cleanly away.

There's usually around 2m of water at low tide and the bottom is hard and steeply shelving. There are ladders on the staging and the harbour authority thoughtfully supplies fender boards to straddle the piles. Remember to leave them behind on departure.

A further eight visitor berths are available alongside two floating pontoons adjacent to the Harbour Office.

Take care turning round in the harbour. There are stagings on both sides of the river, but opposite the visitors' moorings the S bank is clear and it is recommended that bigger boats should turn here, using full power plus propeller kick to turn tightly in the space. A local trick is to put the boat's stem into the muddy bank opposite and let the tide swing her round, but it takes some courage to do it first time.

Above the moorings is a low bridge taking the footpath from Southwold across to the village of Walberswick. Boats have been known to end up against the bridge, carried there by the fierce tide. The bridge is lit with a yellow light on the centre support and great care needs to be taken at night or in bad weather when manoeuvring in its vicinity.

Southwold from SE showing recommended track

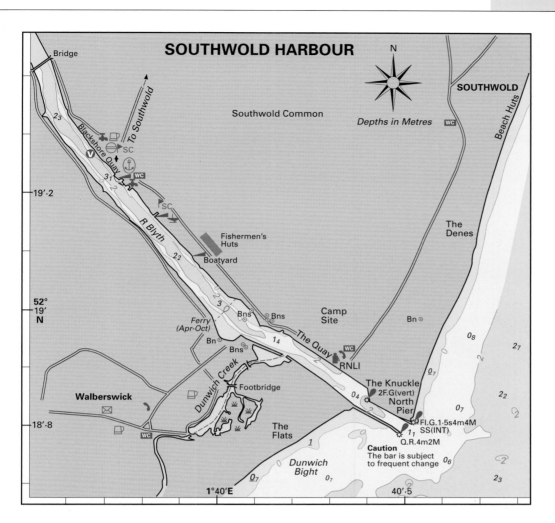

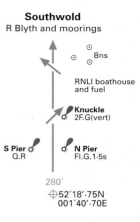

Landmarks

The town of Southwold lies 1M N of the harbour entrance, which is the mouth of the River Blyth. A white lighthouse (Fl.10s.37m24M, MMSI 992351019) stands in a prominent position on top of the low cliff on which the town stands. Also prominent is a Norman-style church built by wealthy local wool merchants. The seafront is marked by rows of colourful beach huts and, further inland, at the back of the marshes, is a large conspicuous concrete water tower.

Approach

From any seaward direction there is clear and deep water to within a short distance of the entrance. Along the coast in both directions the depth runs from 5m close in to 10m or more ½M out. There are no off-lying marks or buoys, so aim for the landfall waypoint. From there the entrance bears about 280°.

Approaching Southwold from N

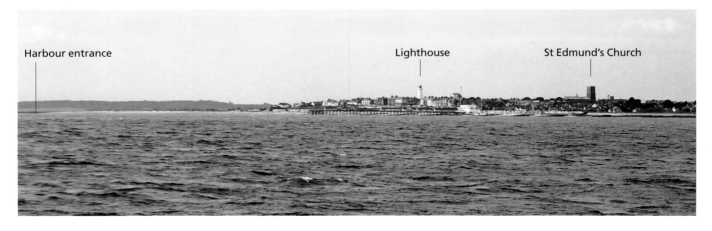

S pier · The Knuckle · RNLI crane · RNLI building · Traffic lights on N pier

Southwold harbour entrance

RNLI · Fuel · Ferry

Southwold harbour looking E from the boatyard

Bridge · Sailing club · HM, WC, Showers · Club slipway

Southwold harbour looking W from the boatyard

Entry

ENTRY SIGNALS:
Three vertical F.R lights or, during daylight, two red flags, mounted on a pole at the end of the N Pier, indicate 'harbour closed'. If displayed, contact Southwold harbourmaster or, if outside the listening hours of 0800–1700, contact Humber Coastguard for advice. Three vertical greens or no flags means it's clear to enter

Entrance is best attempted from 30 min before HW or, if there is sufficient depth, near LW when the coastal tide cross stream is at its slackest. HM will advise on depths over the bar.

The North Pier is marked with a light (Fl.G.1·5s) and the South Pier with a Q.R. Do not stray into the bay N of the North Pier where the water is shallow and the sand bank keeps moving.

Enter along the centreline of the channel parallel to the S pier. The entrance is narrow, 36m, and the stream runs hard both ways, reaching 3-4kn on flood and 5-6kn on ebb. In addition, the coastal tide flows at right angles across the entrance, both rising (southward) and falling (northward) at anywhere between 2·5 and 4kn.

Keep to the middle between the piers as far as the Knuckle (2F.G.(vert)), at the landward end of the N Pier, marked with a 4kn (through the water) speed limit sign mounted on a post, which is in turn mounted on an iron frame jutting out into the entrance.

Just past this, turn hard to starboard and aim to be close alongside and parallel to the concrete retaining wall on the starboard side of the river just before the RNLI station and RIB launching crane. Follow this wall almost to its end then head back into the middle of the river. Keeping close to the wall avoids sand and shingle that's building up on the S side of the channel, but take care to maintain steerage way above the tidal flow, otherwise eddies can swing the boat and push her against the wall. Usually there is at least 2m of water along the wall. At the far end of the wall, a sand spit juts out into the stream to catch the unwary.

Despite the sign on the Knuckle indicating a 4kn speed limit, the Harbour Authority has imposed a maximum speed limit of 'dead slow'. This is described as the minimum speed at which steerage and progress can be maintained and applies from the Knuckle to the bridge at the top of the harbour. The bridge, which carries a yellow

There's a new fuel station on the new north wall

SOUTHWOLD HARBOUR IP18 6TA

Harbourmasters ☎ 01502 724712 (0800–1700H in season)
Contact VHF Ch 12
Callsign *Southwold Port Radio*
   Out of hours call Humber Coastguard on VHF Ch 16
   Email peter.simmons@eastsuffolk.gov.uk
Access 24hr depending on tide, draught and weather
Berthing On stagings and floating pontoons adjacent to Harbour Office. Additional berths can be arranged with Harbour Marine Services ☎ 01502 724721
Facilities WC, Showers
   (Both at Harbour Office and caravan site near harbour entrance, accessed with mooring receipt)
Slipways At boatyard and SC
Electricity Connection points on staging.
Water Taps and hoses on the staging, use cans or own hose
Gas Calor and Gaz at chandler
Repairs 30-T travel hoists and large slip at boatyard
Fuel Arrange with HM. Fuel station close to lifeboat station on N entry wall; red and white diesel
Chandler Next to boatyard at seaward end of foreshore
Phone At pub. Emergency phone at RNLI station
Provisions Some from café near chandler. Shops 1M in town
Pub/restaurant The Harbour Inn ☎ 01502 722381 and in town
Taxi ☎ 01502 722111

The Harbour Inn and visitor moorings

light on the central support, links Southwold with nearby Walberswick on the other side of the river. Vessels exceeding this speed limit will be considered as not complying with ColRegs Rule 6.

All skippers are requested to navigate with caution and to avoid excessive wash, especially near the rowing ferry that operates across the River Blyth about 3 cables from the entrance to the Harbour during summer months. Warning signs are positioned 100m either side of the ferry crossing.

Vessels moving in the harbour are required to keep a listening watch on Ch 12 and to report their intentions and movements to the HM.

SOUTHWOLD

4. Rivers Ore and Alde

⊕ **Landfall waypoint**
52°01'·56N 001°28'·20E Within sight of Orford Haven SWB

Charts
Imray 2000 series, C28
Admiralty Leisure Folio 5607, 2052 and 2695

Tides
Orford Haven Bar Walton -0028
Orford Quay Walton +0040
Slaughden Walton +0105
Iken Cliff Walton +0130

ECP Honorary Port Pilot
(Orford and Ore / Alde entrance)
Philip Attwood ☎ 07528 092635 or
Email orford@eastcoastpilot.com

Main hazards

The entrance to the Ore and Alde is subject to frequent quite massive changes, especially following E gales. Latest information is available via www.eastcoastpilot.com and should be consulted before a planned entry to the rivers. The buoys are taken away for the winter and placed in new positions each spring following a new survey. An entrance chartlet can be downloaded from the *ECP* website.

Ideal time to enter the Ore is about 2hr before HW.

Ore entrance shoals (2014)

Entrance to river Ore Summer 2014

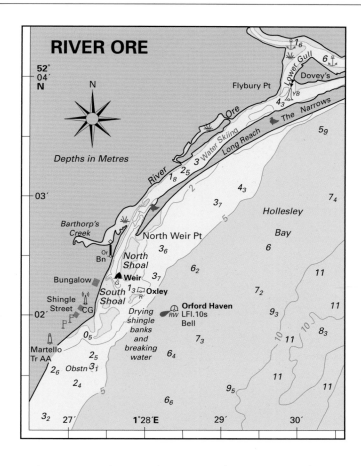

RIVER ORE

52° 04′ N

N

Depths in Metres

03′

02′

Flybury Pt

Lower Gull

Dovey's

1.6

6

4.3

The Narrows

5.9

Hollesley

Bay

7.4

4.3

3.7

5

6

11

Barthorp's
Creek

North Weir Pt

3.6

6.2

North
Shoal

Or
Bn

Bungalow

Weir

3.7

7.2

11

Shingle
Street

South
Shoal

CG

1.3

Oxley

Orford Haven
LFl.10s
Bell

9.3

11

Drying
shingle
banks
and
breaking
water

7.3

10

11

8.3

0.5

6.4

Martello
Tr AA

2.5

2.6

Obstn

3.1

11

11

2.4

9.5

3.2

27′

5

6.6

1°28′E

29′

30′

Streams in the river run strongly, at up to 5kn on spring floods and over 6kn on the ebb.

Entry should not be attempted in strong SE or E winds when seas can break heavily.

Landmarks

Orfordness Lighthouse is prominently conspicuous, especially from N, while the bluff of Bawdsey Cliff, topped with a lattice radar tower, stands out to the S. Trinity House has discontinued the light at Orfordness, although the lighthouse tower itself remains as a good daylight landmark. We do not recommend entry to the Ore after dusk.

Approaching the Landfall Waypoint, the hamlet of Shingle Street appears behind the steep gravel bank due W. To the S stand three Martello towers: the one furthest S stands on the N end of Bawdsey Cliffs, the middle one has a distinctive glass pagoda-like top and the northernmost stands W from the Orford Haven buoy at the S end of the hamlet of Shingle Street. A row of white painted ex-coastguard cottages with a CG radio mast is prominent to the N of the hamlet and marks the entrance.

Entry

From both N and S there's clear and deep water to within a short distance of the entrance. Along the coast in both directions the depth runs from 5m close in to 10m or more only ½M offshore.

Crossing Hollesley Bay from the N, pass the Ness in about 8m of water and about a cable (200 yards) off the shingle and set a course of roughly 235° towards the Orford Haven SWB (RW L.Fl.10s), which should keep you well clear of the Whiting Bank that runs on your port side roughly parallel with the coast.

Pick up the Orford Haven SWB and make directly for the Oxley PHB (unlit) and then to port of the Weir SHB (unlit). It is essential that the first time visitor finds the Orford Haven SWB (L.Fl.10s Bell) and then spots the Oxley PHB to the W and beyond it the Weir SHB close in on the far shore. Follow the buoys in until passing the Weir SHB and turn up river, keeping close to the W shingle bank until approaching Weir Point on the E side of the river. Angle across, keeping an eye on the depth, and run up the E side of the river until past the entrance to drying Barthorp's Creek on the W side of the river, then move over to the centre for the best water.

With wind against tide, heavy seas build up off the entrance and the depth over the bar can alter drastically after SE gales. Obtain the latest available information about the entrance before attempting it and avoid it entirely in strong onshore winds.

Keep well N of the Oxley PHB on approach

Oxley PHB

Weir SHB

Orford Haven SWB

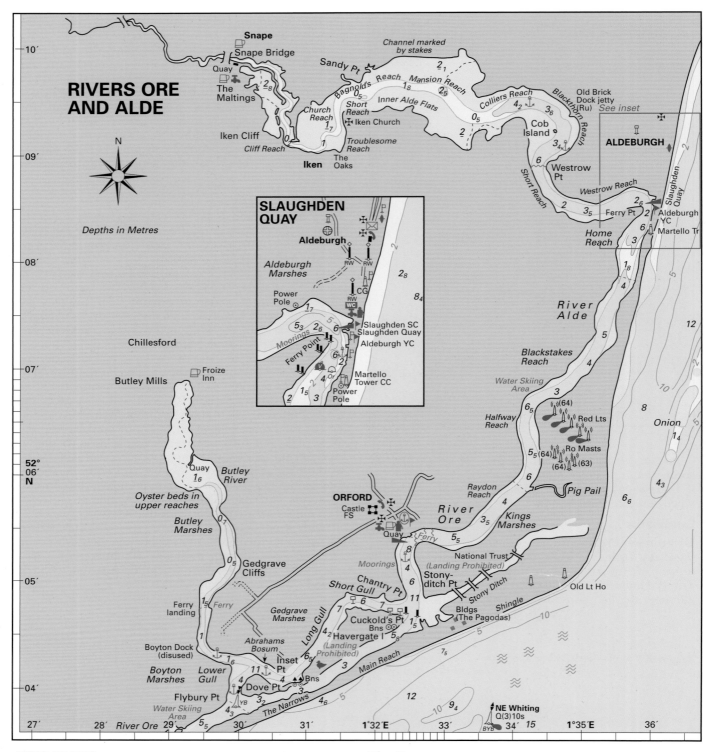

RIVERS ORE AND ALDE

TWO RIVERS

Although one long river, navigable from the entrance right up to Snape Bridge, alongside the famous Snape Maltings concert hall, it's a waterway with two names. From the entrance to about 1M above the village and quay at Orford it's the Ore; from this point in Halfway Reach up to Snape it's the Alde.

The Ore

For much of its length, the Ore divides around Havergate Island, a bird sanctuary that's home to a great variety of wading and marsh birds, including one of the biggest breeding colonies of avocets in Britain. Landing is prohibited.

Having successfully negotiated the entrance to the Ore, the first major landmarks are the incinerator chimney and buildings of the Hollesley Bay Prison on the W bank. There is a short drying creek called Barthorp's

Butley river
entrance.
Keep close to the
N bank

Creek in the W bank, which was used by barges taking produce from the prison farm to London.

The rather featureless Long Reach is a straight stretch of water running NE inside Orford Ness and is a favourite area for water skiing. At the top end of the reach is a SCB marking the S end of Havergate Island. Leaving the buoy to starboard leads you into the Lower Gull where there is a good anchorage under the port bank.

The Butley River branches off NW just beyond the Lower Gull anchorage, but there's a sand spit jutting out from the W bank and the entrance to the creek is well over against the N shore. The channel is marked with withies topped with old paint cans and there are oyster beds in the top half of the creek above the ferry landings, but there's a good anchorage in a little over 2m at LW in the lower reaches of the creek below the disused Boyton Dock.

You can also find good holding ground above the Dock, where the river turns due N for ½M before curving to starboard towards Gedgrave Cliffs, which is about as far as a sea going yacht of any noticeable draught will want to venture. From here on up the riverbed is home to oysters and anchoring is forbidden. Down river of the Cliffs are a number of moorings and it takes a bit of care to wend your way through them, and two long jetties stick out from either side into the river from which an occasional foot ferry operated by volunteers carries walkers and cyclists across.

Past the Butley River entrance, the river runs briefly SE then NE through Long Gull and turns E into Short Gull before joining once more with the other branch that flows S of Havergate Island through Main Reach. There's a good anchorage in Abraham's Bosum, just upriver of the Butley River, and in both Gulls under the lee of Havergate Island. Main reach is virtually a straight cut through the marshes and forms a shorter, but less interesting, route to Orford. Deeper water in this reach is to be found on the E side. There are gradually sloping mudflats extending from the Island.

ORFORD

Approaching Orford from S, the 90ft high Norman Keep, which is all that remains of the once royal castle, stands out to the left of the village, while in the centre is the church proud on the crown of the hill.

The main channel is clearly marked by two lines of moorings each side of the river. There are five moorings laid for visitors, each with an orange pick-up buoy marked 'single visitor'. To find a vacant mooring is sometimes difficult and if you do pick one up, leave someone aboard, don't leave the boat unattended and don't raft up either. Call the Orford HM as you approach the lower moorings and seek his advice.

Don't anchor within the area of the moorings, where the bottom is foul, and don't anchor between the two danger signs either side of the river at the N end of the moorings. These mark pipelines laid in the riverbed taking services

Orford Castle

Comfortable anchorage off Boyton Dock in the Butley River

Orford visitor mooring

Orford Sailing Club

ORFORD   IP12 2NU

Harbourmaster and Quay Warden ① 01394 459950
 ① 07528 092635
 VHF Ch 08 or 16, call sign *Chantry* (0930–1700 in season)
 Email quay@jollyorford.co.uk
Water From standpipes on the quay
Fuel In cans from Friend's garage 0·5M on Front Street
Provisions In village
Pubs/restaurant Several in the village
Post Office/stores/cafe Pump Street
Scrubbing posts Near quay
Telephone Cardphone in car park at back of Orford SC
Slipway At quay. Club slipway at Orford SC
Club Orford SC ① 01394 450997 www.orfordsail.org.uk
Transport Buses to Ipswich and surrounding area

to the National Trust buildings on Orford Ness. It's best to anchor well above or below the main areas of moorings and go ashore by dinghy, but be careful of the swiftly flowing tide. You can stay for a short time alongside the quay, up to an hour or so either side of HW, but watch for the ferry that runs from the quay across to the landing stage on the Ness; other riverboats also use the quay.

Continuing up river from Orford, the next prominent feature is the nest of large BBC World Service radio transmitter masts to starboard. The National Trust owns the marshes surrounding them and landing is strictly forbidden.

It is here, at Pigpail Sluice, that the Ore becomes the Alde.

Orford town quay

The Alde

Under its new name, the river continues in a winding, but generally N direction through rather dull, flat marshland up to Slaughden Quay, which is on the outside of a hairpin bend inland. The first prominent landmark is a Martello Tower on the starboard side where the shingle bank between the river and the sea is hardly more than 50 yards wide. The tower is known as 'CC'.

Slaughden Quay

Slaughden is sited on the apex of the bend in the river, which, having run NNE, now swings almost due W as it heads inland.

Don't anchor at Slaughden within the area of the moorings. A good anchorage can be found in the bay 150 yards S of the club. There are also five visitor moorings just downriver of the club. Visitors are welcome at the club, Aldeburgh YC, and can land at the floating pontoon. There's water available via hosepipe at the end of the pontoon. There's a crowded beaching area between the clubhouse and Slaughden Quay. There are two boatyards: Upson's on the quay and Aldeburgh Boatyard, which lies further back and is a new building, the old one having been burnt down with the loss of some classic yachts early in 2010. Behind Upson's lies the clubhouse of Slaughden SC, which again welcomes visitors when open.

For a longish stay it's worth contacting either Brian Upson or David Cable (see information panel) for a mooring, but expect to have either a longish row or to use an outboard, as the tide is quite strong. Although facilities are limited at Slaughden it's a fairly short walk into the town of Aldeburgh and its well-stocked High Street.

From Slaughden up to Westrow Point the river is lined on either side with moorings and, at the point itself, is crossed by an underwater power cable. Above that, the river turns NE in Island Reach and good places to anchor can be found between Cob Island to port and the Old Brick Dock to starboard or round the corner in Collier's Reach. The steel post on the end of Cob Island has a distinctive swan emblem as a topmark.

At Cob Island the river swings W and widens out into a shallow lake with the winding channel marked by withies. Here too the character of the riverbanks change to well wooded rolling countryside interspersed with arable fields and church steeples reaching skyward, all so characteristic of the Suffolk countryside.

Iken church from Church Reach

From left to right Cob Island post, withies with stbd and port marks

Boats of medium draught can anchor off Iken Church, The Oaks and Iken Cliffs in 1m and 2m of water at low tide. Landing on the Iken shore is restricted and there's only a footpath along the bank to Snape.

Above Iken Cliffs the river winds N and finally NW to the quay and bridge at Snape where the world famous Snape Maltings concert hall stands. It is possible to lie alongside the quay, but it dries at low tide and fender boards are recommended, because the face of the quay is quite rough. Do not moor outside a barge or other flat-bottomed boat, because the ground here slopes and if the inner boat slides, the outer could be pushed over.

SLAUGHDEN QUAY (ALDEBURGH)   IP15 5NA

Boatyards Upson's Boatyard ☏ 01728 453047
    Aldeburgh Boatyard ☏ 01728 452019
Fuel Diesel from Upson's boatyard, petrol in Aldeburgh town
Chandler Aldeburgh Boatyard
Rigger Aldeburgh Boatyard
Visitors' moorings Contact Upson's Boatyard ☏ 01728 453047 or David Cable ☏ 01728 452569.
Electrical engineer Upson's Boatyard
Mechanical engineer Upson's Boatyard
Slipway Upson's Boatyard
Facilities (All at Aldeburgh YC) WC, Showers, Telephone
Club Aldeburgh YC ☏ 01728 452562 www.aldeburghyc.org.uk
Bar/food Aldeburgh YC
Pubs/restaurants Several in town
Water Standpipe on quay and Aldeburgh YC pontoon
Provisions Aldeburgh (about 1M)
Taxi ☏ 01728 833621 and 452142

When planning a trip up river above Cob Island, aim to begin as early on the flood as possible. By doing so, the channel can be picked out more easily and the channel markers understood. Note that these markers come and go from season to season, so once the mud is covered, there may be no marks to guide you or they may be confusing. Starting early may also make a stop at Snape for lunch and a drink at the Plough and Sail possible before hurrying back down to deeper water.

The Maltings   Snape Quay

Snape approaches

5. River Deben

⊕ **Landfall waypoint**
   51°58'·25N 001°24'·20E Near Woodbridge Haven SWB
Deben Entrance
   (Positions July 2014)
   Woodbridge Haven 51°58'·10N 001°23'·70E
   West Knoll   51°58'·28N 001°23'·42E
   Mid Knoll   51°58'·68N 001°23'·38E

Charts
Imray 2000 Series, C28
Admiralty SC5607, 2693

Tides
Woodbridge Haven HW Walton -0002
Waldringfield HW Walton +0020
Woodbridge HW Walton +0040

ECP Honorary Port Pilot
John White ✆ 01394 270106, 07803 476621 or
VHF Ch 08 call sign *Odd Times*
Email deben@eastcoastpilot.com

Hazards

The Deben entrance is subject to frequent changes, especially following E gales. It is essential to obtain the latest information from www.eastcoastpilot.com (which carries a chartlet drawn from the most recent Trinity House survey), the specialist Deben and Ore site www.debenestuarypilot.co.uk or the Woodbridge Cruising Club's site www.woodbridgecruisingclub.org.

The Woodbridge Haven SWB was at 51°58'·10N 001°23'·70E during 2014, but may have been moved since if there have been major changes to the banks. It is essential for the first time visitor to check current information before approaching the entrance and we suggest calling the Felixstowe Ferry HM and *ECP* HPP, John White, for pilotage or advice (see contact details in Felixstowe Ferry or River Deben information panels).

The local boatyard now runs the ferry, which will also act as a water taxi to and from the moorings between its runs across the river. It operates from 1000–1800 throughout the summer months (see River Deben or Felixstowe Ferry information panels for contact details).

The ideal time to enter is about HW -2hr. Streams in the river mouth are quite strong. Entry should not be attempted in strong SE or E winds or at night. Unless you have considerable spare engine power don't try entering against the ebb either, which can run at up to 5kn on springs.

Deben entrance in 2014

Deben Haven

Deben W Knolls

Landmarks

The tall lattice frame of the last remaining radar tower at Bawdsey is the best landmark close to the entrance to this most beautiful river. The entrance lies between Bawdsey Manor, visible in the trees on the E bank and two Martello Towers on the W side of the river.

Entry

From the Woodbridge Haven SWB (Mo(A)15s) steer a course that leaves the West Knoll PHB to port and the Mid Knoll SHB to starboard. *Beware of very strong cross currents, especially on the S going flood, which can push boats onto the S-side shingle spit.*

As you pass the Mid Knoll SHB and turn up river, keep over towards the W shore and, close to the beach, make a hard turn to starboard then keep close in under the shingle bank until at least halfway to the large Deben PHB marking a shingle bank off the Felixstowe Ferry SC.

Felixstowe Ferry approach from seaward

Felixstowe Ferry SC   Felixstowe Ferry landing   Visitor moorings   Deben PHB   Bawdsey landing

At first sight this buoy appears to be almost on the E shingle shore.

Keep well clear of a line of steel posts topped with PH marks standing out from the shingle beach. These mark the ends of groynes and recent erosion has meant they are now well out from the bank. About half way along this waterfront you need to work your way over towards the starboard shingle bank to pass through the relatively narrow deep water gap between the Deben PHB and the Bawdsey shingle shore. (Don't be tempted to follow the local fishermen and shallow draught boats through the gap between the Felixstowe Ferry pier and the Deben PHB – there's not a lot of water and the tide runs very hard just there.)

After passing the Deben buoy, keep over on the starboard bank for the deeper water and slightly less fierce tidal stream. The relatively narrow entrance channel between the shingle banks then opens out into Felixstowe Ferry itself. Close by the Bawdsey shore is a line of four or five visitor moorings, often with boats on them, but the bulk of moorings lie in the channel to the W of Horse Sand.

FELIXSTOWE FERRY

On the W bank lies Felixstowe Ferry with Felixstowe Ferry SC prominent on the bank, just down river from the ferry steps and the slipway to Felixstowe Ferry Boatyard. Close by is an assortment of shacks, mostly used by local fishermen for gear storage, although one is a good fresh fish shop and there's another fresh fish shop at the head of the ferry landing. There's a pair of scrubbing posts on the upstream side of the slipway. There is no public access to the river; launching licences are available either from the harbourmaster or from the boatyard office.

The famous Ferry Café, reputed to serve some of the best fish and chips on the East Coast, stands behind the boatyard, while the yard's owners have opened a new café at the head of the ferry jetty.

On the opposite bank of the river, at Bawdsey, is Bawdsey Manor, which is now a school but was once the centre of radar research. There's a jetty and dinghy slipway and a clean sandy beach. The one-time servicemen's houses along the front are now holiday homes.

FELIXSTOWE FERRY — IP11 9RZ (Ferry Boatyard)

Harbourmasters John White and Stephen Read
℡ 01394 270106 or 07803 476621
VHF Ch 08
Call sign *Odd Times*
Water taxi VHF Ch 08, call sign *Deben Ferry* or ℡ 01394 282173
Facilities WC behind FFSC
Water From standpipe by the boatyard
Chandler At boatyard (limited stock)
Provisions Some at café, otherwise shops in Old Felixstowe 2M
Pubs/restaurant Ferry Boat Inn ℡ 01394 284203
Ferry Café ℡ 01394 276305, fish & chips and all-day breakfasts
Winkles Café
Repairs Felixstowe Ferry Boatyard ℡ 01394 282173
www.felixstoweboats.co.uk
Crane At head of slip. Contact boatyard
Scrubbing posts Close to slip. Contact boatyard
Slipway Contact Harbourmaster
Club Felixstowe Ferry SC ℡ 01394 283785, www.ffsc.co.uk
Telephone Payphone near Ferry Boat Inn
Visitors' moorings Contact Harbourmaster
Taxi ℡ 01394 277777, 275555

Do not anchor in the main channel where the holding is highly suspect and the tide runs extremely strongly. A visit to either Felixstowe Ferry or Bawdsey involves finding a mooring – call the HM for an allocation – or anchoring a mile up river in good holding mud in Sea Reach with a long trip to and fro in the tender.

Above the Ferry, just about in mid-stream, lies the Horse Sand. The deep water channel is on the E side, while the shallower channel on the W side is crammed with moorings. This channel has silted up in recent years restricting the size of boats it can accommodate.

The stretch of water above the last of the moorings and almost as far as the next bend in the river is the only section to which a universal 8kn speed limit does not apply. It is a designated water ski and speedboat area and on the W bank is a semi-pontoon and ski ramp.

The river is clearly defined by the banks here and any buoys are racing marks for either FFSC or the up river Waldringfield SC. This section of the river is also the least exciting visually where it runs between high sea defence banks through Falkenham Marsh to port and low-lying arable land to starboard.

HM   Ferry landing   FFSC   WC   Fish shop   Slipway   Ferry Boat Inn   Café   Chandler   Boatyard

Felixstowe Ferry at twilight

Horse Sand

Sunset over the Deben Horse

At Green Point, where the river turns N and the view of Ramsholt opens out, the Deben reveals its true character with gently rolling slopes covered in woodland and well tended farmland.

RAMSHOLT

Ramsholt stands on the E bank and consists of an old stone barge jetty and a pub, the Ramsholt Arms (IP12 3AB ☎ 01394 411229), plus a red telephone box. There are no services there, but it's a pleasant spot to stretch the legs and 'take refreshment'. For information about moorings contact the HM, George Collins, ☎ 01394 384318 (evenings) or 07930 304061 during the day when he's usually to be found on his own boat *Brio* on a mooring opposite the jetty. There are over 200 moorings at Ramsholt and the fairway is sometimes difficult to identify, but there is good holding in the middle, if you wish to anchor, so long as you don't mind the wash from passing craft.

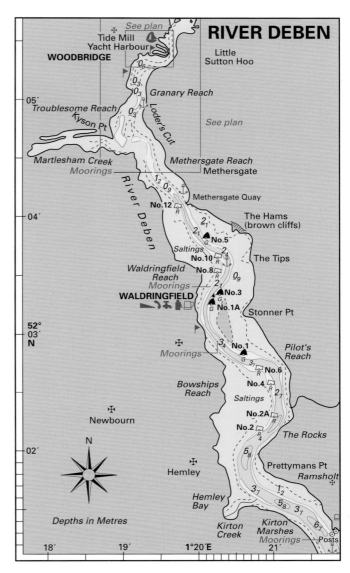

Drying out alongside the jetty by Ramsholt Arms

RIVER DEBEN

Sailing along the wooded shore at The Rocks

THE ROCKS

Above Ramsholt, the channel swings gently W round Kirton marshes, where the drying Kirton Creek joins the river, before heading NE round Prettyman's Point into an area below Ramsholt Woods known as The Rocks, because the riverbed is strewn with them. There is a low sandy cliff forming a sheltered anchorage with a sandy beach for swimming and picnicking, but it's often crowded at weekends. There are no roads or facilities and visitors are requested not to cut down trees to make fires.

Opposite the Rocks is the first of the river buoys, which continue right up to Melton.

The first four buoys are PHBs marking the edge of mudflats extending out from the W shore, pushing the channel well over to the E side of the river until it sweeps back to the W side above No.1 SHB below Waldringfield. Give Nos.4 and 6 a good berth, because the mud and sand spit they mark is growing. Note that all the buoys above Felixstowe Ferry are unlit.

WALDRINGFIELD

No.1 SHB marks the downstream extremity of Stonner Island where the main channel bears to port and is marked by triple lines of moorings all the way through Waldringfield itself.

Vacant moorings are hard to find, however the owners of Waldringfield Boatyard have introduced a novel scheme, using moorings vacated by clients, to each of which is attached a 12ft orange-painted rowing boat with Visitor clearly marked on the sides; oars and rowlocks are attached. Alternatively, ask the HM if he has a spare mooring. Anchoring in the main channel is not recommended, because it is quite narrow, there is much traffic, the bottom's foul and the holding's suspect.

If there is not a vacant mooring available, go up as far as No.3 SHB, at the top of the moorings, and anchor roughly in line with it. Again, such is the pressure for all-tide moorings that this area is now being populated with moorings as well, so be careful anchoring and use a trip line for safety.

There is clean landing on the beach at Waldringfield and there are some pretty walks around the area, but services are limited. There is a pontoon jetty reaching out from the boatyard to which dinghies can be moored during a stroll ashore or a drink or meal at the Maybush, and a river trips boat moors across the end of the pontoon.

WALDRINGFIELD   IP12 4QZ (Boatyard)

Harbourmaster ☎ 01473 736291 / 07925 081062
    Email waldringfieldhm@btinternet.com
Boatyard Waldringfield Boatyard ☎ 01473 736260 VHF Ch 80
Water From taps at boatyard quay or outside sailing club
Fuel Diesel at boatyard (HW only). Petrol in cans from garage 1M up the Woodbridge road
Boat repairs Slipway and 40T crane
Scrubbing posts In front of sailing club
Chandler At boatyard
Telephone Public box near inn
Pub/restaurant The Maybush ☎ 01473 736215
Club Waldringfield SC ☎ 01473 736633
Provisions None
Transport Bus or taxi into Woodbridge or Martlesham

Waldringfield visitor moorings

WOODBRIDGE

Above Waldringfield the river becomes increasingly attractive with wooded banks. It also shallows and, below half tide, great care is needed not to ground. From No.3 SHB, at the N end of Stonner Island, the river runs into a bay at the N end of which are The Hams, brown cliffs with a fine sandy beach, while to the S a promontory called The Tips marks the bay. A spit from the opposite, W, bank is marked by Nos.8 and 10 PHBs. Landing at The Tips is possible, but only for a short period either side of HW.

Passage upriver passing No.12 with Methersgate on starboard side

The river swings over to the other shore just above The Hams and then straightens for the run up past Methersgate on the starboard side. There's another stone jetty here, Methersgate Quay, which was originally used for loading local farm produce into barges, but now landing is strongly discouraged.

From the Quay and No.12 PHB, almost all the way to Woodbridge, the river is marked with both buoys and moorings. There are now so many moorings that it takes considerable care to identify the main channel. At No.14 PHB the river turns 90° to port in Troublesome Reach and heads W towards Kyson Point, which also marks the entrance to Martlesham Creek (drying), before swinging 90° back N again. The saltings that caused these violent changes in direction were cut through in the 1890s to accommodate barges. The cut, called Loder's Cut, can be used by shallow draught (max 1·5 m) craft at about HW ±1hr.

There is a small boatyard, Martlesham Creek Boatyard (www.martleshamcreekboatyard.co.uk), on the S bank of the W-running Martlesham Creek with pontoons, which dry out, and fresh water and power, plus showers and toilets. The yard can launch boats up to 10 tons and offers boat repairs and both inboard and outboard engine servicing.

Roughly half way up Granary Reach, between No.13 SHB and No.16 PHB, the river almost dries at LW, but deepens again as it passes the Deben YC and Everson's Boatyard. From there, through Woodbridge and right up to Wilford Bridge, just above Melton, the river dries to a mere trickle at low water.

Boats unable to take the ground can find a least depth of 2m inside the Tide Mill Harbour, the main marina at Woodbridge, but the sill restricts entrance or exit to HW ±1½hr. Depth over the sill is indicated by a tide gauge marked in metres on the port side of the sill. Those happy to take the mud can moor at the quay at Bass's

Motoring out past Tidemill tide gauge

DYC — St John's Church — Woodbridge Boatyard — WCC — Bass's Dock

Off Deben Yacht Club

St John's
(conspic.)

Robertson's
Boatyard

Suffolk Sails

Lime Kiln Quay

Bass's Dock

Tide Mill

Tide Mill
Yacht Harbour

Woodbridge and the Tide Mill Yacht Harbour

Dock, behind which can be seen the railway station, or along the front of the old Tide Mill Granary. On the end of the dock is the workshop of the late Frank Knights and round the corner the now derelict Whisstock's Boatyard and slipway with the old Ferry Hard stretching right down to the middle of the river bed. (At low water springs you can wade across in calf-deep water.)

Woodbridge is an historic town with a good shopping centre and easy access by bus, taxi or train to Ipswich and onward. Much of the surrounding countryside is well worth a visit and the Sutton Hoo Viking burial site is a major attraction.

Opposite the entrance to the Tide Mill the river narrows under a wooded bank. There are a number of moorings that can be temporarily picked up while

waiting for the tide to give enough clearance over the Tide Mill sill.

Past the marina the river swings W and opens out into a marshy bay on the W side. This is a good place for over-wintering in mud berths. Here also is Robertson's Boatyard and the remains of an old Lime Kiln and attendant quay.

There are a small marina and a boatyard at Melton: the Granary Marina and Richard Larkman's laying up yard. Craft capable of taking the ground now have a well-buoyed, if rather tortuous, channel right up to Wilford Bridge, the point of final navigation on the Deben. Anyone staying in the Tide Mill Marina should consider taking the dinghy and exploring the upper reaches and even ducking under Wilford Bridge into

Looking up river above the Tidemill

Robertson's Boatyard   Limekiln Quay

Melton

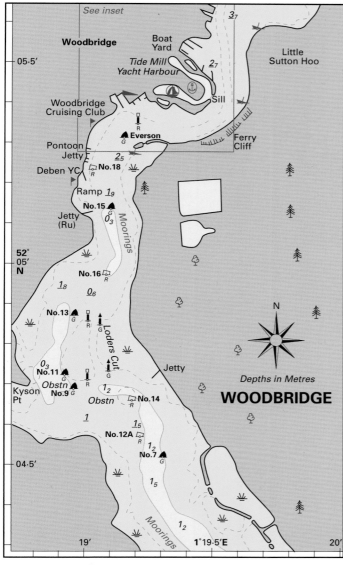

WOODBRIDGE

Depths in Metres

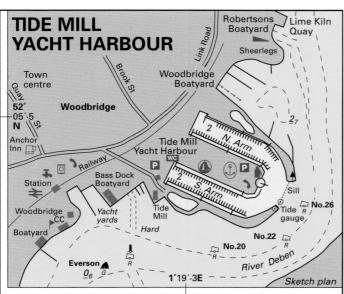

TIDE MILL YACHT HARBOUR

Sketch plan

some pretty countryside up to Ufford. Remember though, the river virtually dries at low water, the mere trickle left being almost fresh water.

TIDE MILL YACHT HARBOUR   IP12 1BP

Contact VHF Ch 80
Callsign *Tide Mill Yacht Harbour*
℡ 01394 385745
Email info@tidemillyachtharbour.co.uk
www.tidemillyachtharbour.co.uk (includes useful daily predictor of heights over the sill)
Access: HW±1½hr
Facilities WC, Showers, Launderette, WiFi (only close to the HM's office)
Water On pontoons
Electricity On pontoons (adaptor required from office)
Gas Calor and Gaz
Telephone At railway station
Boat repairs 16T crane. Several boatyards, see below
Fuel Diesel on berth at entrance
Chandler A few basics on site
Sailmaker Suffolk Sails ℡ 01394 386323 outside marina gate
Rigger Atlantic Rigging ℡ 01394 610324
Provisions: In town, 10 minutes
Pubs/restaurants In town
Taxi ℡ 01394 380034, 386661

YACHT CLUBS AT WOODBRIDGE

Deben YC ℡ 01349 385400
Woodbridge CC ℡ 01394 386737
Facilities WC, Showers, Bar (at weekends only)

BOATYARDS AROUND WOODBRIDGE

Woodbridge Boatyard ℡ 01394 385786
Crane, slipway

Robertson's ℡ 01394 382305
Boat repairs Two slipways, crane, rigging
Facilities WC
Water On quay
Electricity On quay

Granary Yacht Harbour (Melton) ℡ 01394 386327
www.granary-yacht-harbour.co.uk
Boat repairs 36-T boat hoist
Berthing By prior arrangement.

R Larkman, Melton ℡ 01394 382943
Wintering yard with small chandler
Crane 9-T crane for lifting boats over sea wall
Limited facilities

6. Harwich

⊕Landfall waypoint
  51°55'·23N 001°18'·39E SW of Landguard NCB (Q) on
  recommended yacht track

Charts
Imray 2000 series, C1, Y16
Admiralty SC5607, 1491, 2693

Tides
Walton HW +0005

Harbourmaster
Harwich Port Control Ch 71
Call sign *Harwich VTS*
Harbourmaster ✆ 01255 243030

Port control

Harwich Harbour is accessible at all times, but it is imperative that small craft keep clear of the main shipping channels and berthing manoeuvres of container ships. The harbour authority maintains a round the clock radar and radio watch (on Ch 71) and all yachts are requested to listen on this channel from Landguard to Fagbury, on the River Orwell, and to past Erwarton Ness bn on the Stour. Call on Ch 71 only in an emergency, such as being unable to get out of the way of an announced shipping manoeuvre.

The authority also produces an excellent yachtsmen's guide detailing the recommended yacht tracks, which is available from local marinas and chandlers or by writing to Harwich Haven Authority, Harbour House, The Quay, Harwich CO12 3HH ✆ 01255 243030. Harbour launches also patrol the harbour.

Approaches to Harwich and recommended yacht track

Colchester smack *Quiz* sailing in Harwich Harbour

Landmarks

Harwich Harbour is the largest container port in the UK and following extensions to the Felixstowe quays is bigger and busier than ever. The most prominent landmarks are the huge blue cranes that stretch the length of the Trinity and Felixstowe South Quays, all along the E side of the harbour.

On a clear day, from the Landfall Waypoint, the disused lighthouse on the Dovercourt Beach is visible, looking rather like a pale coloured, over large dovecote on stilts at the back of the beach. The tall steeple of Harwich Town church, together with the white roof of the Ro-Ro shed on the end of Harwich Quay make good aiming points. On the E side of the entrance is a beacon

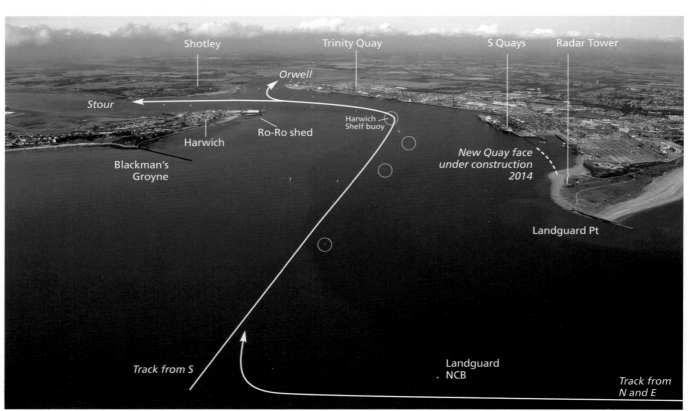

(SCM) on the tip of Landguard with, just inland, the lower fortifications of Landguard Fort, as well as one of the several radar towers (white) that are dotted about the harbour.

Main hazards

Big ships and ferries.

Work on the building of Felixstowe South Quay, on the E side of the harbour, has resulted in an almost uninterrupted quay face from Landguard Beach to the N end of Trinity Quay opposite Babergh PHB in the mouth of the Orwell. From several miles out to sea the veritable forest of blue container cranes make the harbour conspicuous. Beware of big ships swinging round to face seawards when berthed.

Look out for and keep well clear of large container ships using the deep water channel and turning onto and off berths in the harbour

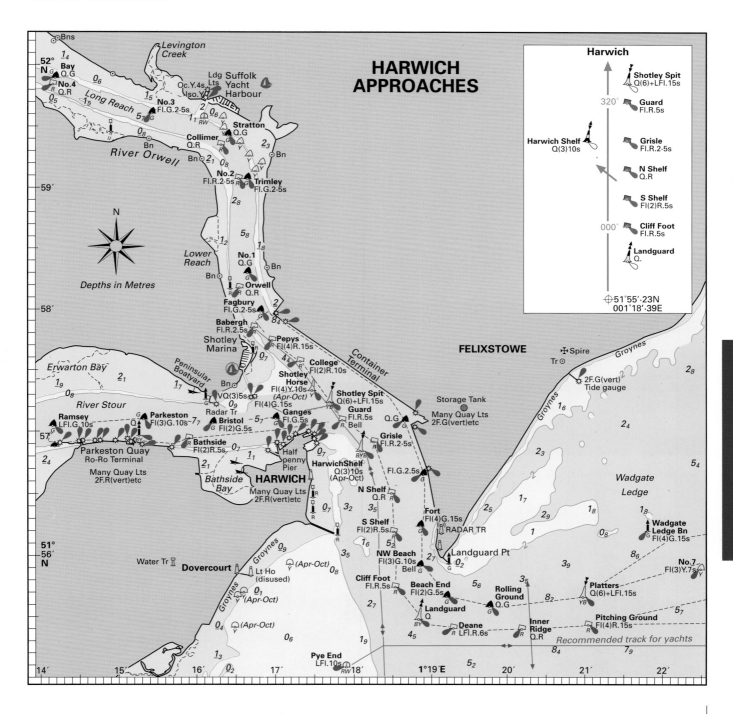

Harwich Shelf ECB is hard to spot, especially at night

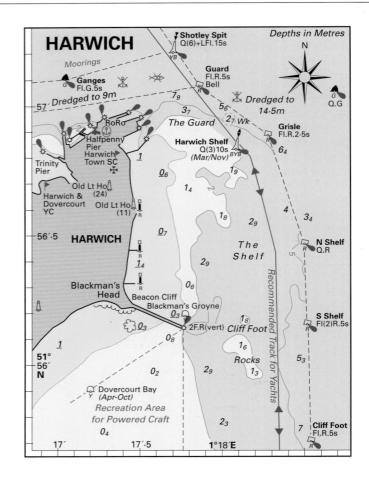

There are areas of shallow water in the harbour that need care and attention, including the Harwich Shelf on the W side of the entrance and the Shotley Spit, which is marked by Shotley Spit SCB (Q(6)+LFl. 15s) in the centre of the harbour.

At the entrance to the harbour, beware the Cliff Foot Rocks patch E of the end of Blackman's Breakwater on the W side of the approach. The bottom is foul at LW and there are strong eddies. Further in, keep to starboard of the seasonal (March to November) Harwich Shelf ECB (Q(3)10s), which marks the E limit of the Harwich Shelf – at LWS it all but dries in the centre.

Approaches

The approaches to Harwich are well marked. In particular, the deep water shipping channel is heavily buoyed, but, because of the number, tonnage and size of shipping using the channel, there are recommended yacht entry tracks shown on charts, which must be used. All of them converge on the Landfall Waypoint, roughly halfway between the Landguard NCB (Q) and Pye End SWB (L.Fl.10s).

Harwich RoRo shed is a conspicuous landmark

Harwich town beach from Guard buoy

Once round Landguard and squaring up to enter harbour, a good point to aim for is the white roof of the Ro-Ro shed at the seaward end of the Navy Yard at Harwich. About opposite the Redoubt Fort marked on the chart, turn a few degrees to starboard and aim for the Harwich Shelf ECB. It's quite a small buoy and is often difficult to spot against the background of ships and quays. Although lit (Q(3)10s), it's drowned at night by the working lights on the container quays and care is needed to identify it.

The working lights on the quays and ships themselves can be seen many miles out to sea and make a night entrance difficult, especially from the N and E. If in serious doubt, make S to the Medusa SHB (Fl.G.5s), which lies E from Walton on the Naze, and return N towards Harwich using the Medusa Channel past the Stone Banks PHB (Fl.R.5s). It adds distance but can be the easier approach.

In spite of the background light pollution problems, Harwich is an all-weather, all-tide, 24hr, remarkably easy harbour to enter.

From seawards In daylight and after a North Sea crossing, yachts will pick up the Cork Sand Bn (Fl(3)R.10s) or the nearby Cork Sand Yacht Bn NCM (VQ) and, keeping S of the deep water channel, proceed to pass well to port of Landguard NCB (Q) to keep well clear of the bend in the shipping channel.

From N Perhaps having departed the Rivers Ore and Alde or Deben, pass close to Wadgate Ledge SHM (Fl(4)G.15s) and cross the deep water channel at right angles between the Platters SCB (Q(6)+L.Fl.15s) and the Rolling Ground SHB (QG) to join the recommended yacht track coming in from E.

Harwich Haven Authority recommends crossing the deepwater channel between waypoints 51°55′·83N 001°20′·29E on the N side of the channel and 51°55′·23N 001°20′·39E on the S side, to give the shortest right angle crossing.

Approaching from S Follow a course of about 345° from the Medusa SHB (Fl.G.5s) through the Medusa Channel to pass close to the Stone Banks PHB (Fl.R.5s) and join the recommended yacht track at the Landfall Waypoint or, at most, three cables S of Landguard NCB (Q).

Yachts approaching Harwich from almost due E and from the direction of the Galloper will have to negotiate the Sunk Gyratory System. Navigate in this area using only the latest charts on which the system's buoyage and traffic separation lanes are marked. Close approach (pilotage) to Harwich Harbour will be by either the S route through the Medusa Channel or the N route via Cork Sand Yacht Bn.

Inside the Cork Sand to the E and the shipping channel to the N and extending SW into Dovercourt Bay are a number of yellow seasonal racing marks.

Entry

Progress through the harbour must be via the recommended yacht tracks shown on current charts. At the Guard PHB (Fl.R.5s Bell) either turn W along the Harwich waterfront to reach the moorings at Halfpenny Pier or cross the mouth of the Stour to Shotley Spit SCB (Q(6)+L.Fl.15s).

At that buoy, turn W either to enter Shotley Marina or to proceed on up the River Stour, keeping to the Shotley side until clear of Parkeston Quay, or continue N from Shotley Spit into the River Orwell. Keep close watch on the depth anywhere near Shotley Spit.

HARWICH HARBOUR

The only facilities for yachts at Harwich are at Halfpenny Pier. From the Guard PHB make W past the Ro-Ro terminal and Halfpenny Pier lies to port. The approach is clear, but beware of swells from passing ships while going alongside.

There are two yacht clubs based at Harwich: Harwich Town SC, which is a dinghy racing club with a clubhouse overlooking the main harbour, and Harwich and

Berthing at Halfpenny (above) and skipper's eye view of approach to the pier with entrance to basin on the right (below)

Foot ferry berth   Town Hall   Entrance

HARWICH

HARWICH AND DOVERCOURT SC

Contact ☎ 01255 508408 www.hdsc.org.uk
Clubhouse on landing barge (LBK6) alongside quay
Access HW±2hr
Visitors' moorings Two
Facilities WC
Water On quayside
Telephone In club
Provisions In nearby town centre

HALFPENNY PIER   CO12 3HH

Harbourmaster ☎ 01255 243030
Berth Alongside pontoons. Watch for wash from passing ships.
    No charge for short stay, but charges apply overnight
Facilities Water and electricity on pier and showers by
    arrangement, see HM
Provisions In town
Pubs/restaurants Nearby in town
Sailmaker Dolphin Sails ☎ 01255 243366
Chandler In town
Taxi ☎ 01255 503000
Note Harwich Navy Yard has no facilities for yachts. The pilots
    and harbour launches use it

Dovercourt SC, which is a cruising club. Its headquarters are at the top of Gashouse Creek, a drying gutway between the Trinity House jetty and Bathside Bay.

There is a water taxi between Harwich Town, Felixstowe (Landguard beach) and Shotley Marina. Details and timetable from Harwich Harbour Ferry Services ☎07919 911440 www.harwichharbourferry.com.

SHOTLEY MARINA

On reaching the centre of Harwich Harbour close to Guard PHB (Fl.R.5s Bell), a low building will be seen off the port bow, which carries the word 'Marina' in large letters. It's at Shotley Marina. Other landmarks behind the marina include a tall white mast at the old HMS *Ganges* naval base and a huge once-green water tower.

Entry to Shotley is via a dredged channel (2m at MLWS) and a lock providing 24hr access. Approach from Shotley Spit SCB, running parallel to the deep water channel towards Ganges SHB (Fl.G.5s). When close to this buoy, turn to starboard and pass between a pair of top-marked beacons, which are lit Fl(4)G.15s on the starboard hand one and VQ(3)5s on the port hand ECM. From these beacons, the channel into the lock runs on a bearing of about 340°.

Locking into the marina is governed by traffic lights (red and green) and there is a waiting pontoon, which is also used by the water taxi, to port on the outside of the entrance. There is an INOGON directional leading light mounted on the starboard lock knuckle with lit arrows to keep approaching craft on line up the narrow approach channel. If the arrows point to the left, steer to port, or if they point to the right, steer to starboard, to maintain your track up the channel.

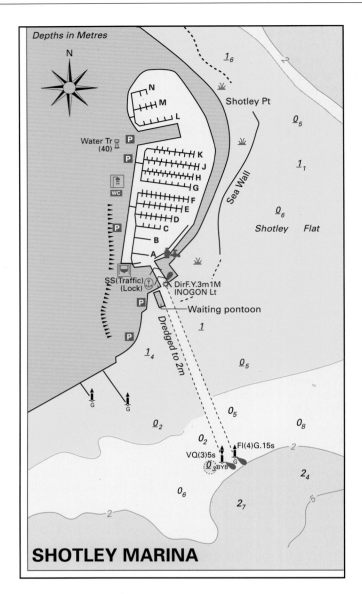

SHOTLEY MARINA

Locking in to Shotley marina

SHOTLEY MARINA

IP9 1QJ

Contact ☎ 01473 788982 VHF Ch 80
Call sign *Shotley Marina*
 www.eastcoastmarinas.co.uk
 Email miriam@shotleymarina.co.uk
Max Size (lock) 20m x 6.5m x 2.2m, (berth) 20m
 on hammerhead only
Facilities WC, Showers and baths, Launderette,
 WiFi
Water On pontoons
Electricity On pontoons
Gas Calor and Gaz
Chandler On site
Fuel From berth immediately to starboard inside lock (24hr)
Provisions From chandler in summer, local shop/PO at Shotley
 Gate 10 mins walk
Bar/restaurant The Shipwreck ☎ 01473 788865
Boat repairs Shotley Marine Services ☎ 01473 788982.
 40-T boat hoist, 20-T crane
Transport Water taxi to Harwich and Felixstowe ☎ 07919 911440
 www.harwichharbourferry.com
 Bus service from Shotley Gate (10 mins walk) to Ipswich
Taxis ☎ 01473 222222, 01473 407777, 01473 255555

HARWICH AREA CONTACTS

Harwich Haven Authority ☎ 01255 243030
Harwich Harbour Control (VTS) ☎ 01255 243000

Radio watch

Inbound to Harwich from the landfall waypoint, the Pye End buoy or Wadgate Ledge beacon, yachts should monitor VHF Ch 71 and maintain a listening watch until they pass Fagbury on the Orwell or Erwarton Ness beacon on the Stour. In the Orwell, monitor Ch 68 above Fagbury.

Entering Shotley Marina lock

Entrance to Shotley Marina lock,
green traffic light and Inogon directional light

7. River Stour

⊕ **Landfall waypoint**
51°55'·20N 001°18'·50E SW of Landguard NCB on
recommended yacht track

Charts
Imray 2000 Series, C28
Admiralty SC5607, 1491, 1594, 2693

Tides
Walton HW
Mistley Quay HW Walton +0025

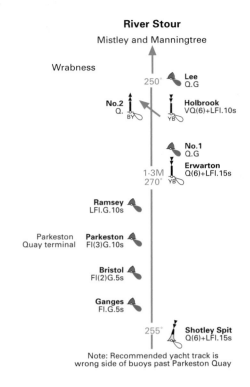

Introduction

The Stour, which forms the boundary between Suffolk
and Essex, is one of the most attractive waterways on the
East Coast, arguably running a close second to the River
Deben. Less populated than the latter it is nevertheless an
integral part of the 20-odd square miles of sheltered
water within the Harwich Haven area. When winds
blow hard from E or W you take to the Orwell, but if it's
blowing from N or S, the Stour comes into its own,
offering sheltered anchorages and good holding for most
of its length.

Entering the Stour from Harwich Harbour

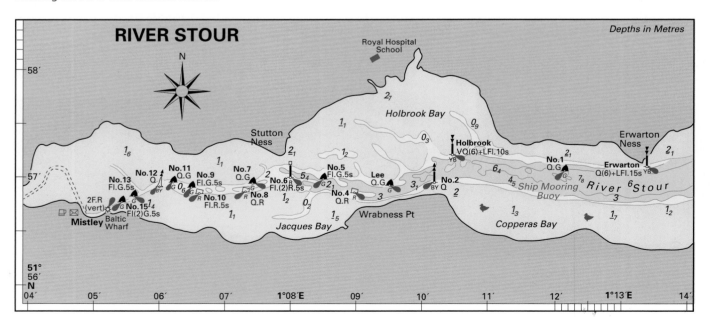

The old Ganges Pier with its white radar tower

Landmarks and Approach

After crossing to the N side of the main shipping channel at the Guard PHB (Fl.R.5s Bell), turn W at Shotley Spit SCB (Q(6)+L.Fl.15s). Pass Shotley Marina control and workshop buildings to starboard (the roof of the workshop is marked MARINA in big black letters), below the Ganges Cliff, on top of which is a conspicuous pale green water tower.

The next landmark to starboard is the old Ganges jetty with a white radar tower on the seaward end. Between Shotley Spit and the jetty are a number of unlit ships' mooring buoys, often with a couple of Trinity House light vessels awaiting refit.

Around the Ganges and Shotley jetties are several yacht moorings that extend up river into Erwarton Bay. Over on the S side of the river is the Harwich International Port (Parkeston Quay), where the ferries berth. At the lower end is a wind farm rig berth and at the up river end is an oiling wharf with a major fuel storage depot behind it. This area marks the change from Harwich Harbour to the River Stour proper. The river here is subject to an 8kn speed limit.

River Stour to Erwarton Ness

Continue W outside the N edge of the deep water channel, leaving the two SHBs Parkeston (Fl(3)G.10s) and Ramsey (L.Fl.G.10s) to port. This course gives ships room to swing when entering or leaving their berths.

The river is at its widest here where it opens out into Erwarton Bay on the N side. You may find a couple of ungainly looking rigs anchored in the bay just below Erwarton Ness. Don't go too close, because they lie to four anchors, one at each corner. Watch out too for tug traffic in the area.

Sailing past the oil depot on the Stour's S bank

At the W end of Erwarton Bay is Erwarton Ness with a SCM (Q(6)+L.Fl.15s). Erwarton is a popular anchorage, although it lacks shelter in either E or W winds. There's good holding up river from the beacon, but take care down river where there can be patches of kelp. There's good clean landing on a sand and shingle beach at HW ±1½hr and a slightly muddy landing can be made at other times using an old barge hard that extends out from the shore to the base of the Ness Bn, almost to LW. There are several footpaths along the foreshore, one of which goes N across the fields to the village of Erwarton.

In S winds, if the Erwarton anchorage becomes uncomfortable, it is possible to find shelter across on the S shore in Copperas Bay in 4-6m of water.

From Erwarton the river runs almost straight for a good two miles with the deepest water a little N of the centre line with only one particular hazard to watch out for – a large ships' mooring buoy on the S side of the channel, W of Erwarton Ness.

Erwarton SCM

Ramsey SHB at start of Stour

Erwarton to Wrabness

About ¾M W of Erwarton Ness SCM is the first SHB, No.1 (Q.G). Around 1M further W there's a pair of beacons. One is the Holbrook Beacon SCM (VQ(6)+L.Fl.10s) to starboard and the other is No.2 Beacon NCM (Q) to port. The pair acts as a gateway to Wrabness.

The Holbrook Beacon also marks the entrance to the drying Holbrook Creek. This little waterway meanders N across Holbrook Bay towards the palatial buildings and prominent clock tower of the Royal Hospital School

Royal Hospital School, Holbrook, dominates the N shore

Holbrook Creek and moorings

No 2 NCM E of Wrabness

standing on the N shore. At the top right corner of the bay are a popular wind- and kite-surfing area and moorings for local boats.

There are two or three moorings laid in the lower reaches of the Creek. Anchoring positions are best found below half tide and by careful depth sounding.

WRABNESS

There are many moorings at Wrabness, which is marked by a plethora of beach huts under a low cliff on the wooded S bank. It is usually possible to pick up an empty mooring for a short stay and anchoring in the main channel is not recommended, because the holding is poor and it's used by small coasters bound to or from the Baltic Wharf at Mistley.

On the other side of the channel, opposite the cliffs, lies No.3 SHB (Q.G.), designated Lee. Do not stray N of this mark, because it shallows very quickly and even at high tide there's little depth of water.

Most other parts of the river offer good holding in some wonderfully glutinous East Coast mud and some of this can be found above the Wrabness moorings towards No.4 PHB (Q.R).

Wrabness can be uncomfortable in E or W winds against tide

No.6 PHM

Wrabness to Mistley and Manningtree

The river is well marked all the way to Mistley, largely to assist the coasters that use the waterway, and it is essential to avoid sailing too far away from the buoyed channel, because the whole area dries extensively. This is another East Coast area where visitors are advised to set off up river before the mud banks are covered and to be awarethat buoys can be blown across the banks they are marking.

Leaving Wrabness and carrying the tide with you, pass No.5 SHB (Fl.G.5s) to starboard and aim for the No.6 beacon (Fl(2)R.5s) about ¾M above the Wrabness moorings. It marks the N edge of the Smith Shoal, which moves the channel and best water well over towards the N side of the river at Stutton Ness. There's a good anchorage opposite No.6 under Stutton Ness, which has a sandy beach that can be reached by dinghy and is popular for picnics.

Leaving No.6, the channel is well buoyed and fairly straight with the buoys all well within sight of each other. Deeper draught boats should keep pretty well to the channel, although it's often tempting to follow a small bilge keel or centreplate cruiser gaily tramping across wide expanses of open water between Smith Shoal and Ballast Hill. Unless you have good local knowledge or are sure of your depth sounder and have an adventurous spirit, don't try it. You could find yourself stuck on some really sticky mud or some very hard gravely ground from which the aptly named Ballast Hill

gets its name. In days of yore barges would settle on the hill and load shingle ballast.

The channel now dives SW towards Mistley Quay at the No.12 NCB (Q) at Ballast Hill. Head for Nos.13 (Fl.G.5s) and 15 (Fl(2)G.5s) SHBs and the Quay lies straight ahead. Keep close to the quay, because the whole area to starboard dries at low water.

Yachts used to lie alongside Mistley Quay at HW ±1½hr, depending on draught, the bottom being fairly level soft mud, but landing is now strictly forbidden and made impossible by a 6ft high steel mesh fence installed along the outer edge of quay. Unfortunately the bollards are within this fence, so finding a ring or projection to secure to and rest before heading back down river is nigh on impossible.

Mistley Marine (VHF Ch 71, ☎ 01206 392127, 07850 208918) runs a small drying marina on the S bank just down river from the Baltic Wharf (where small coasters unload building materials and general cargoes). Mistley Marine also runs a small boatyard and marine engineering works and operates a dredging barge. River moorings and quayside moorings dry out. There are no toilet or shower facilities.

With care and a shallow draught, it's possible to reach ½M beyond Mistley to Manningtree at HW and visit the Stour SC (CO11 1AU ☎ 01206 393924, website www.stoursailingclub.co.uk) with its waterfront clubhouse, small hard jetty and slipway. Visitors are few, but increasing, as people get to know about this attractive little town that has all a crew needs close to hand, including pubs, restaurants, shops, banks and a train service to London.

Approach Manningtree by following the channel buoys carefully and remember that the whole area dries soon after HW. Boats with a draught greater than 1·5m need to avoid a nasty sand bank some 50m in front of the Stour SC clubhouse and quay. The advice is to skirt along the line of moorings.

Manningtree is the head of the navigable Stour and is also on the doorstep of the Dedham Vale and 'Constable country'.

No.12 NCB

Landing at Mistley Quay is no longer allowed. A local haulage firm has closed it off by installing a steel mesh fence

8. River Orwell

⊕ **Landfall waypoint**
51°55'·20N 001°18'·50E
SW of Landguard NCB on recommended yacht track

Charts
Imray 2000 Series, C28, Y16
Admiralty SC5607, 1491, 2693

Port Authority
ABP (From Fagbury to Ipswich Wet Dock)
Ipswich harbourmaster ☎ 01473 231010
Ipswich lockmaster ☎ 01473 213526

VHF Channels
Monitor port operations Ch 71 from Pye End to Fagbury
Monitor port operation Ch 68 from Fagbury to Ipswich

Tides
Harwich HW Walton +0005
Ipswich HW Walton +0025

Hazards

The Orwell carries a busy mix of commercial and leisure traffic, everything from general cargo boats to Thames Barges, East Coast smacks and several hundred small craft, all bustling about day and night. The danger for visiting yachtsmen is the commercial traffic, which is very quiet and a sharp lookout must be kept astern. Ships are constrained by draught and yachts must keep well clear. If a ship is manoeuvring near the docks it is frequently best for yachts to heave to and wait until passage is clear again.

The port authority (ABP) has warned of the danger of wash and the subsequent draw down effect from passing ships in the river at LW, especially at LWS. They are particularly concerned about possible swamping of tenders or the temporary grounding of yachts and urge great caution together with the wearing of lifejackets when going to and from moorings and the shore.

If anchoring anywhere in the Orwell, keep clear of the main channel. Remember to display a black ball during the day and a riding light at night, but it is also advisable to do the same if lying to a mooring, because it tells the skippers and pilots of passing ships that there are people on board. This advice is the result of some 'incidents' between ships and moored and anchored yachts in the past.

The river is subject to an 8kn speed limit decreasing to 6kn above Woolverstone.

The Orwell – lower reaches

The River Orwell, or the Ipswich River as it's often known locally, is attractive and remarkably unspoilt, yet increasingly commercial. It is 9M from the end of the Trinity Quay at Harwich to the lock gates into Ipswich Wet Dock and getting on for ½M wide in places at HW.

Because of the commercial shipping, the main channel has been dredged to a depth of 5.6m at LW and is about 400m (2 cables) wide. Gently rising mudflats merge into either narrow sandy beaches or heavily wooded banks on either side.

Entering the Orwell from Harwich Harbour, stay W outside the dredged channel, leaving the Guard PHB (Fl.R.5s Bell) to starboard and, after crossing the narrowest part of the deep water channel, leave the Shotley Spit SCB (Q(6)+L.Fl.15s) also to starboard, then leave the Shotley Horse buoy (Fl(4)Y.10s) close to port. This buoy is a yellow turning mark that allows yachts to turn in deep water without having to go round Shotley Spit SCB and stray into the main harbour channel. From Shotley Horse make about NW towards the College PHB (Fl(2)R.10s).

Leave College close to starboard. It marks the W edge of the deep water channel opposite the Trinity container berths and is there for big ships. There's plenty of depth between the buoy and the Shotley Spit, which runs out from Shotley Point (roughly half way along the marina retaining wall) to Shotley Spit SCB.

The changeover from Harwich Harbour Authority to Associated British Ports is at the Fagbury SHB (Fl.G.2·5s) off Fagbury Point, close N of the container berths. Nearby is a clearly marked underwater cable, which must be avoided if anchoring to await the tide.

The river is well buoyed and generally there is plenty of room and water outside the channel to avoid large vessels (which have total right of way and often use their horn to assert it). Remember most of them have to do 8-10kn just to maintain steerage way in what is quite a winding and confined channel.

The deep water channel has been pushed further over to the Shotley bank by developments and extensions of the Trinity Quay and a PHB, Babergh (Fl.R.2·5s), has been installed between the Pepys and Orwell PHBs, almost opposite the first SHB, Fagbury (Fl.G.2·5s). Once past the end of Trinity Quay you are in the Orwell proper.

To port, a little N of Shotley Marina, the river opens out into a gentle bay, called Stone Heaps, the name being a legacy from the old barging days, which offers a good anchorage, if a little rough when ships pass. The holding is good, water is plentiful at all states of tide and a shingle beach offers clean landing for a walk round the back of the marina to shops at Shotley Gate.

Sailing gently up the pretty River Orwell

Trimley Marshes

Trimley Marshes lie on the E side behind a raised flood protection bank. Once a marshy bird sanctuary, they have been excavated and flooded by breaching the sea wall to make a proper wetland for wading birds. A walk along the wall with binoculars is always rewarding for birdwatchers.

Upriver of the opening in the sea wall is the start of a line of small boat moorings, which leads into Trimley Bay. Landing is possible at HW on a sandy beach backed by cliffs. It's a popular place to picnic and swim, but the bay is also a designated speedboat and water-ski area.

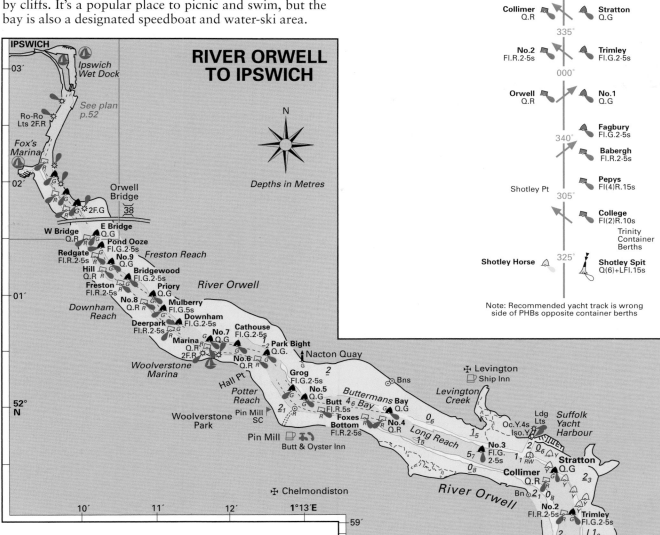

The down river end of Trimley Bay is marked by the Trimley SHB (Fl.G.2·5s) and on the opposite (W) side of the channel is No.2 PHB (Fl.R.2·5s), which marks the start of the NW bend in the river round Collimer Point.

Off Collimer Point is a PHB marked Collimer (Q.R) and a SHB marked Stratton (Q.G). On the W bank also is a tide gauge giving the depth of water over the natural riverbed. Inshore of it are the remains of one of the many old barge hards once in regular use on the river. The river turns NW at this point.

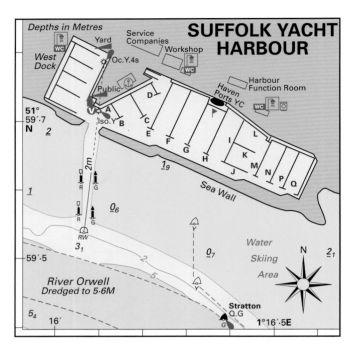

SUFFOLK YACHT HARBOUR

Depths in Metres

West Dock
Yard
Service Companies
Workshop
Oc.Y.4s
Public
Harbour Function Room
Haven Ports YC
51° 59'.7 N
Iso.Y
A
B
C
D
E
F
G
H
I
J
K
L
M
N
P
Q
2m
R
G
R
G
RW
Sea Wall
2
1 9
0 6
3 1
59'.5
1
Water Skiing Area
N
2 1
0 7
River Orwell Dredged to 5·6M
5 4
16'
Stratton Q.G
G
1°16'·5E

SUFFOLK YACHT HARBOUR   IP10 0LN

Contact VHF Ch 80
Callsign *Suffolk Yacht Harbour*
Harbourmaster ☎ 01473 659465/240
   Email enquiries@syharbour.co.uk
   www.syharbour.co.uk
Access 24hr
Facilities WC, Showers, Launderette, WiFi (PAYG)
Water On pontoons
Electricity At each berth
Fuel Diesel and petrol from berth at entrance
Chandler On site
Provisions Some from chandler
Gas Calor and Gaz
Boat repairs Slipways (two), 80-T and 10-T boat hoist, 20-T crane
Scrubbing posts At head of West Dock, turn to port at entrance
Shipwrights On site
Sailmaker On site
Electrical engineers On site
Rigger On site
Engineer On site
Electronics On site
Club Haven Ports YC (in old light vessel in marina)
   ☎ 01473 659658
Pub/restaurant Ship Inn, Levington (1 mile) ☎ 01473 659573

Suffolk Yacht Harbour (SYH)

The first major landing point on the river is at Suffolk Yacht Harbour, a few hundred yards down river from the entrance to Levington Creek (drying) on the starboard bank. The entrance to the marina is a well dredged, 30m wide by 2m deep (at LWS) channel, marked with a SWB at the start of the approach channel then port and starboard hand posts with fluorescent topmarks along the channel. Tides set across the channel and care is required not to be pushed onto the posts, especially at springs. They are substantial steel tubes and will do serious damage to topsides.

At night there are leading lights (outer Iso.Y and inner Oc.Y.4s); the lower light is on a post behind and slightly to port of the visitor's berths and the upper on a taller post near the head of the West Dock, their transit gives an approach up the starboard side of the entrance channel (see chartlet) from the SWB. Changes to the security lighting in the marina have made them easier to distinguish at night.

Visitors' berths and the after hours harbourmaster's office lie directly opposite the entrance with the fuel berth just to starboard. To port is the main slipway and the entrance to the West Harbour used by large yachts.

Suffolk Yacht Harbour nestles behind a raised sea wall

SYH is in an isolated location 1M from the nearest bus stop to Ipswich and Felixstowe, but food and drink are available to visitors in the marina aboard LV87, the lightship home of the Haven Ports YC. There is also the Ship Inn at the village of Levington 1M away.

SYH has an imposing harbour office combining chandler and commercial offices.

Levington Creek

Leaving SYH and travelling up river, the next buoy, No.3 SHB (Fl.G.2·5s), lies off the entrance to Levington Creek. Visitors can pick up a vacant mooring and, approaching HW, take a dinghy up to the old barge quay at the top. From there it's a short walk to the Ship Inn at Levington. The channel in the creek is marked with withies, but watch out for old iron posts and strapping near the quay.

Above Levington Creek, almost as far as the high level Orwell Road Bridge, both shores of the river are lined with moorings between the deep water channel and the drying banks.

West Harbour | Leading lights | HM out of hours

Suffolk Yacht Harbour approach and entrance

Nacton

The Nacton Foreshore runs between Levington Creek and Potter Point, the next major landmark on the N side. The flat mud runs up into a narrow sandy beach, popular for picnics and teaching youngsters to swim, because the water gets very warm as it comes in over the mud in mid-summer. It's a good place to see cormorants standing on mud humps at LW with their wings held spread out to dry.

Butterman's Bay

On the charts Butterman's Bay is correctly shown as the reach up to Pin Mill itself. However, locals usually refer to Butterman's Bay (properly Colton Creek) as the wider stretch of river opposite Levington Creek, on the W side, where there are a number of yacht moorings and a recognised anchorage for sailing barges. During the summer there're often one or more of these stately craft anchored there.

At the top end of the Bay, nestling under the end of a wooded cliff, sits a prominent, solitary white cottage, called Clamp House, which is reputed to have been a smuggler's den. Off the cottage is No.4 PHB (Q.R) on the W side of the deep water channel and, opposite that, the Bay SHB (Q.G). Upriver from both these buoys are double and triple rows of moorings, with a wide open space in the lines of moorings under the trees on the S side, which is a good anchorage, sheltered from S and SW winds. On the S bank, lies one of the jewels of East Coast sailing, Pin Mill.

Pin Mill

Much has been written about Pin Mill and the famous boatbuilding yards of Harry King and Fred Webb, though even more column inches have probably been given over to the riverside pub the Butt and Oyster, which has one of the finest views of the river in both directions from the bar window.

Getting ashore at Pin Mill requires a dinghy and a pair of boots, because there's a lot of mud, especially at LWS. A long hard is laid out from the shore almost to LW mark, so landing is possible at most states of the tide, but, if you go ashore at LW or early on the flood, pull the dinghy all the way up. There's a small rill – the Grindle – that runs down the upstream (W) side of the hard, enabling dinghies to float a long way up.

Pin Mill waterfront with barge on hard outside Butt and Oyster and Grindle to right of causeway

Sailing barge *Thalatta* making her way up the Orwell past Pin Mill

PIN MILL   IP9 1JW

Moorings Contact King's Boatyard, operators of Tony Ward Moorings Ltd, ✆ 01473 780258

Pub/restaurant Butt and Oyster ✆ 01473 780764

Provisions From shops in Chelmondiston. Early closing Wednesdays

Water Tap at Pin Mill SC

Boat repairs Two boatyards: FA Webb ✆ 01473 780291 and Harry King & Sons ✆ 01473 780258

Scrubbing post Contact King's Boatyard

Telephone In car park 100 yards up road

Club Pin Mill SC ✆ 01473 780271 www.pmsc.org.uk

WOOLVERSTONE

The clubhouse of the Royal Harwich YC, which has its own jetty and 54 deep water pontoon berths on the S bank, is the next port of call. During the summer the club welcomes visitors, who can use the showers, bar and restaurant in the clubhouse.

Snuggled into the trees between the club and the marina lies the fabled Cathouse, another smugglers' den. It is said that, when the coast was clear, a lamp was shown, but when the Revenue men were prowling, a white cat sat in the window as a warning.

Next door, up river, is Woolverstone Marina, an open-river 235-berth marina with pontoons held by massive piles driven into the riverbed in a deep pool S of the main channel. Its situation under the wooded shore is attractive, but it suffers from strong tidal streams through the berths and almost constant swell from passing traffic. Recent developments have included the

Similarly, if landing at HW or on the ebb, be prepared for a long drag back down. A vacant mooring may usually be used for an hour or two, if one can be found, but for longer stays, call King's Boatyard.

Pin Mill is a small, unspoilt hamlet that lies in a steep valley running back from the shoreline up to the nearby village of Chelmondiston, from which buses run regularly to and from Ipswich. There's a grocer, a butcher and a post office at 'Chelmo', as it's known locally. Apart from the Butt and Oyster, Pin Mill itself offers nothing for the visiting yachtsman – even the 'pay and display' car park halfway up the approach lane does not allow overnight parking.

The barge hard and posts are still used by Thames barges and almost invariably there is one being worked on at weekends.

From Pin Mill, the river turns more N up Potter Reach and then back NW at Hall Point between the Park Bight SHB (Q.G) and the No.6 PHB (Q.R) into Cathouse Reach with the channel tucking under the wooded slope that shelters Woolverstone Marina and the Royal Harwich YC from SW winds.

Opposite Woolverstone marina is the Cathouse SHB (Fl.G.2·5s).

Royal Harwich YC (above)

Approaching Woolverstone Marina from south

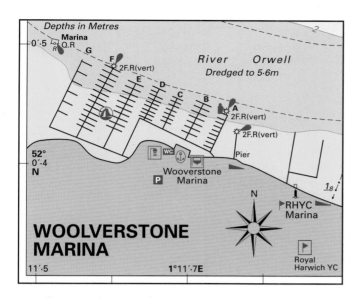

Depths in Metres

River Orwell
Dredged to 5·6m

WOOLVERSTONE MARINA

WOOLVERSTONE MARINA   IP9 1AS

Contact VHF Ch 80
Call sign *Woolverstone Marina*
Harbourmaster ☎ 01473 780206
　　　☎ 07803 968209
　Email woolverstone@mdlmarinas.co.uk
　www.mdlmarinas.co.uk
Access 24hr
Visitors' berths As available. Swinging moorings with taxi service
Facilities WC, Showers, Laundry, WiFi (PAYG)
Water On pontoons
Electricity On pontoons
Fuel Diesel from fuel station on pontoon A hammerhead
Gas Calor and Gaz
Chandler On site
Boat repairs Crane, boat hoist, slip
Engineer On site
Pub/Restaurant On site
Provisions Basics on site. Shops in Chelmondiston

ROYAL HARWICH YC   IP9 1AT

RHYC ☎ 01473 780319
Berthing Master ☎ 07742 145994
VHF Ch 77 (1200 Friday to 1600 Sunday)
　　www.royalharwichyachtclub.co.uk
Visitors' berths By arrangement
Access 24hr
Facilities WC, Showers, Laundry, Pump-out
Water On pontoons
Electricity On pontoons
Scrubbing posts By arrangement
Bar/Restaurant In clubhouse
Slipway

installation of a new fuel berth on the hammerhead of the first pontoon. Alongside it is a wide slip called the Cathouse Hard, also belonging to the marina.

The marina also has 110 swinging moorings in the river and runs a water taxi service on demand.

From Woolverstone up river, leave the No.7 SHB (Q.G) to starboard and the Marina PHB (Q.R) to port into Downham Reach. Here the channel begins to narrow markedly with unspoilt Suffolk parkland to be seen on either shore. Up ahead and spanning the river is the high level Orwell Road Bridge.

On the W shore of Downham Reach stands Deer Park Lodge, nestling in the woods with its own landing stage, and then the Stoke SC clubhouse and moorings providing a foreground to a Victorian folly. Called Freston Tower, the folly was reputedly built by one of the Paul family (famous for their barge fleet) as a garden dining room for entertaining guests to fine food and wine and views of the company's vessel's plying up and down the river. Others say it was built for the education of their daughter with one floor for each day of the week.

The channel here is quite narrow but extremely well buoyed. When a ship is sighted, keep just outside the line of buoys on either hand until she passes. At the bridge itself, the channel narrows down to 92m (300ft) between

Fuelling berth at Woolverstone Marina

the artificial islands that protect the bases of the eight piers carrying the bridge. The air draught is 43·07 m (141ft) at LWS (128ft – 38M at HWS). Do not attempt to pass under the bridge at the same time as a ship, whatever her size.

Ostrich Creek

Once through the Orwell bridge – and do look up when passing under it, the deck is made in two sections with a considerable gap between them – there is a SHB E Fen (Fl.G.5s) marking the E side of the channel between the bridge and the down river end of the Cliff Quay complex. Opposite is the West Power PHB (Fl.R.5s) and this should be left very close to starboard to stay just W of the deep water channel and clear of the shipping activities at Cliff Quay. About ¼M further N is the No.12 PHB (Q.R) that also marks the entrance to Ostrich Creek where both Fox's Marina and the Orwell YC are to be found.

Enter Ostrich Creek from the No.12 PHB, passing between the posts topped with R and G markers. The Orwell YC, on the N shore, has some drying moorings and water can be obtained from the clubhouse or from a floating pontoon. Fuel and oil are available at a garage adjacent to the clubhouse. There's a regular bus service into the centre of Ipswich.

HM Chandler
Fox's Marina YC
Visitors
Fuel berth
Orwell YC moorings

Fox's Marina and Orwell YC moorings

FOX'S MARINA
IP2 8SA

Harbourmaster ☎ 01473 694680 ☎ 07805 038314
Email john.jonas@foxsmarina.com
www.foxsmarina.com

Contact VHF Ch 80

Call sign *Fox's Marina*

Access 24hr, dredged to 3m MLWS

Boat sizes Max 25m LOA, draught 3m

Facilities WC, Showers, WiFi (free)

Water On pontoons

Electricity On pontoons

Telephone On corner of YC at head of pontoon gantry

Chandler On site ☎ 01473 688431

Gas Calor and Gaz

Fuel Diesel from fuel berth on S side of entrance

Club Fox's Marina YC www.fmyc.org.uk

Pub/Restaurant On site

Provisions Shops nearby

Boat repairs and all services On site up to 70T, masts to 110ft

Opposite Orwell YC, on the downriver side of Ostrich Creek, lies Fox's Marina and Boatyard, home of Oyster Yachts. The yard has one of the largest chandlers on the East Coast, a club and a restaurant.

Ipswich Wet Dock

Although there are a number of buoys on the approach to the lock gates into the Ipswich Wet Dock, there is deep water from quayside to quayside and sufficient lighting to see when going in at night. The port's working channel is VHF Ch 68 and the call sign is *Ipswich Port Radio*. Call from about buoy No.9 (below the Orwell Bridge) if wishing to enter.

Although originally designed for commercial shipping, the lock has been refurbished and fitted with rope travellers on the high wall on the port side and a floating pontoon to starboard (when going in) for yachts to moor against as they progress through (you will need to set fenders low for this pontoon). On the very rare

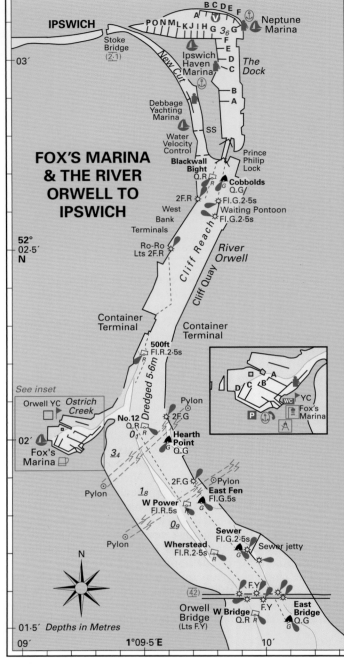

occasion that a ship or large vessel (a sail training ship for example) passes through they have priority and the pontoon is slipped and towed out while the vessel locks through.

There is a waiting pontoon to starboard, just upstream of Cliff Quay on the approach to the lock, if you have to wait long, but most boats prefer to jill about – a lot of ducks and gulls use the pontoon with clear consequences. The lock holds up to 20 x 9·75m yachts at a time, but usually it takes between six and 12.

Visual signals for entering or leaving the lock, which opens virtually on request, are a set of red and green traffic lights located above the Orwell Navigation Service's building on the E side of the lock.

IPSWICH HAVEN MARINA

IP3 0EA

Contact VHF Ch 80
Call sign *Ipswich Marina*
Harbourmaster ✆ 01473 236644
  www.ipswichhavenmarina.co.uk
Facilities WC, Showers, Laundry, WiFi
Water On pontoons
Electricity On pontoons
Boat size Max 80m
Boat repairs Crane, 70-T boat hoist
Fuel Diesel from fuel berth between pontoons A and B
Gas Calor and Gaz
Telephone In office lobby
Electronics On site
Engineers On site
Chandler On site
Bar/restaurant On site and nearby
Provisions Shops 10 minute walk
Taxi ✆ 01473 298298

NEPTUNE MARINA

IP4 1AX

Contact VHF Ch 80
Call sign *Neptune Marina*
Harbourmaster ✆ 01473 215204
  Email enquiries@neptune-marina.com
  www.neptune-marina.com
Facilities WC, Showers, WiFi (hotspot)
Boat repairs Crane, 30-T boat hoist
Water On pontoons
Electricity On pontoons
Diesel From fuel berth by hoist and workshop to starboard of final approach
Gas Calor and Gaz
Repairs All boatyard services available
Provisions Shops 10 minute walk
Taxi ✆ 01473 298298

Approach to Ipswich Wet Dock

Locking into Ipswich Dock

Once inside the wet dock, aim for the far end (it's actually a dogleg), where the Neptune Marina lies ahead on the starboard side with the Haven Marina to port, visitor moorings for the latter usually being allocated near the office, which is round the bend to port and several hundred yards further on at I pontoon. Both marinas offer the usual facilities and are equidistant from the town centre shops, a 10 minutes walk away in the town itself. Haven Marina has its own bar and restaurant, while the N dockside is steadily being redeveloped with bars and restaurants; it is a pleasant walk right round to the lock. Ipswich itself boasts restaurants, pubs, cinemas, a large park and a highly regarded theatre.

The New Cut

To port of the entrance to the Wet Dock is a stretch of water called The New Cut. It is the point at which the river Gipping (from which Ipswich got its original name of Gyppeswick) joins the Orwell. Here Debbage Yachting (✆ 01437 601169 / 07774 694226 *Email* office@debyacht.co.uk) has a yard and small marina situated about halfway between the entrance and the Wherstead Road Bridge, above which navigation is by dinghy only. Boats lie alongside stagings and dry out. You can obtain fuel and water. A flood relief gate crosses New Cut. Normally it lies on the riverbed, but when required it is raised to close the Cut. There are large warning signs and three vertical red traffic lights indicate when it is raised and that access to boats is denied.

9. Walton Backwaters

⊕ **Landfall waypoint**
51°55'·1N 001°17'·9E Close N of Pye End buoy
Charts
Imray 2000 series, Y16
Admiralty SC 5607, 2695
Tides
HW Walton
ECP Honorary Port Pilot
Alec Moss ☎ 01255 850266 *Email* walton@eastcoastpilot.com

Main hazards

The Walton Backwaters lie S of Harwich, well protected by the Pye Sand and Sunken Pye on the seaward side of the narrow Pye Channel approach. This sand is very hard and grounding must be avoided, particularly in onshore winds or when a swell is running. In fact it would be unwise to attempt entry to the Backwaters at all in strong NE winds when big seas are running.

Approaches

It is imperative that the Pye End SWB (L.Fl.10s) is located and identified before approaching the Backwaters. The buoy is of good size and, with the help of GPS, is fairly easy to find, even in choppy seas, although a good pair of binoculars will be useful. This is especially true at night when the light may be hard to identify against the background of Felixstowe and the deep water channel marks if an approach is made from SE. It can also be hard to spot from the NE against the late afternoon sun.

The two main landmarks when approaching the Harwich area are the cranes of Felixstowe container terminal and the Naze Tower standing on the cliffs just N of Walton on the Naze. Either or both is likely to be in sight from several miles away, but in misty conditions they may quickly disappear.

From N When approaching the Backwaters from Harwich, it is best to follow the charted yacht track to stay W of the deep water channel until near Cliff Foot (Fl.R.5s) before turning more SW towards the Pye End Buoy. This course avoids the Cliff Foot Rocks and the shallow waters over the Halliday Flats off Dovercourt.

From NE Following the coast S from the Deben or Ore, cross the Harwich deep water channel by way of the charted yacht track to arrive at Inner Ridge PHB (Q.R) on the S side, then alter course W for the Pye End buoy.

Pye End SWB must be located for entry into Pye Channel

Walton Backwaters from N. Stone Point in centre with Walton Channel all the way to Walton; Twizzle branches off to right for Titchmarsh Marina and Horsey Mere. Line of sunken barges on N shore of Horsey Island; Hamford Water running off to right past them

Walton Pier   W&FYC Twizzle   Titchmarsh Marina   The Wade   Kirby Quay

Hamford Water

Walton Channel   *Stone Point*   *Sunken barges*   *Pye Channel*

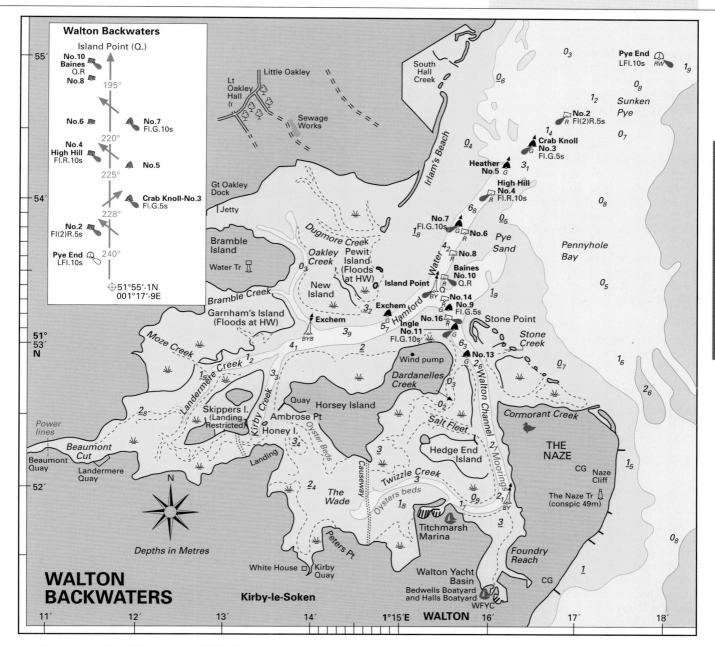

Walton Backwaters

Island Point (Q.)

No.10 Baines Q.R
No.8
195°
No.6 / No.7 Fl.G.10s
220°
No.4 High Hill Fl.R.10s / No.5
225°
Crab Knoll-No.3 Fl.G.5s
228°
No.2 Fl(2)R.5s
240°
Pye End LFl.10s

⊕ 51°55'.1N
001°17'.9E

WALTON
BACKWATERS

Depths in Metres

Kirby-le-Soken

WALTON

Looking W up Hamford Water with Walton Channel and sunken barges on Horsey Island at left.
Kirby Creek branches off to left and Oakley Creek to right. Pye Channel runs in from right

From E If arriving from across the North Sea, the likely approach to Harwich is via the Sunk. After negotiating the Sunk Gyratory System, continue parallel to the Harwich deep water channel, on the S side, until reaching the Inner Ridge (Q.R) or Deane (L.Fl.R.6s) PHBs or even Landguard NCB (Q), which is sometimes the easiest to sight. From there make a turn SW towards the Pye End buoy.

From S When arriving from the Blackwater, Colne or Crouch via the Wallet and the Medusa Channel in clear weather, the Naze Tower and the cranes of Felixstowe docks will be sighted while still S of Walton Pier.

Pass the Medusa SHB (Fl.G.5s), which is positioned 2¼M seaward of Walton Pier, and Stone Banks PHB (Fl.R.5s), while aiming for the Felixstowe cranes. This course should keep you E of the Pye End buoy but bring you close enough to spot it and identify it.

Once N of Walton Pier, all the way to Pye End, keep a sharp lookout for pot markers and fishing floats.

Entry

It is usual, when entering the channel, to pass the Pye End SWB on the landward side, leaving it close to port. From the buoy, shape a course of about 240° for just under 1M to reach the PHB No.2 (Fl(2)R.5s).

At this stage a look ahead will show no sign of a break in the coast; the Backwaters do not reveal themselves until much closer in. Not for nothing did Arthur Ransome name his famous book *Secret Water*.

The next buoy to make for is Crab Knoll No.3 SHB (Fl.G.5s), distant ⅓M, followed closely by an unlit SHB No.5.

The lit PHB High Hill No.4 (Fl.R.10s) marks the N end of a deeper section of the channel towards the lit SHB No.7 (Fl.G.10s) and unlit PHB No.6. From there pass No.8 PHB and head directly for PHB No.10 Baines (Q.R) and look for the small Island Point NCB (Q), which is not always easy to find and often appears to be out of position to the W. Major changes have taken place at the junction of the Pye Channel with Hamford Water and the Walton Channel. Massive sand shifts meant the twisting channel around Stone Point had to be dredged and re-buoyed. The new channel is narrow and steep sided and ebb tides at springs can run to a fierce 6kn at peak flow (in the second hour). At LWS there is around

No.10 PHB Baines

Passing Island Point NCB bound for Hamford Water

No.16 PHB marks narrowest part of Channel

0·6m over chart datum, but the bottom is uneven with ridges left from plough dredging operations.

First time visitors should keep a close eye on the depth and not stray outside the marks; the sand is as hard as concrete! Small boats in particular should be wary of a swirl or mini whirlpool that forms on the upriver side of Stone Point on the flood and again on the down-river side on the ebb. Both are strong enough to cause a sudden change of direction if not expected.

The channel is narrowest opposite No.16 PHB and care must be taken when passing a vessel going the other way, especially on the ebb, which runs strongly. Take your time and follow the buoys carefully.

It is common to enter the Backwaters in the afternoon and the sun's glare on the water at that time can mean a very hard time spotting and identifying buoys until almost upon them. Polarising sunglasses may help and binoculars always do.

Because the Pye Channel is so narrow, running between banks of hard sand, the tide funnels through it and can easily reach speeds of more than 2kn, particularly on the early ebb.

Departing the Backwaters at night can also be an interesting experience, because the buoys that are lit tend to be hidden among the background lights of the docks at Felixstowe, while the unlit ones simply disappear in the darkness. It's essential to work out rough courses to steer. This is one occasion when a chart plotter can be of real benefit.

The Naze Tower dominates the Backwaters and is one of the best coastal daymarks for navigation

Ingle No.11 SHB at NE corner of Horsey Island

care must be taken not to disturb birds or damage plant life. Indeed, since the whole of the Backwaters is a Site of Special Scientific Interest (SSSI), such care must be taken throughout the area.

W of the anchorage is a SHB No.11 Ingle (Fl.G.10s) a short distance N of where a shallow creek branches off to starboard around the E end of Horsey Island. The Walton Channel starts here with lines of moorings showing where the best water is and extending S for almost 1M to the Spit NCB. This NCB marks the end of a spit between the Walton Channel, which runs on S past the buoy as Foundry Reach, and The Twizzle, which turns W towards Titchmarsh Marina and Horsey Mere. The spit is extending so if turning from The Twizzle into Foundry Reach stand well out round the mark.

Walton & Frinton YC

To reach the Walton & Frinton YC, leave the Spit NCB to starboard and continue S into Foundry Reach.

The W&FYC has buoyed and marked the channel right up to its clubhouse, but the channel is tortuous, occasionally shallow and some of the buoys can be hidden by nearby moored boats, revealing themselves only at the last moment.

There is a good hard and concrete ramp for dinghies right under the front of the clubhouse (its N side) where the end of the concrete landing is marked by a red topped PHM post, which must be left to port if going alongside the club quay.

It is wise to wait until above half flood before heading up Foundry Reach, but then enter it by leaving the Spit NCB to starboard and heading straight through the 'gate' formed by No.2 PHB and No.3 SHB. Ahead you'll see a landing place on the E bank at No.5 SHB, but this is not for public use and does not offer access to the town.

Follow the port and starboard hand buoys in careful sequence. You will see the W&FYC clubhouse ahead from around No.7 SHB, but continue to follow the channel buoys as far as No.8 PHB. At that buoy, if you intend to lie alongside the W&FYC quay on the W side of the clubhouse or to visit Bedwell's boatyard, turn to starboard between a green topped SHM post and a small flat topped buoy painted black over yellow with 'N cardinal' written on it. Be sure to leave this NCB to port (i.e. stay N of it). Then leave a red-topped post PHM to port and make for the quay ahead to port or turn to starboard, keeping close around boats in mud berths, and head on for Bedwell's quay. The W&FYC quay is accessible at or near HW and there is a two-hour time limit on boats lying alongside it.

The Walton Yacht Basin is entered through a 12ft wide break in the sea wall from the creek on the E side

Speed limits

Please note that there is an 8kn speed limit in the approaches and within Hamford Water. This limit is reduced to 6kn in creeks and channels leading off Hamford Water and to 4kn in congested areas.

The Walton Channel

When bound up the Walton Channel towards Titchmarsh Marina or Walton town, leave the Island Point NCB (Q) to starboard and bear round SE to follow the line of unlit red PHBs. These and the No.9 SHB (Fl.G.5s) mark the way past Mussel Scarfe where the channel is narrow and, at LW, the buoys are often blown well out of position and lie over the banks or in the channel. Careful consideration has to be given to tide and wind direction before deciding how close to pass these buoys and a sharp eye should be kept on the depth, which varies considerably.

The channel runs very close in to the beach around Stone Point where that side is steep to and forms a popular anchorage off the sandy beach. The water is relatively deep and tides run fast (3–6kn on a spring ebb), so care must be taken when setting an anchor. On occasion this may be tricky and more than one attempt may be needed to ensure a good grip. Nonetheless, it's a popular anchorage.

Landing is possible at all states of the tide and the beach away from the point is good for swimming or having a picnic, but there is a nature reserve nearby and

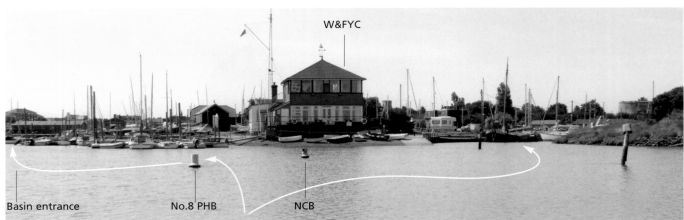

Basin entrance   No.8 PHB   NCB

Approaching W&FYC from Foundry Reach

Approaching quay at W&FYC

New extension to W&FYC

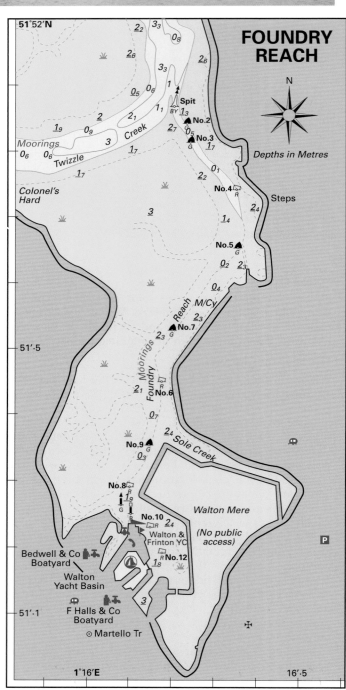

FOUNDRY REACH

Depths in Metres

of the W&FYC. A retaining gate (opened by arrangement) is lowered to the creek bed to allow entry or exit for a short time at HW when there is 2–2·5m over it. A tide gauge is positioned beside the gate. Contact Bedwell & Co (☎ 01255 675873) or W&FYC (☎ 01255 675526). It may not be possible to open the basin's gate on low neap tides.

If you have made arrangements with the club or Bedwell's to enter the yacht basin or are planning to approach the Frank Halls boatyard, turn to port round No.8 PHB, leaving the NCB to starboard, and follow the

Entrance to Walton Yacht Basin with gate raised

Walton Yacht Basin gate warning sign

PHBs to No.12 (keep close to the end of the W&FYC pontoon at No.10 PHB for the best water). From No.12 locate some thin white poles leading into the narrow entrance to the gated basin. As you approach, your view of the entrance between sheet piling will open up and so too will the channel between the white poles. If you see a triangle on top of a pole in the centre of the entrance to the basin, do not attempt entry – this mark stands on top of the raised gate. Only enter when the gate and its mark have been lowered beneath the water and sufficient depth is shown on the tide gauge beside the gate.

W&FYC with the basin behind the clubhouse. Bedwell's and the club quay on the left of the club; Halls and the basin entrance on the right

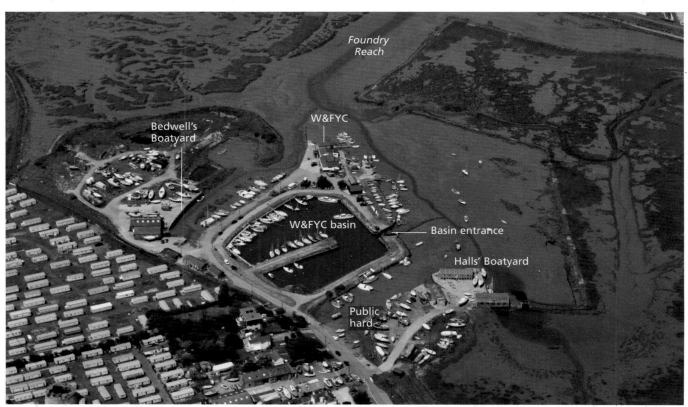

WALTON ON THE NAZE   CO14 8PF

Club Walton & Frinton YC ☎ 01255 675526/678161
    www.wfyc.co.uk

Access HW ±2hr

Facilities at W&FYC: WC, Showers

Slipway (contact club)

Water At W&FYC and in basin

Electricity On pontoons in basin

Provisions In town

Telephone At W&FYC

Post Office In town

Boat repairs Frank Halls ☎ 01255 675596
    Bedwell & Co ☎ 01255 675873
    Both located by W&F YC with cranes/slips

Pub/Restaurant W&FYC and many in town

Pharmacy ☎ 01255 675900

Taxi ☎ 01255 675910, 676887, 674444

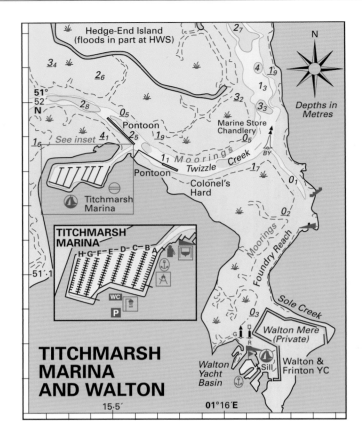

Titchmarsh Marina

The Twizzle (or Twizzle Creek) runs W and NW from the Spit NCB, in the Walton Channel, along the S shore of Hedge End Island and W into Horsey Mere. Titchmarsh Marina is cut into land on the SW side of the channel.

From the Spit NCB, moorings continue on both sides of the creek and, just over a cable in, there are pontoons on the SW side (just as the creek turns NW) where boats berth alongside. Watch your depth passing the start of these pontoons, as boats lying alongside take the ground at low water and there are shoal patches in the channel. The entrance to Titchmarsh Marina is between the NW end of the pontoons and the SE end of a second line further up the creek, also on the SW side. A tide gauge on the SE end of the further pontoons shows the depth in the marina's entrance channel.

Turn in as soon as the entrance opens up. There's a slipway to port with the fuelling pontoon beside it (at the head of 'A' pontoon) and the marina offices are in the building above. Once past the fuelling berth the channel turns hard to starboard past the ends of each pontoon. 'A' is nearest to the marina office, 'H' the furthest away.

Horsey Mere

Above Titchmarsh the Twizzle continues to wind its way NW and then W out into the open area of Horsey Mere. It is navigable to the W end of Hedge End Island by shoal draught boats at most states of the tide, but care must be taken to avoid grounding on oyster layings marked by withies.

At HW the Mere is a large expanse of shallow sailing water, but at LW it is just a sea of mud. A causeway, The Wade, crosses the middle of the Mere from the mainland to Horsey Island. Boats with a draught of not much more than 1m can cross it, but it must be close to HW, preferably on spring tides. There is no obvious point at

Entering Titchmarsh Marina with fuel berth to port and depth gauge to starboard

Depth gauge at marina entrance

TITCHMARSH MARINA

CO14 8SL

Contact VHF Ch 80 (0800–2000 in season)

Call sign *Titchmarsh Marina*

Harbourmaster ☏ 01255 851899

Marina Office ☏ 01255 672185
Email info@titchmarshmarina.co.uk
www.titchmarshmarina.co.uk

Access HW±5hr (1·2m in entrance at LWS)

Fuel Diesel and LPG at berth in entrance

Facilities WC, Showers, WiFi

Water Taps on pontoons (no hoses, but can be borrowed from office). Also on fuelling berth where hoses are provided

Electricity On pontoons

Gas Calor and Gaz

Phone Overlooking marina by office block

Chandler Marine and Outdoor ☏ 01255 676411, on site

Slipway Contact marina office

Provisions In town plus some basics at chandler on site

Post Office In town

Boat repairs 35-T Travelift, 25-T mobile crane, engineers and electronics on site

Scrubbing berth Against wall near fuel berth

Pub/Restaurant Harbour Lights on site ☏ 01255 851887

Taxi ☏ 01255 675910, 676887, 674444

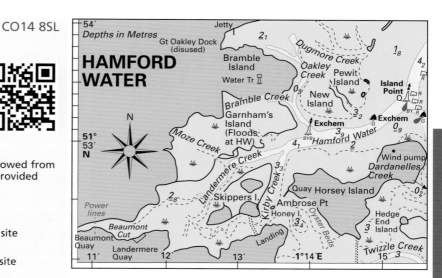

Withies mark the way across Horsey Mere

which to cross the Wade or where you can expect the greatest depth of water; it's a case of watching the depth sounder and taking it gently while being prepared to retreat.

At HW springs, if heading westward across the Mere, take care on the approach to Kirby Creek where it's hard to spot the submerged, marshy extremity of Horsey Island.

Stand well off the island until you're sure you're into the deeper waters of Kirby Creek.

On the W side of the Wade, Kirby creek leads away NW and runs round the W end of Horsey Island to join Hamford Water. An even less well-defined arm of the creek heads off S towards Kirby Quay. Readers of Arthur Ransome's book set in the Backwaters, *Secret Water*, will recognise Kirby Quay as Witch's Quay and Horsey Mere as the Red Sea with Hamford Water as the Secret Water of the title. Unfortunately, Kirby Creek, where it winds S to Kirby Quay, is not so well marked as in the book, but it still provides a wonderful area to explore by dinghy.

Hamford Water

Hamford Water – sometimes known locally as the West Water – runs SW from the Island Point NCB (Q) at the S end of the Pye Channel (the entry channel to the Backwaters). Leave the Island Point buoy to port and Hamford Water opens up ahead.

Walton Backwaters from S. Harwich in background, Walton Channel running up to W&FYC with basin and Twizzle going off to Titchmarsh Marina. Caravan parks are not so obvious from water level

Depths are good up past the SHB marked Exchem, where the channel bends more to the W, and on as far as the ECB, also named Exchem, at the entrance to Oakley Creek. This is a popular reach in which to anchor, but can be uncomfortable if the wind picks up from NE or E. An anchor ball or riding light is strongly advised.

Oakley Creek

The Exchem ECB, which carries a radar reflector, marks the end of a spit out from Garnham's Island on the W side of the entrance to Oakley Creek. Leave the buoy close to port to avoid the mud on the E side when entering Oakley. Silting has created a bar across the entrance joining the E bank to a NW/SE horse on the W side of the creek, but it's not enough to prevent entry after half flood (earlier with shallow draught). Seals often bask on the exposed mud inside the entrance.

Oakley creek runs in a generally N direction between Bramble Island and Pewit Island with a branch, Bramble Creek, turning off W along the S side of Bramble Island, while the main creek rounds the E end of the island and turns NW along its N side. Freighter traffic (often at weekends) to and from the explosives factory at the head of the creek, combined with the narrowness and lack of water above Bramble Creek make Oakley a place where it is inadvisable to anchor. However, if you enjoy exploring creeks and gutways on the tide with a good chance of seeing plenty of seals, it's worth visiting as the tide rises, even if only by dinghy.

Posts topped with red squares or green triangles mark the winding channel in from the entrance and must be followed carefully. Bramble Creek branches off W about ¼M in with a wooden jetty just inside on the N side of the channel.

Oakley Creek continues to wend its way N with a branch off to starboard

Exchem ECB at entrance to Oakley Creek

where seals often swim and sunbathe on the point of Pewit Island. Above that, the creek tends W and approaches the Great Oakley Dock (landing prohibited) in a short N arm and ends in a dredger berth opposite the dock. (You may be requested to leave the area if a coaster, which carries a hazardous cargo, is berthed or is due.) A large yellow post stands on a mud spit between the arm to the jetty and the one to the dredger berth. These upper reaches dry and a return down the creek should be made immediately after HW.

Back in Hamford Water, the short stretch between Oakley Creek and the entrance to Kirby Creek is a popular anchorage with good depths.

Kirby Creek

Running S from Hamford Water, between Horsey Island and Skipper's Island, Kirby Creek turns SE around the corner of Horsey out into the Mere. One part heads E towards the Wade (and so to the Twizzle), while another winds S to Kirby Quay.

When approaching the entrance to Kirby Creek, keep a close eye on the depth, but it is best to enter from E along the Horsey Island shore to avoid the long spit out from the NE corner of Skipper's Island, which is unmarked and seems magnetic to yacht keels.

As Kirby creek opens up, some moorings appear at the S end on either side of Honey Island. A small buoy with a board topmark labelled 'Fishery Buoy' shortly within the entrance to Kirby Creek marks the start of oyster layings that go right through to the moorings. It is possible to anchor short of the fishery buoy when conditions are rough in Hamford Water, but space is restricted.

Kirby Creek divides around Honey Island (both branches are shallow), before heading E into Horsey Mere. Anchorage can be found on the W side of Honey Island with a landing by dinghy possible on the mainland shore opposite the SE corner of Skipper's Island. From there it's a sea wall walk of about 1½M to Kirby-le-Soken for shops and a pub.

Approaching Honey Island moorings from Horsey Mere

Looking W from the moorings in Landermere Creek towards Landermere Quay

Landermere Creek

Immediately W of the entrance to Kirby Creek there is a mud bar where the spit from Skipper's Island has broadened across the main channel. Depending on draught, it may be necessary to wait until above half tide to cross this bar into Landermere Creek itself. Once over it, there is a ½M reach in which to find depth enough to anchor before the creek turns sharply SW around the corner of Skipper's Island towards Landermere Quay.

In the reach along the W side of Skipper's Island there are four or five moorings, but still plenty of room to anchor N of them. Immediately S of the moorings the creek divides with one arm rounding the SW corner of Skipper's Island and returning E to join Kirby Creek, and the other continuing W towards Landermere Quay.

For going ashore at Landermere Quay it is best to anchor or borrow one of the moorings then go in by dinghy, because the approach is not clear and is unmarked.

Towards HW it is also possible to explore by dinghy above Landermere Quay, even reaching Beaumont Quay, the most W'ly point of the Backwaters. This quay is best approached via Beaumont Cut, a straight, dug channel, but it is crossed by low power cables, preventing anything much larger than a dinghy with a mast from reaching the quay. Guy's Hospital, London, built the quay in 1832 using stone from the old London Bridge, which was demolished in that year; Essex County Council bought it in 1920 and a preserved limekiln can still be seen at the eastern end.

The sad bones of the old sailing barge *Rose* lie in a pool just above the quay, providing a reminder of the days when remote docks such as Beaumont formed a vital trade link to the sea.

Access to Beaumont Quay, the westernmost point of the Backwaters, is limited by power cables across Beaumont Cut

10. River Colne

⊕**Landfall waypoint**
  51°44'·0N 001°05'·4E Immediately NE of Knoll NCB
Charts
Imray 2000 series, Y17
Admiralty SC5607 and 3741 for Colne N of Brightlingsea
Tides
HW Walton +0025
Harbourmaster VHF Ch 68 Call sign *Brightlingsea Harbour*
☎ 01206 302200 ☎ 07952 734814

Main hazards

The main hazards to be avoided when approaching the Colne are the long NE–SW stretch of the Gunfleet Sands and Buxey Sand, followed by the shoals of the Knoll, Eagle, Priory Spit, Colne Bar, Bench Head and Mersea Flats.

Channels through or around these hazards are well buoyed, but navigators must identify each buoy carefully and ensure that progress is made from one to the next in the correct sequence. It may be tempting to cut corners, but it's rarely worthwhile. It may appear that you are in clear water with good depth, but wander off course and that can change with little warning.

Buoyage does move and is changed to take account of shifts in banks and shoals. It is wise to keep your charts up to date.

Approaches

Mariners can approach the Colne from the NE (Harwich and rivers to the N), the SE or S (across the Thames Estuary or from the Crouch and Thames), and from the W (River Blackwater). If crossing the North Sea, the likely approach would be via the Sunk, round the NE end of the Gunfleet and through the Wallet, effectively resulting in an approach from NE.

Whatever your direction of approach, you will sight the white turbines of the Gunfleet Wind Farm from many miles away. In that sense they are a useful navigational mark.

From the NE, SE or S All routes from seaward converge on the Knoll NCB (Q), which should be left to port. From there, shape a course to leave first the Eagle (Q.G) and then the Colne Bar buoy (Fl(2)G.5s) to starboard with the NW Knoll (Fl(2)R.5s) to port.

When sailing round from Harwich, a course close to the coast enables vessels to pass N (inshore) of the N Eagle NCB (Q) and from there to make for the Colne Bar buoy. Above half flood a course direct from the N Eagle to the Inner Bench Head buoy may be considered, but this means crossing the Colne Bar, which can be rough in stronger winds and should be avoided on the ebb. Be aware too that the tide sets strongly to the W here on the flood (and E on the ebb).

Inner Bench Hd buoy

Looking N up Colne channel with Brightlingsea harbour on right and Pyefleet on left

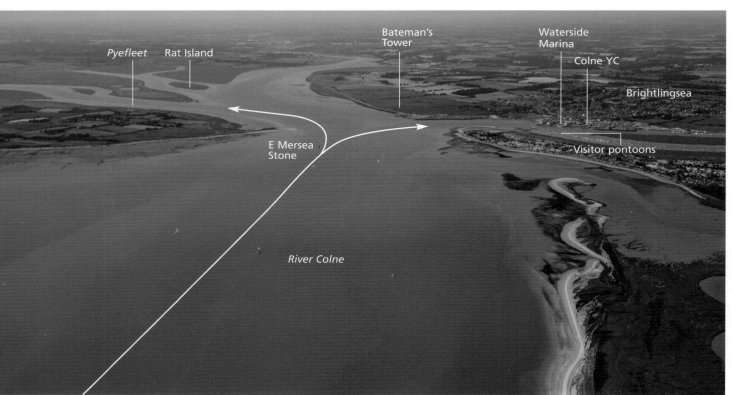

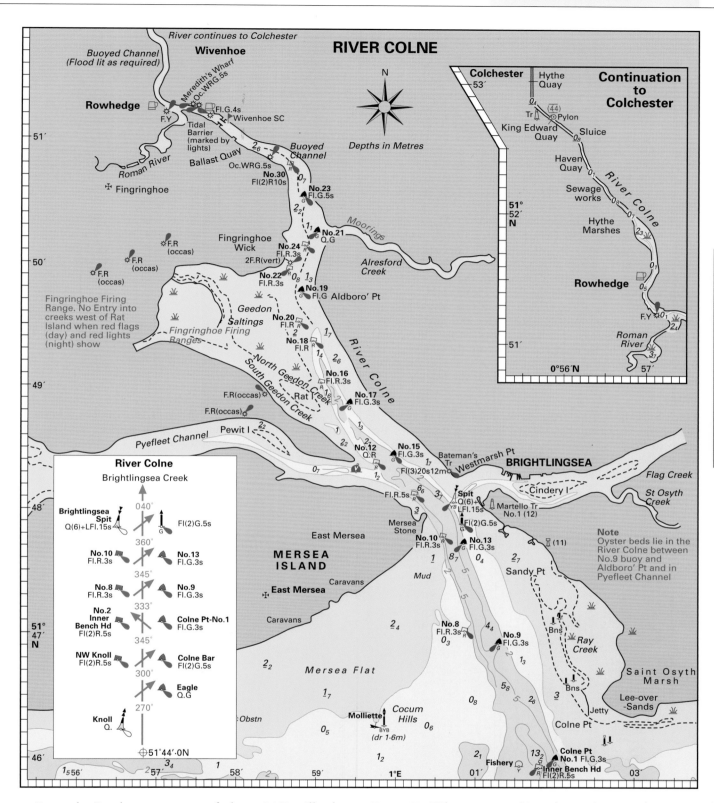

From the Bar buoy a course of about 345° will take you to Colne Pt No.1 SHB (Fl.G.3s) and the Inner Bench Head No.2 PHB (Fl(2)R.5s).

The Inner Bench Head is a very tall pillar buoy that marks the beginning of the deepwater Colne channel. Few buoys are now used to mark the channel and the next buoys are a mile distant. These are the No.8 (Fl.R.3s) PHB and the No.9 (Fl.G.3s) SHB.

From W When approaching from the W (the River Blackwater), sea state, tide and draught will dictate how far off the Mersea Flats you need to stand. With a deep draught and rough seas at low water (last of the ebb out of the Blackwater, first of the flood up the Colne) you may need to sail out round the Bench Head SHB (Fl(3)G.10s), towards the Colne Bar buoy and then N towards the Inner Bench Head to avoid the very extensive Bench Head Shoal.

With less draught or more water and better sea conditions a course across the shoal directly to the Inner Bench Head may be possible. If taking this approach, beware the large unlit 'Fishery' yellow spherical buoy positioned about a cable W of the Inner Bench Head buoy.

Finally, with shallow draught or towards HW with calm water, an inshore course can be set to skirt the Mersea Flats, keeping S of the Molliette ECM wreck beacon on the Cocum Hills. From there a course of about NE will lead to the No.8 PHB (Fl.R.3s) and the deep water Colne channel.

The Mersea Flats, inside the Molliette ECM, are indeed fairly flat, but only cross them above half tide and with shallow draught in calm conditions. It does shorten the passage to the Colne, but by surprisingly little.

When approaching the Colne from the Blackwater at night, it's best to do so via the Bench Head and Colne Bar buoys. It might be a longer route than you would take in daylight, but it follows the deep water and you have the benefit of lit buoys. Similarly, from other directions, finding the Knoll then approaching from there means a lit approach in deep water all the way. It's certainly a good plan in rough weather at the bottom of the tide.

Entry

Once into the Colne deep water channel, it is marked with pairs of port and starboard lit buoys. The sides are steep to (more so on the W side), so if tacking, keep an eye on the depth and it will be quite apparent when you leave the channel across the line of buoys.

Once past No.8 PHB and No.9 SHB, the shingle bank of East Mersea Stone will be seen ahead to port, probably with a few craft at anchor, and the town of Brightlingsea ahead to starboard with its prominent block of waterfront flats making a clear landmark.

From No.10 PHB (Fl.R.3s) and No.13 SHB (Fl.G.3s) onwards, the river can be quite busy, particularly if there are dinghies out racing, so a sharp lookout is needed to avoid other craft as well as to pick out the necessary navigation marks. Note also that coasters carrying gravel frequently run up or down the Colne on the tide and there is plenty of commercial traffic in and out of Brightlingsea.

The main place for mooring and re-supplying on the Colne is Brightlingsea, while the main anchorage is across on the W side in the Pyefleet. It's just after No.13 SHB that the courses of inbound vessels diverge according to destination with most going to Brightlingsea.

BRIGHTLINGSEA

From No.13 SHB, in reasonable daylight, a pale coloured tower with a dark conical roof can be seen on the shore beyond the Brightlingsea Spit SCB on Westmarsh Point – Bateman's Tower (Fl(3) 20s). Once past No.13 SHB, keep out in the deep water channel with Bateman's Tower clear to the left of the Brightlingsea Spit SCB (Q(6)+L.Fl.15s) until that buoy is almost abeam and you have gone a short way past a green SHM (Fl(2)G.5s) off the Point Clear shore. Only then is it time to turn into Brightlingsea Creek.

Brightlingsea harbour from SW with mooring pontoons, landmark flats and waterfront

Landmark flats · Waterside Marina · Town jetty · Colne YC · Visitor berths · Fuel berth · Cindery Island

Spit SCB | Leading marks | Spire | SHB | PHB | BSC | Flats | Depth gauge

Looking into Brightlingsea Creek from the Colne. Spit buoy to port, stbd-hand depth gauge to starboard and leading marks in line with spire

Brightlingsea Spit SCB and Bateman's Tower

Leading marks | Spire | BSC

SHB | PHB

The depth gauge, with channel buoys and leading marks beyond

Leave the Brightlingsea Spit SCB to port and the SHM beacon, which has a gauge on it showing depth in metres over the bar, to starboard. Refer to the depth on the gauge as you enter, because once past the Spit buoy and in the creek, there is slightly less than 1m for the first 100 yards or so at LWS.

Make good a course of about 040° to keep the two leading marks on the shore in transit. These, to W of Brightlingsea SC's white clubhouse, are lit at night with 2 F.R. lights, but by day they are vertically striped white/red/white panels on white posts. (They can look like white/black/white if the light is poor or the sun behind them.) They can be hard to see from a distance, but look for a tall spire that stands up behind them, but not quite in line.

Keeping the leading marks in transit, leave a green SHB (Fl(3)G.5s) to starboard and continue towards a red PHB (Fl.R.5s). As you approach this PHB the creek and harbour will open up to starboard. When about 25m from the buoy, turn to starboard, leaving it on your port side, and head towards Brightlingsea Hard with the NCM on the end of the first mooring pontoon to starboard. A second pontoon is moored parallel to the first and N of it. Head between this second pontoon and the Waterside PHB Fl.R.6s on the N side of the creek.

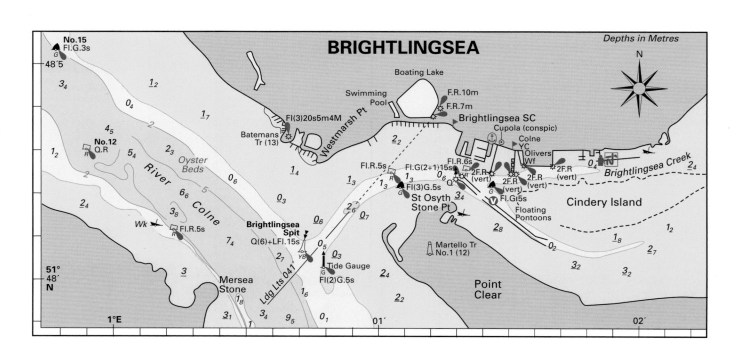

Brightlingsea entrance with leading marks and 'gateway' buoys

At night you may have trouble sorting out all the lights. There's the block of flats to port, the Waterside PHB Fl.R.6s, and lights beyond on the end of the long town jetty (Fl.R.3s) and pairs of fixed red vertical lights on the Colne YC hammerhead, as well as the wharf just upstream, while ahead to starboard you will see the pontoon NCM (Q), and the second pontoon Fl.G(2+1) 15s.

A variety of timber ships and wind farm vessels visit the wharf in Brightlingsea Creek, north of Cindery Island, especially near HW. Keep a sharp lookout for them when entering or leaving the creek, because some of the wind farm vessels are high speed craft and the ships are constrained by their draught, so you must give them adequate room to manoeuvre. Several of the wind farm vessels moor on the two seaward pontoons.

Brightlingsea is a crowded and popular harbour where anchoring is prohibited, so it's essential to try, during daylight hours, to make contact with the HM (Ch 68 Brightlingsea Harbour) and request a berth on the floating pontoons or, alternatively, call the Waterside Marina (the berthing complex in front of the flats) on Ch 80. The HM (or an assistant) will often be out and about on the water to help, advise and guide visitors to a harbour pontoon berth and will probably come out to meet you in a harbour launch (with Harbourmaster written on the topsides) during working hours, just to seaward of the pontoon NCM.

Approaching the first pontoons in Brightlingsea.
HM's launch is approaching with berthing instructions

You may also need to avoid the Brightlingsea/Point Clear/East Mersea Stone ferry, which plies to and fro across the harbour.

The speed limit within the harbour is 4kn.

Beyond the first two pontoons, there are a further two in parallel, which are very long indeed. If you arrive out of harbour office hours, leave the first pontoons to starboard and berth in a visitor's berth at the seaward end of the northern of the two longer pontoons about 150m beyond the NCM.

At LW there is limited depth on the inshore side of the pontoons, so be careful when turning. Tides run swiftly in the creek (up to 2kn) and must be taken into account when berthing alongside or departing.

A water taxi service (Ch 37) makes trips ashore from the pontoons easy and it's much safer than crossing from the shore in a laden dinghy when the water is choppy. If the water taxi is not running, call the Harbourmaster on Ch 68 who may be able to help.

Approach to the marina is past the Waterside PHB and a port hand withy. Depth gauges face in and out at the entrance

The Waterside Marina has a drying sill at 1m over CD, and has silted inside in recent years; dredging back to its original depth of 2m is expected before the 2015 season. There is a clear sill depth gauge at the entrance, displayed inwards and outwards. Access is around HW±3hr. Enter by leaving the Waterside PHB to port – there may also be a port hand withy between the buoy and the entrance. The marina has the obvious advantage of ready access to shore, unlike the harbour pontoons, where visitors must use a dinghy or the water taxi. There is a prominent notice on the seaward side of the wall beneath the flats showing contact details.

Brightlingsea has an attractive waterfront with the Colne YC prominent at the top of the busy hard and a lovely timbered building, now converted to flats, with a cupola on the roof. The older part of the town, between the hard and the shopping centre, has retained its nautical air with various marine companies dotted about and boats appearing over garden walls. It is the home of James Lawrence Sailmakers (largely for traditional craft), the Colne Smack Preservation Society (next to the CYC pontoon) where several smacks are berthed and the Pioneer Sailing Trust. Sadly the old shipyards have gone now, but boatyards remain busy.

The Hard is a popular launching place for all sorts of craft, but is also the location of some of the busiest scrubbing posts on the East Coast. To use them, talk to the Harbour Office (☎ 01206 302200) or make

Brightlingsea water taxi runs from pontoon to shore

The hard and its scrubbing posts

BRIGHTLINGSEA   CO7 0AX

Harbour pontoon moorings (harbourmaster)
Contact VHF Ch 68
Call sign *Brightlingsea Harbour*
Harbour office ☎ 01206 302200
    www.brightlingseaharbour.org
    Email mail@brightlingseaharbour.org
Access HW ±5hr
Water Taxi VHF Ch 37, 07535 508537
Weather Recorded daily inshore waters message
    ☎ 0844 499 2681
Scrubbing posts and slipway (Town Hard) call harbour office
Fuel Diesel by arrangement with harbour office, sited by
    pioneer Sailing Trust shed
Facilities (at Colne YC) WC, Showers, Laundry (ask in office).
Pump-out By diesel berth, as above, by arrangement with
    harbour office
Water CYC hammerhead. Activated by a coin in slot on box on
    E end wall of CYC
Foot ferry ☎ 07981 450169
Colchester ferry ☎ 07534 552681
Gas Calor and Gaz from chandlers
Chandler Two nearby
Provisions In town
Post Office In town
Boat repairs At nearby yards
Engineer French Marine Motors ☎ 01206 302133
    www.frenchmarine.com;
    D B Marine ☎ 01206 304391 www.dbmarineeng.co.uk
Sailmakers In town, Lawrence ☎ 01206 302863
Clubs Colne YC CO7 0AX ☎ 01206 302594
    Email waterside@colneyachtclub.org.uk
    www.colneyachtclub.org.uk
    Brightlingsea SC CO7 0BA ☎ 01206 303275
    www.sailbrightlingsea.com
Pub/Restaurant Several nearby, in town and at
    Colne YC (weekends and some weekdays)
Taxi ☎ 01206 305006, 307355

enquiries at the white hut at the top of the Hard. The same applies for launching on the hard if you wish to launch a trailer-sailer.

The town jetty, just upstream from the block of flats and marina, has a 24m-long hammerhead. A Thames barge often picks up and discharges passengers from the berth, but yachts may lie there for up to 15mins to load or unload, although it's best to check first with the HM. Tenders and small craft can be secured inside the

WATERSIDE MARINA

Contact VHF Ch 80
Call sign *Waterside Marina*
Harbourmaster ☎ 01206 308709
    ☎ 07584 474675
    www.watersidemarina.net
    Email office@watersidemarina.net
Access HW ±3hr
Facilities Public WC in apartment complex, closes at 2200H; keys
    to Colne YC WC and showers in box at foot of pontoon
    ramp. WiFi
Water On pontoon with hoses
Electricity On pontoons
Pump-out See Brightlingsea harbour details above

Waterside Marina entrance, Brightlingsea

ST OSYTH

Access HW±1½hr
Facilities WC
Water At boatyard
Provisions In village – ¼M
Post Office In village
Boat repairs St Osyth Boatyard, CO16 8EW ☎ 01255 820005
Slipway At boatyard
Pub/Restaurant Several in village

hammerhead or on the access walkway for up to 2hr, but beware the inside may be dry at LW. The jetty is the terminus for the water taxi and the Point Clear foot ferry, and is very popular with children for crabbing.

The small 12-passenger foot ferry operates from the jetty to Point Clear (St Osyth) and East Mersea Stone from Easter to the end of October. For details of service times see www.brightlingseaharbour.org/ferry.html or phone the operator on ☎ 07981 450169.

A second route operates between the jetty and Colchester, stopping at Wivenhoe and Rowhedge, but must be booked with the Harbour Office by 1300h on the day of travel. The ferry operator is on ☎ 07534 552681.

St Osyth

St Osyth Creek runs SE off Brightlingsea Creek where the two arms meet at the E end of Cindery Island. It is a narrow, tortuous creek with best water at the entrance between the little Pincushion Island and the S bank of the creek.

The creek is sparsely marked, but leads to the St Osyth Boatyard beside the road bridge at St Osyth. The village is known to have been a port as far back as 1215

and the bay beside the road bridge is full of houseboats and some barges in for repair. There is a line of mud berths at stagings along the waterfront below the boatyard.

Boats of up to 1·5m draught can reach the quay at HW, but must either seek a berth alongside and dry out or return down the creek in good time, because it more or less dries at LW. For a berth contact St Osyth Boatyard.

East Mersea Stone

Sometimes known as East Mersea Head, the point has a steep shingle beach with clean landing and the attraction of the Dog and Pheasant pub about a mile inland (☎ 01206 383206). The foot ferry from and to Brightlingsea also lands and picks passengers up from here. It is a convenient way to go shopping for stores in Brightlingsea while lying at anchor off the Stone.

The Brightlingsea – Point Clear – East Mersea Stone foot ferry

Boatyard beside the road bridge at St Osyth

Wreck

East Mersea Stone, looking NW to the entrance to Pyefleet Creek

The shore is steep to and if the anchorage is busy it may be necessary to anchor in relatively deep water or just around the point, but the holding is good and an evening stroll ashore pleasant. It is occasionally useful too as a waiting anchorage if catching a tide early in the morning, but do keep as close to the Point as possible and show a riding light, because plenty of yachts come and go at night and coasters run up and down the Colne.

The Pyefleet

Pyefleet Creek or The Pyefleet, which runs along the N side of Mersea Island, eventually reaching the Strood (the causeway to the island), is the main anchorage on the River Colne and is a favourite amongst East Coast yachtsmen, which means it can become very crowded during summer weekends.

The entrance lies about 2 cables N of the PHB (Fl.R.5s) marking the wreck of the SS *Lowlands* on the W side of the River above Mersea Stone. Sailing barges often anchor in the mouth of the Pyefleet and several smacks and bawleys have moorings there. Indeed there are now a lot of moorings in the Pyefleet off the Colchester Oyster Fishery's landing, including a number of large white-buoyed visitor moorings belonging to the Fishery. There is a fee payable for using these – details are marked on a tag on each buoy. There is room, however, to anchor above these moorings between the Mersea shore and Pewit Island, but much beyond that and you come into an area of oyster layings, which you must not anchor or ground on. The creek also shallows rapidly, W of Pewit Island, making it hard to find a hole to lie afloat in clear of the layings.

Holding in the Pyefleet is generally good, though in places the mud is very soft and boats do drag their anchors unexpectedly. In fact Pyefleet mud seems to have a character of its own and delights in sticking firmly and in great quantities to both anchor and chain, making recovery a messy business. It is common to see boats motoring seaward as their crews expend much energy dipping buckets and scrubbing the mud off ground tackle, decks, topsides and selves.

The Pyefleet has great charm and a place in the heart of most East Coast sailors, but it can also prove a particularly uncomfortable berth in the wrong conditions. Should the wind draw into either the E or W and blow hard against the tide, the whole creek cuts up rough with boats pitching and tossing all over the place. It occasionally becomes so bad that a boat will dip her head under at times.

A further attraction for a lot of visitors to the Pyefleet is the presence of the Colchester Oyster Fishery's sheds on the S shore from where it is possible to buy oysters and cooked crabs and lobsters (☎ 01206 384141 *Email* info@colchesteroysterfishery.com www.colchesteroysterfishery.com).

Pyefleet visitor buoy with payment instruction tag

Sunset over the Pyefleet

Looking into Alresford Creek. The entrance is well buoyed from the No.21 river buoy

Pyefleet to Alresford

Leave the No.12 PHB (Q.R) to port when leaving the Pyefleet to head seawards or to cross to Brightlingsea or to continue up the Colne.

Half a mile up the Colne, the N and S Geedon Channels open up on the W side to surround Rat Island. These channels lead in towards the Fingringhoe firing ranges, where activity is indicated by numerous red flags on the seawall, and cannot be used much, but there is a small hole that local craft sometimes anchor in, just inside the mouth of the S channel.

After passing No.17 SHB (Fl.G.3s) follow the line of red PHBs from No.16 at North Geedon up to No.24 (Fl.R). Pass fairly close to each (as river traffic allows), because they lie along the W edge of the channel while the E side, which shelves gradually, is unmarked until No.19, N of Aldboro Point. Keep a close watch on depths when tacking in this area and beware the dogleg in the channel around No.18.

SHB No.19 (Fl.G) off Aldboro Point is at the apex of a long right hand bend extending from N of No.18 PHB round to No.21 SHB. In the middle of the bend on the W bank, at Fingringhoe Nature Reserve, there's a disused jetty inshore from No.22 PHB.

The next landmark is the gravel works and jetty in Alresford Creek on the E side of the river.

Alresford Creek

Alresford Creek is entered from immediately upstream of No.21 SHB (Q.G) with a line of small port hand pillar buoys and starboard hand conical ones showing the line of the narrow channel.

Laid and maintained by a group of local yachtsmen who have moorings in the creek, these marks are clear and easy to use, but the creek dries out almost completely and there is little space for visiting craft to lie.

Within the creek there is a disused jetty on the N side from which ballast was loaded for many years (the ballast is now taken out by road) and a hard landing at a ford. From the landing it is about a mile to Alresford where there's a pub, the Pointer (☏ 01206 824378), a Post Office and a train station.

Alresford to Wivenhoe

Above Alresford, the Colne continues between wooded banks with Alresford Grange nestling among the trees on the E bank just where the channel runs closest to that shore before sweeping W towards the very active Fingringhoe ballast quay. Small coasters load and depart from the quay on the tide and when they are manoeuvring in the area they use the whole channel and yachts must keep well clear.

Approaching Wivenhoe, the ballast quay on the left, with Wivenhoe SC in the distance on the right bank

Ballast quay   Traffic lights   St Mary's Church   Wivenhoe SC

Wivenhoe Flood Barrier and the town beyond. The SC is on the right, with its moorings

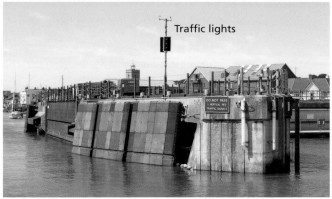

Passing through the flood barrier

There is a line of fore and aft small craft moorings along the E edge of the channel opposite the quay, making this a busy bottleneck area. It is within sight of the Wivenhoe tidal barrier and Wivenhoe itself.

Immediately below the barrier, on the E bank, is the Wivenhoe SC (CO7 9WS), which has a slipway and floating pontoons where vessels of under 2m draught can lie alongside at about HW ±1hr before drying out in soft mud. Visitors are welcomed. ① 01206 822132
Email clubsecretarywsc@gmail.com
Web www.wivenhoesailing.org.uk.

WIVENHOE

Just above the ballast quay to port and the club to starboard, the river is spanned by the massive structure of the Wivenhoe tidal barrier. It's an unattractive edifice, but the central section is normally open for vessels to pass through unimpeded.

Approach from No.29 SHB with the open section directly ahead. There's a pair of port and starboard hand buoys (Nos.38 and 31), followed by a substantial pair of port and starboard hand beacons (Q.R/Q.G) to guide boats into the passageway through. The barrier is marked on each side by 2F.R/F.G (vert) lights. (These signals are also shown on the upstream side for passage down through the barrier.)

Traffic warning signals on the N pier are arranged to show 3F.R.(vert) lights, directed both downstream and up, which are lit to indicate that the barrier is closed or that a large vessel is in transit. In either case, do not try to pass through.

The opening in the barrier is 30m wide, so two-way traffic is practical, but be careful to pass port to port and at less than 5kn.

Once through the barrier, Wivenhoe waterfront opens to starboard with boats berthed bows on in mud berths

Approaching Wivenhoe from tidal barrier

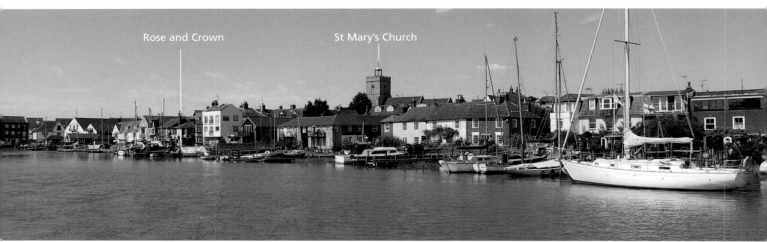

with all activity watched by visitors to the popular Rose and Crown pub. A modern jetty projects from the starboard bank a few yards beyond the barrier but, like the long quay higher up, it has railings along its edge making it unwelcoming to any visiting boats. There is a line of small craft fore and aft moorings to port with some more a little higher up, off the quayside where new houses and blocks of flats overlook the river. Boats can berth briefly on the tide at this quay, but again the railings are right on the edge of the quay, making landing difficult.

There are shops and a Post Office in Wivenhoe, plus pubs and restaurants, doctors, dentists and a chemist.

Sadly, in such an attractive spot, finding a mud berth along the quay is a matter of chance and even then an empty berth may not prove comfortable, once the tide has gone, if your boat's hull does not match the hole made by the resident vessel. It is better to moor at the Wivenhoe SC below the tide barrier.

FINGRINGHOE

There is no buoyage beyond the Wivenhoe barrier, so for best water use charts and/or generally follow the outside of bends. As the river bends away from Wivenhoe, another creek opens on the S shore. This is Fingringhoe Creek, commonly known as the Roman River. It mainly dries and should only be explored by shallow draught vessels near HW, when it is an attractive waterway leading up to Fingringhoe, a once thriving port.

ROWHEDGE

Above the mouth of the Roman River, the Colne takes a turn to the N past a semi-derelict quay and Rowhedge appears on the W bank. Once a busy centre for boat building, plus having a large fishing fleet, the Rowhedge waterfront is now quieter with few obvious signs of its maritime past.

It's still possible to moor along the quayside at Rowhedge, close outside the waterfront pubs, but timing is dependent upon draught and it's likely that you will only have from perhaps HW -2 to HW +1½hr unless planning to dry out there.

There is a floating pontoon at which yachts can berth for a visit to the village, but they share it with the ferry

Drying pontoon for short visits. Ferry berths at the back

from Wivenhoe, although that usually berths on the inside. Boats with a draught of up to 5ft can get alongside at HW ±2½hr, but the pontoon dries completely at LW.

The village, which is right by the river, offers several pubs, including Ye Olde Albion and The Anchor on the quay, as well as a Post Office and shops.

ROWHEDGE TO COLCHESTER

The Colne runs a further two miles from Rowhedge to Colchester and is perhaps of interest only to the curious or the adventurous, although there is a visitor pontoon near the head of navigation. There are attractive tree-lined reaches at first, but soon you are passing rundown industrial wharves and warehouses until you reach King Edward Quay on your port side, at the end of which is a low-level road bridge.

Near to HW there is enough water for a boat of over 2m draught to creep right up to the road bridge, but this would be within an hour of HW and time must be allowed to return down river to deeper water. It is possible to dry out at the King Edward Quay, in gaps you may find between a variety of permanently moored craft, but it should be undertaken with caution – as you might

Rowhedge waterfront – the Anchor pub with the visitor pontoon beyond

Nearing the head of navigation opposite the winding hole, the road bridge in the distance

expect, there is debris around, and you should test the depth each side before committing yourself.

There is also a visitor pontoon by the quay, not far below the conspicuous lightship (home to various activities including local Sea Cadets), and shoal draught boats up to 9m in length should dry out reasonably level in mud beside this pontoon. There was no debris beside the pontoon on our visit, although low tide reveals some wreckage that a shoal draught boat would be well clear of at HW. Rafting out may be uncomfortable for the outside boats where the mud slopes more steeply.

The section of quay close to the bridge has been renovated and provided with bench seats and lighting,

making it far more attractive than it once was. There is electricity and water but no other facilities. The town centre is about a mile away. Colchester Borough Council, responsible for the area, can be contacted on ① 01206 282222.

There is a winding hole to starboard below the pontoon. It was originally intended for turning coasters, but beware – the main area has silted up very badly.

It's worth noting that the plans for the regeneration of the area include the possible provision of more facilities for visitors, but there is no clear timescale for the work.

The visitor pontoon at King Edward Quay, restricted to shoal draught boats up to 9m LOA, shown at HW and LW

11. River Blackwater

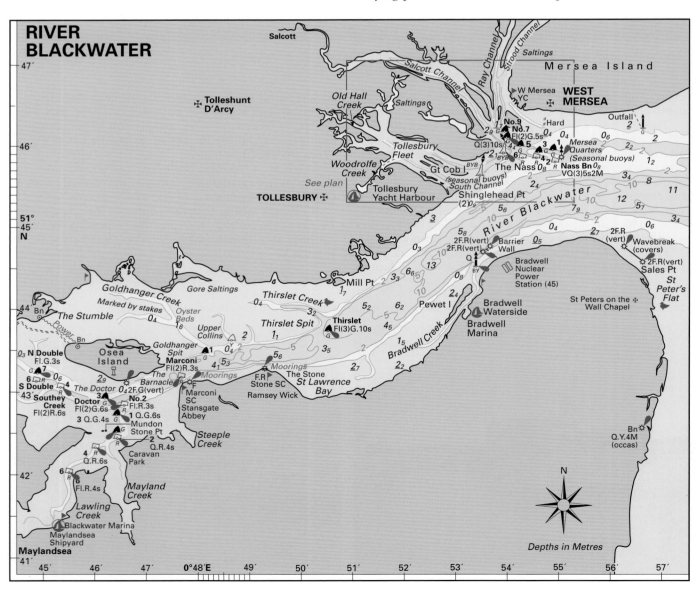

⊕ **Landfall waypoint**
51°44'·0N 001°05'·4E Immediately NE of Knoll NCB

Charts
Imray 2000 series, Y17
Admiralty SC5607, 3741

Tides
Bradwell HW Walton +0030
Osea HW Walton +0050
Maldon HW Walton +0100

Blackwater River Bailiff
Nigel Harmer ☎ 01621 875837 ✆ 07818 013723
Email nigel.harmer@maldon.gov.uk

ECP Honorary Port Pilot
Nigel Harmer ☎ *as above*
Email blackwater@eastcoastpilot.com

Main hazards

The entrance to both the River Blackwater and the River Colne lies W and NW from the Knoll NCB (Q), which in turn stands at the SW end of the Wallet channel, N of the Buxey Sand and W of the Gunfleet Sand. Approaching the buoy is straightforward if arriving from the NE through the Wallet, but from S, either from the Crouch or Thames, it means crossing the sandbanks. As with everywhere in the Thames Estuary, these banks are hazards to navigation and must be treated cautiously.

From the S, the best approach to the Knoll is via the Spitway between the Swin and Wallet channels, which saves a long haul NE to round the NE Gunfleet and return SW through the Wallet.

From the Crouch, small craft may cut through the Rays'n, but even they must cross Swire Hole to avoid drying patches on the Batchelor Spit.

Bradwell power station is an excellent landmark

Once the Knoll is reached, from any direction, navigation becomes less hazardous although compass courses will be needed in poor visibility.

Approaches

From the Knoll NCB (Q) shape a course to leave the Eagle SHB (Q.G.) close to starboard. Alter course then to pass between the NW Knoll PHB (Fl(2)R.5s) and the Colne Bar SHB (Fl(2)G.5s). From there, steer to leave the Bench Head SHB (Fl(3)G.10s) to starboard. The Bench Head buoy is generally thought of as the beginning of the Blackwater.

Craft approaching the estuary from the NE by way of the Wallet may, if tide and weather conditions permit, shorten their passage slightly after passing Clacton by ignoring the Knoll NCB and leaving the North Eagle NCB (Q) on their port side before making for the Colne Bar SHB.

West Mersea with (L to R) Salcott Channel, Thorn, Mersea and Besom Fleets. Hammerhead landing pontoon at right

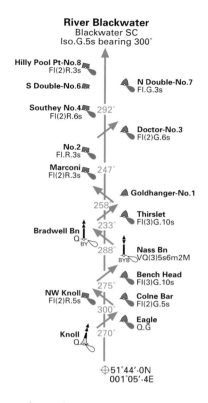

If crossing from the River Colne to the Blackwater, sea conditions, draught and state of tide will dictate your course. It may be necessary to go right out to the Bench Head buoy near to low tide on a rough day, but a more likely route is out round the Inner Bench Head, then on a course made good of about 250° into the deep water channel with the Bench Head buoy bearing about 110°.

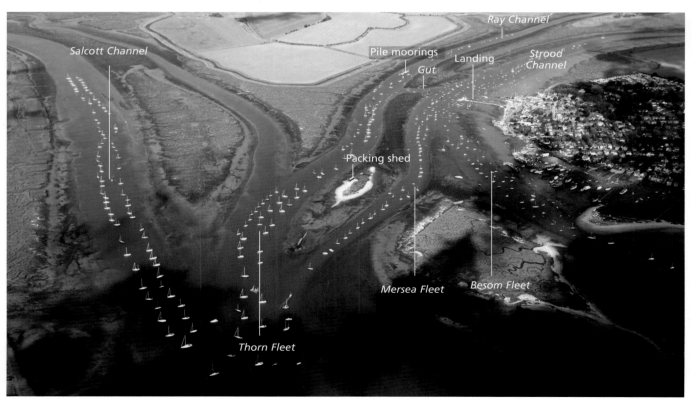

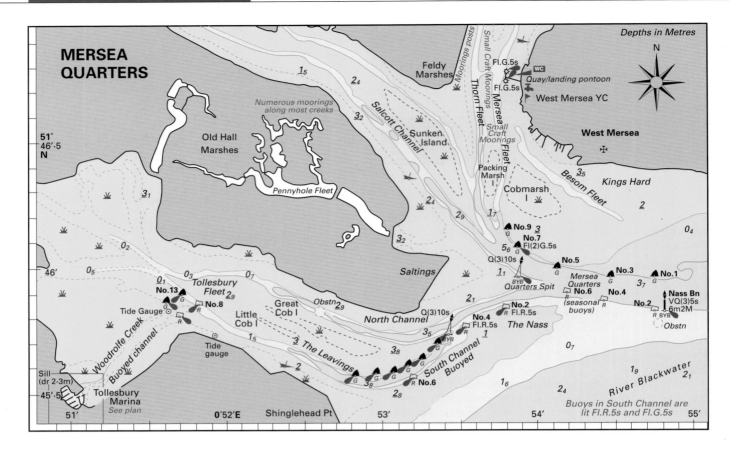

MERSEA QUARTERS

Depths in Metres

Feldy Marshes

West Mersea YC

Quay/landing pontoon

Fl.G.5s

Fl.G.5s

West Mersea

Kings Hard

Besom Fleet

Numerous moorings along most creeks

Old Hall Marshes

Salcott Channel

Sunken Island

Small Craft Moorings

Thorn Fleet

Mersea Fleet

Small Craft Moorings

Packing Marsh

Cobmarsh

Pennyhole Fleet

No.9 G
No.7 G Fl(2)G.5s
Q(3)10s
No.5 G
Mersea Quarters
No.3
No.1
Quarters Spit BYB

Saltings

Mersea Quarters (seasonal buoys)
No.6 R
No.4 R

No.2 R Fl.R.5s

No.2 R BYB

Nass Bn VQ(3)5s 6m2M

Obstn

Tollesbury Fleet
No.13 G
Tide Gauge
No.8 R

Great Cob I

Little Cob I

Obstn

North Channel

Q(3)10s

No.4 R Fl.R.5s BYB

The Nass

Woodrolfe Creek
Buoyed channel

Tide gauge

The Leavings

G G G G G G

South Channel Buoyed

River Blackwater

Sill (dr 2-3m)

Tollesbury Marina See plan

Shinglehead Pt

No.6

Buoys in South Channel are lit Fl.R.5s and Fl.G.5s

Shallow draught boats can leave the Colne S of No.8 PHB and make good a course of about 220° to stay S of the ECM (1M distant) marking the wreck of the *Molliette* on the Cocum Hills. From there they can turn onto about 250° with Bradwell Power Station fine on the port bow until again finding the deep water of the Blackwater itself.

Entry

Once past the Bench Head it is often difficult to identify any marks other than the two massive lumps of Bradwell Power Station on the S shore and a general view of 'that's W Mersea' on the starboard bow. Although the power station has been decommissioned, it seems likely that the landmark buildings will remain in some form for many years.

From the Bench Head, make good a course of about 290° to clear Sales Point and lead you towards the Nass Beacon ECM (VQ(3)5s6m2M) marking the entrance to Mersea Quarters and Tollesbury, with the option of leaving it to the N and going on up the Blackwater. (Keep checking your position, because you will have tide running athwart your course for the full 4M from the Bench Head to the Nass Bn.)

WEST MERSEA

First port of call on the Blackwater is West Mersea. Enter the Quarters from close E of the Nass Bn ECM (VQ(3)5s 6m2M), following the line of mainly unlit port and starboard buoys towards the mass of moorings. A course of about 280° for half a mile will take you from the Nass Bn to the Quarters Spit buoy ECB (Q(3)10s), which must be left to port. Further in, to starboard, you will see No.7

SHB (Fl(2)G.5s). From No.7 inwards you have to rely on the lines of moorings to show where the best water is.

There are boats moored well out in Mersea Quarters, but there is still room to anchor, although it can be rather exposed at HW with a heavy swell if the wind is from E or SE.

Once you're amongst the moorings there is no room to anchor safely and you must seek a mooring. For this it's best to call the West Mersea YC launch, call sign *YC1* on VHF Ch 37, from close to the Nass Bn. The launchman will do his best to find you a mooring and can take you to and from the shore, for which journeys there is a charge, as there is for short term and overnight mooring. (The launch charge may be refunded if you eat or drink in the

Quarters Spit ECB

Nass beacon

Looking N into Thorn Fleet with Packing Shed to starboard

Packing Shed

WMYC launch, call sign *YC1*

Pile moorings in Ray Channel

WMYC.) As an alternative to a swinging mooring, YC1 may ask you to moor fore and aft on the row of piles in the Ray Channel.

Beyond the Quarters, the channel divides into several separate arms. Each of these generally has a clear lane of best water to follow between the lines of moorings, but at slack water boats may lie athwart the channel, making it hard to pick out.

Steering about NW from a position between the Quarters Spit ECB and No.7 SHB will take you up the

WEST MERSEA

Moorings Contact WMYC launch, call sign *YC1* on VHF Ch 37
☎ 07752 309435
Additional Water Taxi *Lady Grace* VHF Ch 72 ☎ 07791 859624 0800-1800H (and evenings by prior arrangement).

Water Bailiff John Welham ☎ 01206 383461

Access 24hr

West Mersea YC CO5 8PB ☎ 01206 382947
Email info@wmyc.org.uk
www.wmyc.org.uk

Fuel Garage in town

Water On pontoon hammerhead

Gas Calor and Gaz from chandlers

Chandlers Marinestore Wyatts ☎ 01206 384745

Boatyards and repairs Peter Clarke's Boatyard ☎ 01206 385905
West Mersea Marine ☎ 01206 382244

Scrubbing posts Contact WMYC

Slipway On waterfront, contact Peter Clarke's Boatyard
☎ 01206 385905

Provisions In town

Post Office In town

Sailmakers Gowen Ocean ☎ 01206 384412
Doug Seaden Sailmaker ☎ 01206 331306

Engineers AB Clarke ☎ 07756 474243
Malseed Engineering ☎ 01206 382457
Ohm Marine Engineering ☎ 07905 243414
Service N Repair (outboards) ☎ 01206 385008

Diver John Welham ☎ 01206 383461

Pub/Restaurant Many along front and in town, including
WMYC (☎ 01206 384463 to book)

Clubs West Mersea YC ☎ 01206 382947
Dabchicks SC ☎ 01206 383786

Transport Buses to Colchester

Taxi ☎ 01206 384666, 385984

Start of South Channel to Tollesbury approaching from the Nass Beacon

Salcott Channel to the W of Sunken Island. Heading a little to starboard, the middle line of moorings leads into Thorn Fleet on the W side of Packing Marsh Island with its distinctive oyster shed. (Following Thorn Fleet will take you to the pile moorings in the Ray Channel.) On the E side of Packing Marsh Island is the shallower Mersea Fleet and the third line of moorings, while way over to the E of Cobmarsh Island is Besom Fleet, which runs right along the West Mersea foreshore.

A narrow channel, The Gut, cuts through from the Thorn Fleet and Ray Channel to Mersea Fleet and the Strood Channel opposite the hard and landing pontoon. The Strood Channel runs on N from the RNLI lifeboat station and Dabchicks SC to turn NE round the back of Mersea Island towards the Strood itself, which is the causeway between Mersea and the mainland. (Beyond this causeway is the head of the Pyefleet, which runs E into the Colne.)

All of the Mersea channels are thick with moorings and their headwaters are really only suitable for exploration by dinghy. Best water is generally found between paired lines of moorings in each fleet or channel. Whatever you do, don't cut across from one fleet to another, the water is shallow and the mud hugs keels. Withies generally mark oyster layings, not good water.

TOLLESBURY

Tollesbury shares a common entrance with Mersea from the Nass Bn ECM (VQ(3)5s 6m2M), its creeks running W from Mersea Quarters. To enter, follow the line of PHBs in from the Nass Beacon and turn to port at No.6, leaving the Quarters Spit ECB (Q(3)10s) to starboard, before following the charted channel W and WSW for several hundred yards to find a small PHB No.2, lit Fl.R.5s.

A word of warning is needed here. In common with many East Coast ports, when entering Tollesbury in the late afternoon, the sun will be low and directly ahead. This makes spotting buoys and/or identifying them extremely difficult, so proceed with caution. New visitors are also advised to follow the buoyed channel and not be distracted by local boats whose draught and local knowledge enable them to cross the Nass at the right state of the tide.

The No.2 PHB is the first of three PHBs placed along the N edge of the Nass sand bank. Depending upon wind and tide conditions, at anything less than HW, these buoys can drift over the bank, so watch the depth and be prepared to stand off them a little. The second PHB, No.4 (Fl.R.5s), is paired to the N with an ECB (Q(3)10s)

Turning NW into the Leavings

White conical waiting buoys for Tollesbury Marina just S of Woodrolfe Creek

at the seaward end of a long spit out from Great Cob Island, forming a 'gate' to the buoyed South Channel. The South Channel, which is the main Tollesbury channel, carries on SW leaving the Great Cob ECB on your starboard side. (You might also see local boats make their way to Tollesbury by leaving the ECB to port, entering the North Channel and then on to Tollesbury via the W end of Great Cob Island.)

Great Cob ECB

Start of buoyed channel into Woodrolfe Creek

Once through the 'gate' into the Tollesbury South Channel, you should find it mainly buoyed along its N side with about five SHBs (the number varies), each showing a flashing light, but there is also the third of the PHBs, No.6, to take note of on the edge of the Nass about 200 yards up the channel. No.6 marks a hard, drying sandy knoll on the Nass, but, although the buoy itself can dry out, once the tide is flooding there is usually deeper water close to it, so tend to pass close to this buoy, remembering that the wind can blow it over the shallows.

At the last SHB, usually No.11, the channel turns sharply to starboard in a NW direction into a reach known as The Leavings, which used to be an anchorage for local fishing smacks, but now sees the beginning of the Tollesbury moorings. Follow the line of these moorings, being very careful of depth if tacking outside the line of starboard hand withies, and Woodrolfe Creek will open up to port. You will see the landmark white blocks of flats over the saltings, together with the masts in the marina and a red light vessel, which is HQ for the Fellowship Afloat Charitable Trust.

There is a landing place half way up the Leavings on the S side, which gives access to a walk along the seawall into Tollesbury. It can be used at most states of tide. There is a tide gauge, marked in feet, on the S bank of The Leavings before you reach Woodrolfe Creek entrance, showing the depth over the marina sill.

Off the mouth of Woodrolfe Creek there are some white conical mooring buoys, which are waiting buoys for use when there is not enough water to get into the marina.

There is a second tide gauge, on the N bank of Woodrolfe Creek not far in from the entrance, again marked in feet. The creek dries and has a narrow, winding channel, but further up it is marked with a few port and starboard buoys, mostly lit Fl.R.5s or Fl.G.5s. The line of moorings also gives guidance as to the best water.

TOLLESBURY MARINA   CM9 8SE

Contact VHF Ch 80 & 37
Call sign *Tollesbury Marina*
Harbourmaster ① 01621 869202/868471
Email harbourmaster@tollesburymarina.com
www.tollesbury-marina.co.uk

Access ±1½hr

Fuel Diesel at berth below crane

Facilities WC, Showers, Laundry, WiFi, swimming pool, tennis courts

Water On pontoons

Electricity On pontoons (chargeable)

Gas Calor and Gaz

Chandler On site

Provisions In town (10 minutes)

Pharmacy and doctor In town

Post Office In town

Boat repairs 20-T boat lift and cranes, three slipways up to 30T. Also 8T crane at Tollesbury Saltings (see text)

Scrubbing posts In marina

Slipway Contact marina office

Telephone At Tollesbury CC

Pub/Restaurant Tollesbury CC on site and in town

Clubs Tollesbury Cruising Club ① 01621 869561
www.tollesburycc.co.uk

Tollesbury SC ① 01621 868218
Email tsc@tollesburysc.co.uk
www.tollesburysc.co.uk

Buses To Maldon, Colchester, or Witham

Taxi ① 07788 480542

TOLLESBURY MARINA

45'.7

N

51°
45'.6
N

P

Quay
Boatyard

Jetties

Jetties

Marked Channel

Boatyard
Tide
gauge

Sill

1₃

(2₃)

45'.5

P

Tollesbury CC

A

V

B

F

G

C

D

E

Tollesbury
Marina

45'.4
Depths in Metres   0°51'E   51'.2

RIVER BLACKWATER

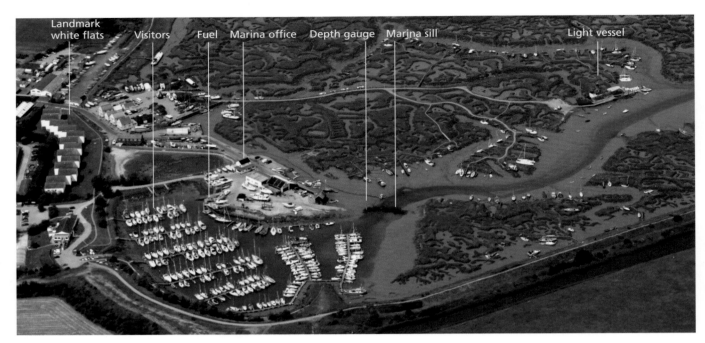

Landmark white flats | Visitors | Fuel | Marina office | Depth gauge | Marina sill | Light vessel

Woodrolfe Creek and Tollesbury Marina near LW

As you pass the light vessel to starboard and approach Tollesbury Marina the entrance is clearly seen to the left of an old black weatherboard granary shed beside the Woodrolfe Boatyard slipway. An arm of water also turns

Landmark light vessel in Woodrolfe Creek

sharply to starboard along Tollesbury waterfront, but it should not be followed without current advice unless previously inspected at LW. It gives access to the self-styled 'natural marina' run by Tollesbury Saltings (☎ 07521 318155 website www.tsl-online.co.uk), where mud berths for visitors may be available on request, accessible close to HW.

A final tide gauge, also marked in feet, is painted on a hefty green starboard hand post sited on top of the sill, immediately outside Tollesbury Marina, to show the depth over it, which is about 2m at HWS and 1·5m on neaps. The sill is hard, uneven concrete.

On entering the marina, the fuel berth is hard round to starboard towards the boatyard crane. You pass pontoon G in the entrance and the visitors' pontoon A is furthest in to starboard. There are bookable scrubbing posts beyond pontoon A.

Tollesbury Marina entrance

Tide gauge on sill

To Marina

To Tollesbury Saltings

Tollesbury Marina starboard hand post with depth gauge

BRADWELL

When entering the Blackwater the outstanding landmark is Bradwell Power Station on the S shore, close to which lie Bradwell Creek and Bradwell Marina. The distance diagonally across the Blackwater deep water channel from the Nass Bn to the isolated power station breakwater, which has 2FR(vert) lights at each end and can often look like a ship from a distance, is a shade under 1½M.

A cable beyond the W end of the breakwater there's a NCM beacon (Q), the Bradwell Beacon, which carries a depth gauge indicating depths in feet at the marina entrance. To enter Bradwell Creek and the marina, leave the beacon to starboard and head in between the red buoys to port and withies to starboard. Shoal patches have been noted near the beacon and close to the third red buoy, so be very careful if entering at LW±1½hr. The

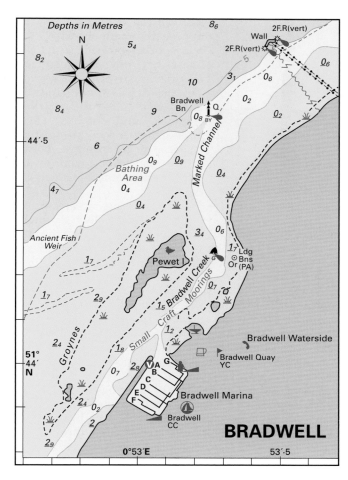

Bradwell Marina and creek with power station and breakwater

Bradwell NCM beacon

tide can run strongly across the approach channel with the buoys being pushed across the bank or into the channel, making it narrower than ever. The depth will vary frequently until well into the marked channel and it is best approached on a rising tide (especially at springs). Better depths tend to be found on the side of the channel marked by the buoys.

In recent years, greater depth of water has actually been found outside (E of) the buoyed channel, so if you need to enter or leave near to LW this may be worth a try, but check our website for up to date information and watch the echo sounder.

At the last PHB bear to port and head for a green conical SHB. The line to this buoy is shown by a pair of leading marks on the seawall – two small red triangles against a white painted patch on the wall. These marks have been adjusted for a change in the channel and are not always easy to make out; binoculars will help. Leaving the SHB very close to starboard, turn hard to starboard and follow the lines of moorings into Bradwell Creek. Best water is between the innermost line of small boat (drying) moorings and the S line of bigger boat moorings. Here the tide runs very strongly through the creek.

SHB and leading marks. *Inset* leading marks on seawall

BRADWELL MARINA CM0 7RB

Contact VHF Ch 37 or 80
  Call sign *Bradwell Marina*
  Harbourmaster ✆ 01621 776235/776391
  Email stuart@bradwellmarina.com
  www.bradwellmarina.com
Access HW ±4½hr
Fuel Diesel and petrol berth at base of tower
  (0830–1700). Tight turning space
Facilities WC, showers, laundry, WiFi, chemical toilet emptying
  point
Water Taps and hoses on pontoons
Electricity On pontoons
Gas Calor and Gaz
Provisions Bradwell Community Shop and PO (✆ 01621 776274,
  www.bradwellshop.co.uk)
Boat repairs 45-T boat lift, self-launch slipway (contact marina)
Pub/Restaurant Marina bar-restaurant on site
  Green Man ✆ 01621 776226, at Waterside
  King's Head ✆ 01621 776224, in village
Clubs Bradwell CC www.bradwellcruisingclub.co.uk
  Bradwell Quay YC www.bqyc.org.uk
    (HQ near the Green Man)
Transport Bus to Southminster train station
Taxi ✆ 01621 783007, 784878

To port will be seen the remains of Bradwell Quay and some scrubbing posts (belonging to the nearby Bradwell Quay YC) beside a public slipway. Off the end of it is a large red beacon that must be left on your port side. Shortly beyond is a single red PHB. Turn to port around this and the marina entrance is open ahead between red and green piles, but remember the tide sets swiftly across the approach.

Pass between the piles and, unless directed elsewhere, the main visitors' berth is on the hammerhead berth dead ahead (row A) with a secondary berth on the hammerhead next to it to starboard (row B). The fuelling berth is ahead on the starboard side of the high jetty beneath the blue and white marina tower.

The marina's entrance channel can be navigated by very shallow draught vessels at all states of neap tides, but at springs all craft must take care and entry timed for 90 minutes or so after LW. The marina itself is dredged to a general 6–8ft (1·8–2·4m).

It is sometimes possible to borrow a mooring in Bradwell Creek, but anchoring is not advisable. When picking up a mooring, be aware of the strong tide.

Bradwell Creek entrance channel and leading marks

Leading marks   SHB

Approaching the entrance to Bradwell Marina

The marina is in the hamlet of Bradwell Waterside, which has one pub and no shops. There is a useful community-run shop and PO in the village of Bradwell-on-Sea, a 20-minute walk away.

If holidaying and staying at Bradwell, it is worth the walk, either by way of the sea wall or through the village, to visit St Peter's on the Wall (www.bradwellchapel.org). Established by St Cedd in 654 AD, it is an extremely simple but calm place of worship, perhaps the oldest surviving church building in England.

Bradwell to Thirslet

When departing Bradwell Creek, be sure to round the beacon, leaving it to port, before turning up river. It is then tempting to make directly towards Osea Island, which appears dead ahead, but between Bradwell and the island lies Thirslet Spit on the N side of the main channel. It is marked by the Thirslet SHB (Fl(3)G.10s), which, when finally located, is quite obvious, but spotting it can be difficult. Thirslet Spit is made of very hard sand and is steep to on its river side. Many, many vessels have grounded on it as they make their way straight up or down the Blackwater. A dog-leg around it is essential, so steer for the moorings at Stone rather than directly towards Osea. (When returning down river, from Osea, keep Bradwell power station fine on your port bow, after passing close outside the Stone moorings, until past Thirslet.)

Thirslet Creek runs NW from the spit buoy and can provide a sheltered anchorage when the sand banks are uncovered. However, once the banks are awash it becomes rather exposed.

Opposite Thirslet, on the S shore, St Lawrence Bay is an area popular with PWCs and water-skiers.

STONE

On the S shore ½M above Thirslet is Stone with a long shingle beach, many moorings and several large, highly active fleets of racing dinghies that criss-cross the entire river from Stone Sailing Club (www.stonesailingclub.org.uk).

Tides run fast through the moorings and it is best to shape a course to pass outside them all.

Stone to Osea

A further ¾M up river, across on the N side, the small No.1 SHB marks the end of Goldhanger Spit and the entrance to Goldhanger Creek. The spit extends from the E end of Osea Island and the Creek cuts NW towards the village of Goldhanger with an arm breaking away to run behind Osea Island towards The Stumble, eventually rejoining the main river and actually making Osea an island. If you choose to sail this area, look out for the isolated danger buoy, approximately 5 cables N of Goldhanger No.1 SHB, marking two wrecks.

A charted causeway runs from Decoy Point on the mainland to West Point on Osea Island and can be crossed by most craft about an hour either side of HW springs.

Osea anchorage with landmark house above the beach

Thirslet Spit SHB

Sailing up river with Marconi SC to port and Osea Island to starboard

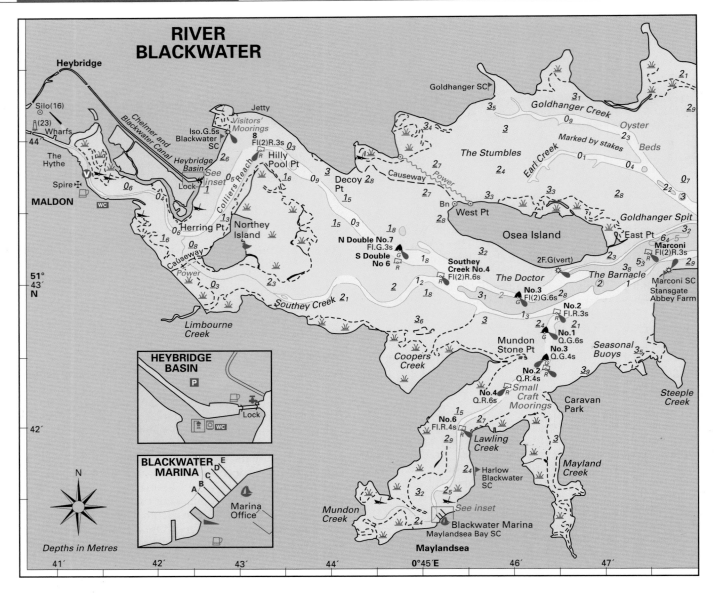

RIVER BLACKWATER

Depths in Metres

There are oyster layings in Goldhanger Creek making it difficult to find an anchorage. Like Thirslet, it only offers shelter once the banks are dry. One or two small craft do lie at the head of the creek where there is also the Goldhanger SC. If your boat can take the ground comfortably then there is a landing and Goldhanger village with its pubs, The Chequers Inn and The Cricketers, a reasonable walk away.

Across on the S shore at Stansgate there are more moorings and the Marconi SC (① 01621 772164 *Email* info@marconi-sc.org.uk www.marconi-sc.org.uk).

NW of Stansgate, at the W end of the Marconi SC moorings, there is the Marconi PHB (Fl(2)R.3s), which doesn't always stand out too well. It is placed in good water, but at a point where the river channel narrows and it should be left to port for safety. The area between Stone and the anchorage E of Osea pier, particularly around the Marconi buoy, is frequently choppy and can be disturbingly rough with wind against tide.

The pier at Osea is now a shadow of its former self, but still carries 2F.G(vert) lights that act as a useful guide. There's good depth and holding E of the pier with the shell beach of Osea a popular place for walking and picnicking. Note however that the island is privately owned and you may not be welcomed above the HW mark. At LW, deep draught boats must beware The Barnacle shoal patch a cable E from the pier.

The Osea anchorage has been used by many different types of craft down the centuries, from raiding Vikings to barges, coasters off-loading into lighters for Maldon and Heybridge and from gentlemen's yachts through to modern cruisers. There's good holding if you set the anchor properly and shelter from N winds, in addition to offering a pleasant place to stretch your legs ashore or swim off the beach – and children can paddle about the anchorage in dinghies, practising their boat handling skills.

Lawling Creek

South from Osea is the No.2 Mayland Spit PHB (Fl.R.3s), which marks the S side of the main river channel, but also the W side of the entrance to Lawling Creek. This creek runs SW to Maylandsea and the Blackwater Marina.

Enter Lawling Creek by leaving the Mayland Spit buoy to starboard (it is a PHB for the river only) and steer to leave the SHB Lawling Creek No.1 (Q.G.6s) to starboard. From there, leave No.3 Mundon Point (Q.G.4s) to starboard and No.2 (Q.R.4s) to port, altering course to about SW towards No.4 Mayland Creek (Q.R.6s) off the entrance to Mayland Creek. Continue to No.6 (Fl.R.4s) from where the Harlow (Blackwater) SC will lie ahead and the moorings offer a guide to the channel up to the Blackwater Marina.

There is a sheltered anchorage on the S side of Mundon Stone Point, but be warned that the mud bank inside the headland is extensive. The small knoll of sand that forms the headland is often used for barbeques by visiting club cruises and is also a frequent perch for herons and cormorants.

Opposite Mundon Pt is the entrance to the drying Mayland Creek, which has a number of moorings in it.

About a mile in from the entrance, on the E bank, where there are more moorings, stands the Harlow (Blackwater) SC ☎ 01621 740300
Email clubsec@harlow-blackwater-sc.co.uk
www.harlow-blackwater-sailing-club.co.uk.

BLACKWATER MARINA   CM3 6AL

Contact VHF Ch 80
Call sign *Blackwater Marina*
Harbourmaster ☎ 01621 740264
    Email info@blackwater-marina.co.uk
    www.blackwater-marina.co.uk
Access HW±2½hr
Fuel Diesel
Facilities WC, Showers
Water Taps and hoses on pontoons
Electricity On pontoons
Boat repairs Slipway, 18-T travel hoist, 15-T crane. Engineers, Rigging
Slipway Contact marina
Gas Calor and Gaz
Provisions In village, five minute walk
Post Office In village
Pub/Restaurant On site and takeaways in village
Taxi ☎ 01621 741621

The club has 35 swinging moorings – the boats on them are afloat at HW ±2hr – and a launching ramp that has water at similar times.

Mayland Spit buoy

Approaching Blackwater Marina

Blackwater SC at Heybridge shines a leading light down river

From HBSC you can see the Blackwater Marina on the port hand, but you must approach by continuing to follow the winding line of moorings carefully until you reach a final green SHB (a blue barrel painted green, so not always obviously green) lying N of the marina, from where the pontoons are clearly visible ahead. These are drying pontoons that can be reached at HW±2hr, but there are also marina owned moorings laid to about half way down the creek.

Approach the pontoons on a direct line from the green SHB with the big, fire damaged shed straight ahead and the slipway on the right. 'A' pontoon is beside the slipway; 'E' is at the seaward end.

Above the marina the creek narrows rapidly and dries completely, but there is an active club, the Maylandsea Bay SC (☎ 01621 740470 *Email* sec@maylandseabay-sc.org.uk www.maylandseabay-sc.org.uk), just upriver. The club manages a few drying moorings (owned by Maldon DC) for its group of cruising members.

Lawling Creek to Heybridge

From Osea, leave No.2 PHB (Fl.R.3s) to port and No.3 the Doctor SHB (Fl(2)G.6s) to starboard. The water along the Osea Island shore looks inviting, but beware the Doctor flats, which have caught the keel of many a yacht trying to take a short cut inside the buoy.

At the Doctor SHB the river turns NW and the next buoy is the No.4 PHB (Fl(2)R.6s) marking the entrance to Southey Creek. This creek winds away W behind Northey Island to rejoin the main Blackwater river opposite Herring Point. It is a broad expanse of water at HW, but quickly narrows and dries as the tide ebbs. You can sail behind Northey on a good tide, but beware the hard causeway between the island and the mainland at the SW corner.

Just above Southey Creek a pair of buoys, the Doubles, mark a distinct narrowing of the fairway, which shoals to less than 1m at LWS. The SHB, No.7 North Double, is lit (Fl.G.3s) and marks the rejoining

Entering Heybridge Lock leaving curved line of withies to port

Lock Master's House   Traffic lights   The Old Ship

Showers · Lock Cottage · Old Ship · Jolly Sailor · Lock Cafe · CRS Marine

Stebbens Boatyard

Heybridge Basin with lock into Blackwater-Chelmer Canal

with the main river of the arm of Goldhanger Creek that has gone round the N side of Osea Island across the Stumble.

The river now runs up to Heybridge between the NE shore of Northey Island to port (site of the Battle of Maldon in 991 AD) and Mill Beach, which stretches from Decoy Point, at the mainland end of the causeway across to Osea Island, up river to Heybridge. The channel off Mill Beach is narrow and there's little water at LW, although at HW on a big spring tide Northey Island now largely floods.

There are moorings all along the Mill Beach foreshore, but the main marks to look ahead for are the towers of the old mill and the Blackwater SC (a long white building with a black roof set behind the seawall), which shows an Iso.G.5s light at night.
The club (☎ 01621 853923
Email secretary@blackwatersailingclub.org.uk
Website www.blackwatersailingclub.org.uk) has a large number of drying moorings, a concrete launching ramp and a floating wooden pontoon that cruisers can go alongside at HW.

Off the BSC the channel turns SW around the No.8 PHB (Fl(2)R.3s) Hilly Pool Point off the N tip of Northey Island. As its name implies, the river bed here is uneven, but best water is found towards the mainland (W) shore.

Heybridge Basin

Half way along this reach, known as Colliers Reach from the days when colliers brought up here, lies Heybridge Basin, the seaward end of the Blackwater & Chelmer Navigation, a canal running inland to Chelmsford. The

HEYBRIDGE BASIN   CM9 4RX

Contact VHF Ch 80

Call sign *Heybridge Lock*

Lock Master Martin Maudsley ☎ 01621 853506, ☎ 07712 079764

Access HWS ±1hr, HWN -1hr; 0600-2000H May-Sept, 0700-1700H Oct-April

Facilities WC, Showers, Laundry

Water Taps, hoses

Electricity At shore points – tokens from Lock Office

Boat repairs Stebbens Boatyard ☎ 01621 857436 / 07974 530269
CRS Marine ☎ 01621 854684 / 07850 543873
www.crs-powerboats.co.uk

Cranes 20-T at basin, 7-T at CRS Marine

Pub/Restaurant The Old Ship ☎ 01621 854150
The Jolly Sailor ☎ 01621 854210
The Lock café on seawall

Provisions Basics from small shop at rear of the Jolly Sailor, open in pub hours ☎ 01621 854210

Transport Bus to Maldon (infrequent)

Taxi ☎ 01621 855111

basin is a traditional wintering berth for yachts, but has also become a popular summer stopover since the end of the timber trade and removal of the stacks of seasoning timber from the canal banks. Its popularity means that prior booking is virtually essential.

Drying moorings extend along the foreshore between the Blackwater SC and the Basin lock, but not much further. The entrance to the lock is readily identifiable by a large clump of trees and white buildings with a space (the lock) between them. It is usually difficult to tell whether the lock gates are open or shut until directly in line with them, but then a red or green traffic light on the left hand side makes it clear.

The approach channel begins at the small Lock Reach SHB and is marked by a curving line of withies to be left close on your port side. There are depth gauges on either side of the lock entrance (shown in metres on the left, in feet on the right) and the lock is worked (at best) for about an hour either side of HW. There is almost always plenty of knowledgeable help with mooring lines once in the lock. Visitors should berth in the basin as directed. The Lock Master's cottage and office stands on the port side of the lock.

Once berthed in the Basin it is a pleasant dinghy trip up the canal (which has a 4kn speed limit) to land at a pontoon behind Tesco's supermarket in Maldon to re-provision. There is also a group of useful shops at Heybridge, reached by walking or cycling about 1M up the towpath and turning right along the road that crosses the canal. These include smaller supermarkets, a pharmacy, PO and small restaurant/takeaways.

As an alternative to locking into the Basin, CRS Marine has drying pontoon moorings just outside the lock on the N side of the entrance, albeit with similar access times to the Basin, and some swinging moorings in the river.

Heybridge to Maldon

From Heybridge Basin, Colliers Reach continues SW to Herring Point where the river turns NW once more, then W, and winds up to Maldon. A few smacks may be anchored opposite Herring Point in the bight off the end of the mole, but they dry out soon after HW.

Leave Herring Point No.9 SHB to starboard and keep following the red and green buoys as the channel first twists to the N, close to the E shore, then back W past the end of the Promenade (mole). Maldon YC (www.maldonyc.org.uk) stands on the W shore just S of the Promenade. A large yellow/black post with a yellow X topmark stands a short way along the promenade marking the inner end of a concrete launching ramp.

Approaching the Maldon Hythe quay

MALDON   CM9 5HN

River Bailiff ☎ 01621 875837(office at Hythe Quay)
   ☎ 07818 013723
   Email rivers@maldon.gov.uk
Access MHWS ±1hr to visitors' pontoon at Hythe Quay
Water Tap
Chandler Marinestore, North St (☎ 01621 854280)
Gas Calor and Gaz at Marinestore Chandlers
Provisions In town
Post Office In town
Pharmacy and doctor In town
Boat repairs Various yards along North St and Downs Road
   including Shipways Boatyard (☎ 01621 854280) 15-T crane,
   slipway, 20-T winch; Hedgecock's (☎ 07836 715685)
   15-T crane.
Rigger TS Rigging ☎ 01621 874861 www.tsrigging.co.uk
Pub/Restaurant Queen's Head ☎ 01621 854112
   Jolly Sailor ☎ 01621 853463
   Many others in town
Club Maldon Little Ship Club ☎ 01621 854139
   www.mlsc.org.uk
Taxi ☎ 01621 850850, 852633, 855111

Lines of drying moorings outside the channel on both the Prom foreshore and the opposite bank, together with the channel buoys, give a good indication of the deep water. A sharp turn to starboard at the No.19 final SHB brings you onto a course parallel and close to the beginning of Hythe Quay. Beware Thames barges motoring to and from the Quay around tide time, because they need the full width of the deep water to manoeuvre in, particularly if they are to be turned to berth at the quay with their heads downstream.

Visitors should lie alongside the floating pontoon set parallel to the N end of the Quay and be prepared to dry out, unless their visit is to be very swift at HW. There is no charge for the occasional overnight stay alongside this pontoon, though a charge may be made for longer stays. It has perhaps 2·5m at HWS and 1·0m at HWN.

Above the Hythe Quay, boatyards and mud berths line the W bank right up to the road bridge at the

St Mary's Church   HM   MLSC   Queen's Head   Visitor Pontoon

The visitors' pontoon at Hythe Quay near HW

Fullbridge, but there are likely to be few available berths. A drying berth may be available on the upstream side of the first pontoons belonging to Shipways Boatyard (☎ 01621 854280), which is immediately above the Queen's Head pub and has Marinestore Chandlers on site. It's advisable to call first and enquire.

Maldon town climbs the hillside with the spire of St Mary's church standing clear above the masts of barges lying in their permanent berths at the Hythe, while further upstream and to the right are the grey buildings of the old timber yards and flour mills. This was once a thriving port with smacks lining the foreshore along the prom, barges being repaired at Walter Cook's yard (where the blocks are still used by barges), and barges and coasters coming and going to the mills, plus a number of busy boatbuilding yards above the town and a sailmaker in between. Today the barges at the Hythe are used for corporate and private charters, and yachts and motor boats fill the mud berths that line the bank from the Hythe right up to the Fullbridge. However, the commercial traffic and smacks have gone, although several yards are still busy with yachts.

Maldon Little Ship Club stands behind the Quay and the Jolly Sailor and Queen's Head pubs serve the needs of thirsty sailors. The River Bailiff has his office at the seaward end of the Quay close to Walter Cook's old black shed. The whole Quay has been 'sanitised', but there is still an East Coast air that thickens as you move up river through the various boatyards, where the charm of mud and old wooden boats still persists.

Looking back down Blackwater from Maldon at LW - note the run of best water between Heybridge and Maldon

12. River Crouch

⊕ **Landfall waypoint**
51°41'·8N 001°08'·3E   Just S of Swin Spitway SWB

Charts
Imray 2000 series, Y17
Admiralty SC5607, 3750

Tides
Burnham-on-Crouch HW Walton +0042

Crouch Harbour Authority
Harbourmaster ℡ 01621 783602
Email info@crouchharbour.org.uk
www.crouchharbour.org.uk

ECP Honorary Port Pilot
Jim Dew   *Email* crouch@eastcoastpilot.com

Main hazards

The Whitaker Channel, leading in towards the River Crouch, runs roughly NE-SW between Foulness Sand (on the S side) and the Buxey and Ray Sands (on the N side). All of these sandbanks are extremely hard and present a serious hazard to any vessel grounding in rough weather. The buoyage in the channel is excellent with marks at frequent intervals – and all of them lit.

There is shoal water between the Swin Spitway and the Whitaker Beacon, across the eastern tail of the Swallowtail bank, and the Swallowtail itself dries between points S of the Swallowtail Nos.2 and 4 buoys. The channel between the Buxey Sand and the W end of the Swallowtail is narrowing but is still deep.

Tides are strong, but follow the courses of the channels without too much set across the sands.

Watchkeepers must keep a lookout for both inbound and outbound ships using the main channel along the S side of the River Crouch. These ships may be bound to or from either the Baltic Wharf, above Essex Marina, or, more frequently, the terminal on Wallasea Island just W of the Roach entrance. This latter traffic, bringing spoil from London's Crossrail excavation to create a wetland area, will end eventually but in 2014 was thought to have some years still to run with more spoil being sought elsewhere.

There are speed limits on different stretches of the Crouch and these are clearly indicated by marked buoys.

Approaches

From NW, N and NE From the Rivers Colne and Blackwater the normal route will be through the Spitway, which is the shallow channel running between the Wallet and the Swin. Identify and pass comfortably close to both the Wallet Spitway (L.Fl.10s Bell) and Swin Spitway (Iso.10s Bell) SWBs before turning SW towards the Whitaker Channel. (See Chapter 20 for more information.)

As an alternative to the longer haul out to the Spitway, shoal draught boats may slip through the shallow inshore Ray Sand (Rays'n) Channel from the Blackwater or Colne. This runs between the Buxey Sand and the Dengie Flats. It is a passage recommended only on a rising tide, above about half tide, and with a close watch kept on the depth sounder. The long established mark is the Buxey Beacon NCM standing on the NW side of the Buxey Sand. At the southern exit from the Rays'n there is an unlit yellow buoy on the S edge of the Buxey Sand. There is no clear channel across the last mile where the

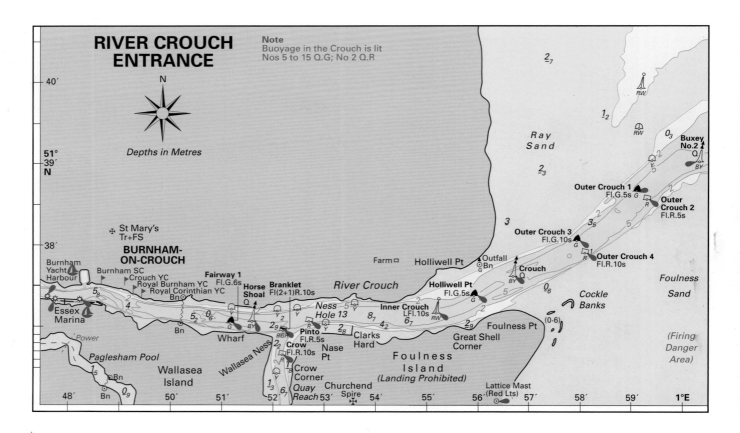

Buxey and Ray Sands (S end of the Dengie Flats) join together, but two SWBs give an indication of where the best water may lie to reach the yellow buoy. Recent unofficial surveys showed no actual channel, but found best water to run N/S to E of the SWBs along the 000°59'·6E line of longitude. However, this may have changed since and the most recent information may be found at www.crossingthethamesestuary.com.

The Rays'n is like a funnel. The E arm runs from the Knoll NCB across the Swire Hole (with its rapidly changing depths), until you reach a point where the Buxey Bn bears S. From there alter course to about SW, leaving the Buxey Bn ½M or so to port. While making towards the tall pylons on Foulness, look for the first SWB (a pillar mark). Then turn S towards the second SWB (a spherical buoy) and the unlit spherical yellow buoy, then SSW towards the Outer Crouch No.1 and No.2 buoys.

A shallow draught boat can use the western arm of the funnel when on passage from the Blackwater. From Sales Point, round the tip of St Peter's Flats then shape a course of about 185°, leaving both of the outer wrecked target vessels about 1M W. After passing the Buxey Bn, which should be about 1M E, head a little more W (around 195°) and make towards the Foulness pylons, to find the SWB pillar and finally turning S as before towards the second SWB and the charted unlit yellow buoy.

The 'middle route', useful if sailing to the Crouch from the Colne, is to head for the NW Knoll (Fl(2)R.5s) and continue S into the Swire Hole, before altering to about SW to leave the Buxey Bn some ½M to port and continuing as described above.

Buxey Beacon NCM

From E, S and SE Coming in from the E means navigating through the off-lying sand banks towards the Inner Whitaker SCB (VQ(6)+LFl.10s) before heading SW into the Whitaker Channel.

From the River Thames or the North Kent coast, the navigator will again have to work through the sands towards the South Whitaker SHB (Fl(2)G.10s).

When using the East Swin for an approach from S, near LW, be sure to reach the South Whitaker SHB (Fl(2)G.10s) before carefully crossing the NE end of the Whitaker Spit. In 2014 the 2m contour had extended to reach a point N of this buoy. At higher states of the tide, skippers may have enough charted depth to start their turn across the Spit once past the West Hook Middle PHB (Fl.R.5s).

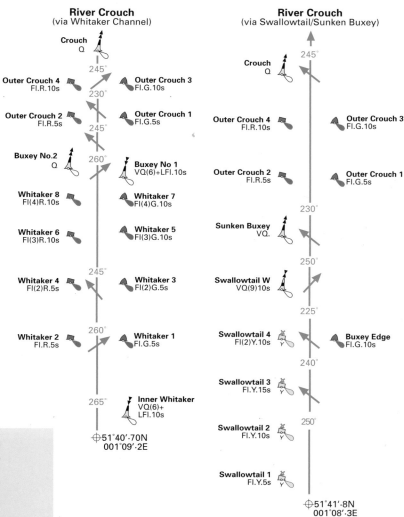

River Crouch
(via Whitaker Channel)

Crouch Q

245°

Outer Crouch 4 Fl.R.10s — Outer Crouch 3 Fl.G.10s

230°

Outer Crouch 2 Fl.R.5s — Outer Crouch 1 Fl.G.5s

245°

Buxey No.2 Q — Buxey No 1 VQ(6)+LFl.10s

260°

Whitaker 8 Fl(4)R.10s — Whitaker 7 Fl(4)G.10s

Whitaker 6 Fl(3)R.10s — Whitaker 5 Fl(3)G.10s

245°

Whitaker 4 Fl(2)R.5s — Whitaker 3 Fl(2)G.5s

260°

Whitaker 2 Fl.R.5s — Whitaker 1 Fl.G.5s

265°

Inner Whitaker VQ(6)+LFl.10s

⊕ 51°40'·70N 001°09'·2E

River Crouch
(via Swallowtail/Sunken Buxey)

Crouch Q

245°

Outer Crouch 4 Fl.R.10s — Outer Crouch 3 Fl.G.10s

Outer Crouch 2 Fl.R.5s — Outer Crouch 1 Fl.G.5s

230°

Sunken Buxey VQ.

250°

Swallowtail W VQ(9)10s

225°

Swallowtail 4 Fl(2)Y.10s — Buxey Edge Fl.G.10s

240°

Swallowtail 3 Fl.Y.15s

250°

Swallowtail 2 Fl.Y.10s

Swallowtail 1 Fl.Y.5s

⊕ 51°41'·8N 001°08'·3E

Note that the NE extent of the Shoeburyness Outer Firing Danger Area covers almost the entire drying area of the Foulness Sand.

Entry

From the area of the Swin Spitway SWB and the Inner Whitaker SCB, the Whitaker Channel runs SW for almost 9M to the Crouch NCB (Q) at Shore Ends. The deeper buoyed channel lies along the edge of the Foulness Sand with good water all the way, although care

Crouch NCB

must be taken in the region of the Sunken Buxey where there is a kink in the channel between Buxey No.1 SCB (VQ(6)+L.Fl.10s) and Buxey No.2 NCB (Q).

An alternative route is along the Buxey side, from the yellow Swallowtail No.1 (Fl.Y.5s) past two more lit yellow special marks, then through a gate formed by the Swallowtail No.4 (Fl(2)Y.10s) and the Buxey Edge SHB

(Fl.G.10s), and on past the Swallowtail W WCB (VQ(9)10s) and the Sunken Buxey NCB (VQ), joining the main channel at the twin Outer Crouch buoys.

Both routes arrive at the Crouch NCB (Q), which marks the start of the River Crouch itself. There is often a sizeable seal colony hauled out on the Foulness Sand shortly before Shore Ends, which makes a fine sight.

Shore Ends to Burnham

From the Crouch NCB the river runs W past the Inner Crouch SWB (LFl.10s) for about 2¾M to the mouth of the River Roach, which opens S. A further PHB (Fl.R.5s) lies 2 cables W of the yellow Clarks racing buoy, E of the Roach entrance. On the W side of the Roach entrance is the red/green/red Branklet 'preferred channel' buoy (Fl(2+1)R.10s), which marks the mud spit out from Wallasea Ness and must be left to port when heading for Burnham or to starboard if heading into the Roach.

From the Branklet buoy a slight dog-leg around the Horse Shoal NCB (Q) should keep you in a dredged section up to the Fairway No.1 SHB (Fl.G.6s), but there

is some doubt about whether this is still a necessary diversion. From Fairway No.1 (marked 'F1') the deep water channel runs past the extensive wharf on Wallasea Island, where ships are constantly unloading spoil, and onwards along the S shore of the Crouch, well up beyond Burnham town. However, once the lines of moorings are reached there is good water anywhere across the river – but be aware of the tide, it can easily run at up to 3kn. Be careful also, when beating up river, not to stray into the breaks in the Wallasea Island sea wall opposite the whole Burnham waterfront. These breaches, made to create a wetland nature reserve on the island, have submerged obstacles in them to prevent navigation and the ebb pours out strongly through the gaps.

Inner Crouch SWB

Looking W along Burnham waterfront to Yacht Harbour

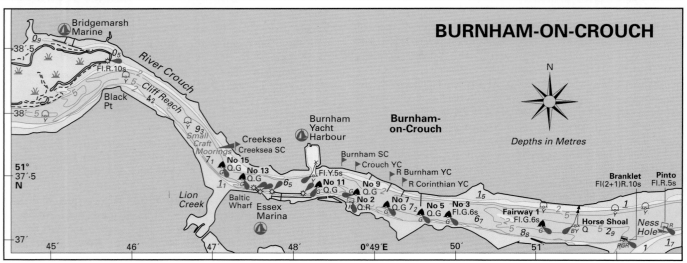

Horse shoal NCB and jetty for spoil dumping on Wallasea island, S of No.1 Fairway SHB, which marks W end of Horse Shoal

BURNHAM

Approaching Burnham-on-Crouch, the first of the long lines of swinging moorings on the N side of the river starts at the Rice & Coles boatyard, identified by a crane on the seawall and a landing pontoon. A group of four large yellow spherical buoys, a short way downstream, marks the crossing point for high voltage power cables and no attempt should be made to anchor nearby. Anchoring is also prohibited anywhere in the Fairway and is to be avoided anywhere within the moorings. Care must also be exercised when spoil barges are arriving at or leaving the Wallasea jetty.

Outside Burnham Week (usually the last week of August) there are moorings available up and down the river. These are looked after by the various boatyards and yacht clubs, which also have their own landing pontoons.

The first landmark for Burnham is the big white building of the Royal Corinthian YC. From there on through the town there are the Royal Burnham YC, The White Harte, The Ship, Prior's boatyard, the Crouch YC and the Burnham SC before reaching Burnham Yacht

Harbour. It's an interesting waterfront steeped in history, but is no longer as busy, with as many active yards, as it once was. However, it is still a main centre for shopping, chandlery, sail and boat repairs or maintenance. A ferry service runs from the Town Quay (by the Anchor pub) across the river to Wallasea at Essex Marina in summer (for details see information panels).

Burnham Yacht Harbour

The harbour is cut into the N shore of the Crouch, just up river from Burnham town, with a yellow pillar mid-channel buoy with an X topmark (Fl.Y.5s) off the entrance. It is important to pass close to this buoy, because the entrance channel is dredged through mud banks that dry.

From this offing buoy, head in towards a big blue-grey shed and pass between a pair of large metal posts, red (Fl.R.10s) to port and green (Fl.G.10s) to starboard.

There is no designated visitors' berth, so call ahead and, if arriving late, request codes for the gate to the pontoons and the door to the ablutions block.

Royal Burnham and Royal Corinthian yacht clubs

Burnham SC and Crouch YC

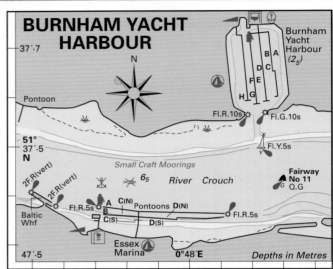

Approaching Burnham Yacht Harbour, No.11 SHB and yellow mid-entrance channel buoy

Entrance to Burnham Yacht Harbour

From the entrance, turn to starboard for pontoon row A and to port for row H. Berth numbers are on ends of fingers with low numbers close to the shore and high numbers near the river. Some fingers, particularly in row A, are shorter than the boats occupying them, which makes finding the numbers difficult.

BURNHAM YACHT HARBOUR — CM0 8BL

Contact VHF Ch 80
Call sign *Burnham Yacht Harbour*
Harbourmaster ☎ 01621 786832 *office* ☎ 01621 782150
   Email admin@burnhamyachtharbour.co.uk
   www.burnhamyachtharbour.co.uk
Access 24hr
Fuel Diesel at berth on row 'F', landward end close to boat lift. Tight turning space
Facilities WC, Showers, Laundry, WiFi (free)
Water Taps and hoses on pontoons
Electricity On pontoons. Charged per night
Gas Calor and Gaz from chandler
Chandler Marinestore, on site, ☎ 01621 783090
   www.marinestore.co.uk
Boat repairs 35-T travelift, 100-T slipway
Sailmakers In town
Provisions At Co-op (Fiveways), about 10 minutes walk up road from marina, or in town, about 15 minutes walk.
Post Office At Fiveways (top of road from marina to town)
Telephone Pay phone in Swallowtail bar
Pub/Restaurant Swallowtail on site, many in town
Pharmacy At Fiveways near Co-op
Ferry Crossings to Essex Marina in season (☎ 07704 060482 www.burnhamferry.co.uk)
Trains Direct to London
Taxi ☎ 01621 784154, 772999, 783007

Wallasea and Essex Marina

On the S shore of the Crouch, slightly upstream from the Burnham Yacht Harbour, is Wallasea Bay with the Essex Marina, whose pontoons run parallel to the river. At the W end of the bay is the Baltic Wharf, which is a busy shipping wharf and watchkeepers must keep a sharp eye out for vessels manoeuvring in the main channel.

Approaching the marina is more a case of not passing it by. A pair of outer and inner pontoons runs parallel to the river with entrances at both ends and a linking

ESSEX MARINA — SS4 2HF

Contact VHF Ch 80
Call sign *Essex Marina*
Harbourmaster ☎ 01702 258531
   Email info@essexmarina.co.uk
   www.essexmarina.co.uk
Access 24hr
Fuel Diesel and petrol from barge at W end beside boat lift
Facilities WC, Showers, WiFi
Water On pontoons with hoses
Electricity On pontoons
Gas Calor
Chandler TCS Chandlery ☎ 01702 258094, on site
Boat repairs 70-T travelift, 100-T slipway
Pub/Restaurant Marina Bar, Essex Marina YC, both on site
Hotel On site
Ferry Crossings to Burnham town quay in season
   ☎ 07704 060482 www.burnhamferry.co.uk
Trains Rochford (4M) for London
Taxi ☎ 0702 200200

Essex marina entrance from down river

Fuel berth and travel hoist at Wallasea and Essex Marina

walkway between them and the shore in the middle. Riverside berths (along arm A) are alongside the main pontoon, while all others are on fingers from the berthing arms. Contact the marina office for berthing instructions and ask whether to enter from downstream (East) or upstream (West) end.

Wallasea to Althorne Creek (Bridgemarsh)

Above Wallasea and the Baltic Wharf the river turns NW through Cliff Reach with shallows along the N shore, so it's wise to leave Fairway buoys 13 and 15 to starboard (both Q.G). Here the Fairway ends, off Creeksea, and the river scenery becomes more rural and interesting when compared to the reaches below Burnham.

The NW section to Althorne Creek and Bridgemarsh Marine, known as Cliff Reach, because of the 40-50ft cliffs along the N shore, offers one of the few places in the Crouch with any shelter from NE winds. Anchorage can be found under the cliffs, but there are some foul patches along the low water line. If the wind goes into the W it can be very uncomfortable here and a move to anchor under the opposite shore may be worthwhile.

Throughout Cliff Reach and indeed most of the succeeding reaches, the best water lies about midway between the banks. Keep towards the outsides of bends as there are often spits and shoals off points and headlands.

To port at the top of Cliff Reach is Black Point where the main river bends back SW and Althorne Creek runs off to the N behind Bridgemarsh Island (no landing allowed). Althorne Creek is the location of Bridgemarsh Marine.

Bridgemarsh Marine

A large red beacon (Fl.R.5·5s) labelled Ada Point, off the E tip of Bridgemarsh Island, is the first sign of Althorne Creek. If entering the creek, leave this beacon to port and, as the entrance opens up, follow the line of red can buoys leading in around the bend W to the marina hidden behind the island. Approaching the marina

BRIDGEMARSH MARINE CM3 6DQ

Office ☎ 01621 740414 / 07968 696815 (manager) or 07802 658398 (Deputy)

Access HW ±4hr

Facilities WC, Showers, Laundry

Water On pontoons

Electricity On pontoons

Gas Calor (Butane and Propane)

Boat repairs General, electrical, mechanical. Slipway and 12T crane.

Scrubbing posts

Boat storage

Pubs In Althorne village, 1½M

Post Office/General store In Althorne village, 1½M

Transport Railway station, 1hr to London, 10 minutes Burnham

Taxi As Burnham

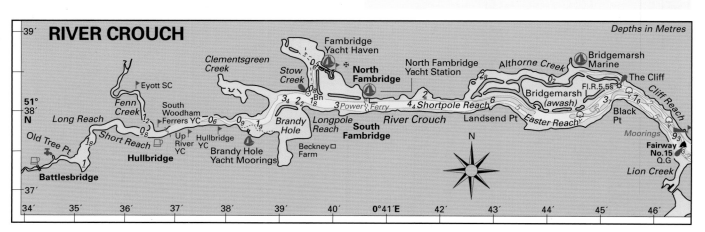

Approach channel and Bridgemarsh Marine

(Bridgemarsh Marine) the end of the main pontoon is directly ahead. A sign indicates that the fairway continues to port along the S side of this pontoon. There is less than 1·0m at the pontoon but the bottom is mud.

A separate, second pontoon stands beyond the first, on the far (W) side of the yard's slipway.

Any intending visitors should call first as spaces are limited.

ALTHORNE TO FAMBRIDGE

From Cliff Reach the main river takes a dive SW past the yellow Canewdon racing mark (summer), then W along the S shore of Bridgemarsh Island, which floods on spring tides, through Easter Reach and NW through Raypits Reach before returning to a W'ly course with Shortpole Reach passing the W end of Bridgemarsh Island. (Circumnavigating Bridgemarsh Island by way of

Entrance to Althorne Creek

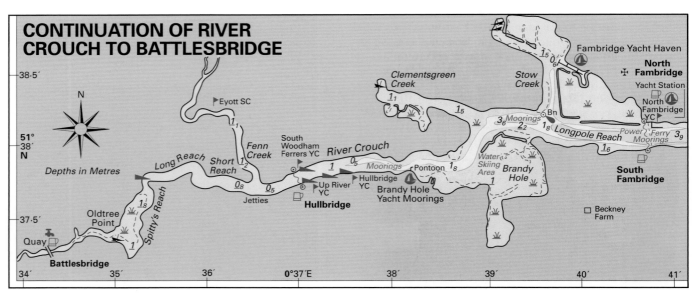

Approaching the long visitors' pontoon at North Fambridge

Althorne and Bridgemarsh Creeks is possible near HWS with a fair wind and a very shallow draught boat or dinghy, but there's an old ford to cross and the channel is tortuous, so it's not recommended.)

A little over 1M above Bridgemarsh Creek (the W end of Bridgemarsh Island) there are lines of moorings at Fambridge, with the North Fambridge YC and North Fambridge Yacht Station on the N shore. The Station is a 120m long floating pontoon outside the North Fambridge YC clubhouse for visiting boats to lie alongside. This and the moorings are operated by the Yacht Haven. Posts at each end of the pontoon are lit Fl(3)G.4s. Anchoring is only advisable above or below the moorings, but there is good depth. Astonishingly, the NFYC clubhouse was designed by Brunel for use as a field hospital in the Crimean War!

As you approach Fambridge from downstream (E), you only see the end of the visitors' pontoon and may not appreciate its length until you are much closer. Berthing is available along both sides (1·2m least depth), as directed, but can be crowded, so call ahead for a berth. (Phone is usually more effective than calling on Ch 80.)

Note The North Fambridge Yacht Station and the Fambridge Yacht Haven are under joint management, hence the duplication of some contact and website details.

Entrance to Stow Creek and Fambridge Yacht Haven

NORTH FAMBRIDGE YACHT STATION   CM3 6LR

Contact VHF Ch 80
Call sign *Fambridge Yacht Haven*
    ☎ 01621 742911
    www.fambridgeyachthaven.com
Access 24hr to moorings/pontoon
Fuel Diesel, jerry can service only
Facilities WC, Showers, WiFi (free with code)
Water On pontoon
Electricity On pontoon
Gas Calor and Gaz
Boat repairs Slip and 18-T hoist
Club North Fambridge YC www.nfyc.co.uk
Pub/Restaurant Ferry Boat Inn at top of yard ☎ 01621 740208
Transport Railway station 1M in village, trains to London or Burnham (complimentary drop-off service provided)
Taxi ☎ 01245 328818, 01621 783007 or ask in office

Fambridge Yacht Haven (Stow Creek)

A little over ½M upstream from Fambridge, Stow Creek branches off to the N with Fambridge Yacht Haven at the top. In the mouth of the creek there's a beacon, known as Stow Post (Q(4)Y.8s), showing a 4kn speed limit sign. This should be left to port when making for the marina, despite some charts still suggesting it should be left to starboard, and there is a small green buoy on the E side of the entrance. It is the shallowest part of the marina approach with a least depth of about 1m.

The ¼M channel is straightforward and is marked with small red buoys to port and occasional small green buoys to starboard. There is a pair of reflective leading mark posts at the N end and you should find least depths

Ada Point PHM   Haven entrance

RIVER CROUCH

Entrance to Fambridge Yacht Haven

FAMBRIDGE YACHT HAVEN   CM3 6LR

Contact VHF Ch 80

Call sign *Fambridge Yacht Haven*
Office ℡ 01621 740370
www.fambridgeyachthaven.com

Access HW ±5hr

Fuel Diesel berth; petrol by jerry can or
available for boats on trailers

Facilities WC, Showers, Laundry, WiFi (free
with code)

Water On pontoons

Electricity On pontoons

Gas Calor and Gaz

Chandler Small stock on site

Provisions Basics on site

Boat repairs Slip and 25-T boat hoist

Pub/Restaurant Ferry Boat Inn, N Fambridge ℡ 01621 740208;
the Ferry Boat Tender café bar on site

Transport Railway station 1M in village, trains to London or
Burnham (complimentary drop-off service provided)

Taxi ℡ 01245 328818, 01621 783007 or ask in office

of 1·5–2m. As soon as the marina opens up to starboard
you can turn sharply in along the long pontoon, the
fairway being on the S side. The fuel berth is just over
halfway along.

Restaurant overlooking Brandy Hole Moorings' landing pontoon

BRANDY HOLE MOORINGS   SS5 6QB

Contact ℡ 01702 231496 or 07788 470718

Access HW ±4hr

Moorings Contact Brandy Hole Moorings

Slipway Contact Brandy Hole Moorings

Landing At pontoon, but shoreside access gate may be locked;
contact Brandy Hole Moorings

Boat repairs Slipway, boatyard, canvas work

Provisions At Co-op, Hullbridge, 20–30 minutes walk

Post Office Ferry Road, Hullbridge

Pub/Food The Anchor (walk up river along sea wall)
℡ 01702 230777
Restaurant @ Brandy Hole ℡ 01702 230320
www.brandyhole.com

STOW CREEK TO BRANDY HOLE

Just W of Stow Creek the main river turns SW past a
small red buoy, while an arm called Clementsgreen Creek
carries on W, but is not navigable for cruisers. The SW
stretch of the river, called Brandy Hole Reach, sees the
Crouch becoming much narrower and shallower. A
notice warns against anchoring above this point because
of shellfish beds. Moorings here and beyond mostly dry
at LW, although some remain afloat in Brandy Hole Bay,
a designated water-skiing area, and near the landing

The Up River Yacht Club on the S shore between Brandy Hole and Hullbridge

pontoon on the S shore where the river once more turns W. The lines of moorings extend for over a mile up stream to Fenn Creek and beyond.

The old Brandy Hole Yacht Station no longer exists as a single entity, because the boatyard, with its slipway and pontoon, is now in different ownership from what was the Yacht Club and is now a restaurant. If planning to visit, phone ahead to the moorings business as they may be able to meet you at the (usually locked) gate off the pontoon.

Brandy Hole to Battlesbridge

We are now so far up river that HW is half an hour after Burnham, yet there are some very active clubs and large numbers of moorings.

The Up River YC has a private slipway and a clubhouse with bar, kitchen and changing rooms, plus moorings in

Battlesbridge moorings looking downstream from the road bridge. Note substantial drying horse in mid stream

the river (① 01702 231654 www.upriver.org.uk). Both the dinghy and cruiser fleets are very active right through the season.

The South Woodham Ferrers YC (① 01245 325942 www.swfyc.com), which shares its clubhouse with the Woodham Ferrers Water Ski Club, stands on the N bank near the ford just E of Fenn Creek and opposite the Upriver YC. The club has cruiser moorings, workshops and a large concrete slipway. There are showers and toilets in the clubhouse.

From Fenn Creek the river runs west for a short distance, through moorings and past houses with shoreside moorings on the S bank. Occasional yellow buoys beyond the last mid-river moorings appear to suggest the best water, although the bottom seems fairly flat. From there, the river follows a winding, narrow route with enough water on a high tide for a boat drawing perhaps 1·5m to reach the old mill buildings and antiques centre at Battlesbridge for a swift pint in The Barge, but do not linger when the tide turns. Should the antiques (or the pints) prove too much of a temptation, it is possible to stay over a tide alongside the concrete wall on the N shore if there is room.

There is also a private small craft landing stage on the S bank just before the bridge where boats of up to 20ft can lie free of charge for a maximum period of 3hr. The ground at the small craft landing is fairly flat, but the mud at the opposite wall slopes outwards and lying there with bilge keels would mean leaning out at an alarming angle, while a single keel boat would need to be leant inwards rather carefully to avoid rigging and guardrail damage. Beware also of a substantial horse in midstream, which is all ready to catch your keel as you turn the boat to head down river. With so little room to turn, only undertake the manoeuvre at or (better) just before HW.

Perhaps the best advice for any newcomer is not to plan on staying over a tide unless you have visited at LW and picked your spot.

13. River Roach

⊕ **Waypoint**
51°37'·0N 000°52'·3E Just E of Branklet buoy

Charts
Imray 2000 series, Y17
Admiralty SC5607, 3750

Tides
Paglesham HW Walton +0040
Rochford HW Walton +0050

Crouch Harbour Authority
Harbourmaster ☎ 01621 783602
Email info@crouchharbour.org.uk www.crouchharbour.org.uk

Roach Sailing Association
Secretary ☎ 07836 344508
Email johnwalmsley@hotmail.com www.roachriver.org.uk/rsa

ECP Honorary Port Pilot
Jim Dew *Email* roach@eastcoastpilot.com

Main hazards

There are two ways of entering the Roach and the only notable hazard is the entry via the Havengore Bridge, which requires good weather and shallow draught, plus permission from the live firing range officials. Otherwise, there are no real hazards within the Roach, provided you follow the channels and avoid spits extending from offshoot creeks.

There are a lot of fishing boat movements in the river, so anchorages need to be chosen with care to avoid obstructing fairways.

There is an 8kn speed limit in the Roach, reducing to 4kn in the creeks and through the Paglesham moorings.

Approaches

The Roach can be entered either from its junction with the Crouch or directly from the sea across the Maplin Sands, then through the Havengore lifting bridge and the inside creeks. The first section of this chapter deals with the approach and entry from the Crouch, and the details of the river and its creeks. The approach and entry from the sea across the Maplin Sands are described later in section 2 of this chapter.

SECTION 1

Approach from the Crouch

When approaching from the Crouch, make for the red/green/red Branklet 'preferred channel' buoy (Fl(2+1)R.10s) ½M E of the Horse Shoal NCB (Q), but remember to leave it on your starboard hand – the Branklet Spit is extensive.

Entry from Crouch

Leave the Branklet preferred channel buoy close to starboard at the entrance in order to keep off the mud bank spreading out from Nase Point on the E shore. Then keep to the middle of the channel, favouring the outside of bends. There are racing buoys, but once past the Crow PHB (Fl.R.10s) further channel marks do not resume until approaching Paglesham.

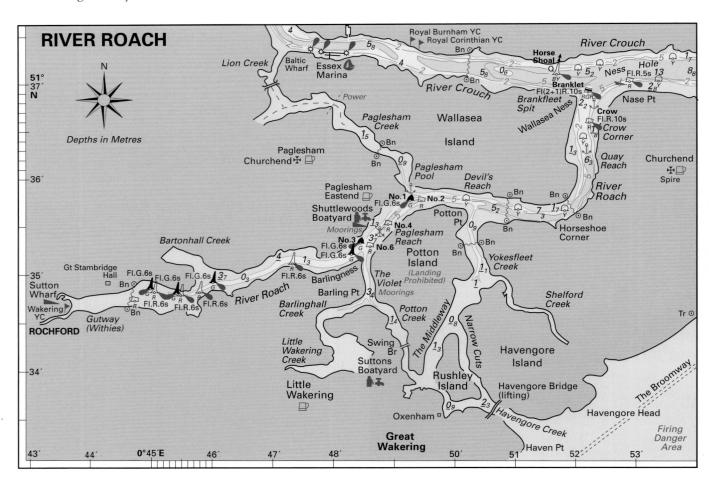

The landing on the East shore of Quay Reach

Branklet to Paglesham

Unlike the Crouch, there is shelter to be found within the Roach from all wind directions. The first useful spot is in Brankfleet at the N end of Quay Reach, just within the mouth of the river, under the W shore, where there is fair depth close in under the sea wall and good holding. Be sure to remain N of the yellow racing buoy Jubilee, because this is positioned off a bay that dries out.

A few boats are occasionally moored on the E side of Quay Reach near a landing on Foulness Island, charted as 'The Quay'. The landing is none too clean and somewhat slippery, but gives access to the hamlet of Church End. It is all MOD land, so you must keep to the footpath then road and the walk is about a mile.

Underwater power cables cross the river at the S end of Quay Reach where the channel bends sharply W. Keep to the outside of this bend where a yellow racing buoy 'Roach' indicates the deepest water. A short way on, in Devil's Reach, more cables cross and immediately afterwards Yokesfleet Creek opens off S to run down the E side of Potton Island. Another sheltered anchorage can be found just inside the entrance under Potton Point, but beware the mud banks on either side of the entrance.

On the N side of the main channel in the area of the Yokesfleet Creek mouth there are sometimes oyster crates marked by small green buoys, which must be avoided. Similarly, beware some oyster layings on the Potton side a little further on.

Looking into the entrance to Paglesham Creek or Pool

Beware long spit

Approaching Paglesham near LW

It's at this point that the river turns SW into Paglesham Reach. On the corner, a narrow creek branches off NW, confusingly known as both Paglesham Creek and Paglesham Pool. There's a small, sheltered anchorage just inside the mouth, protected by the mud spit off the point, but it's best found below half tide with a close eye on the echosounder. The gutway is very narrow. There is a landing just above the pill box on the point, from where it is possible to walk to the Punchbowl (☎ 01702 258376) at Church End (Paglesham) or along the seawall to the much nearer Plough and Sail (☎ 01702 258242) at the top of the lane above the boatyard.

Also on the corner are fairway buoys Nos.1 (Fl.G.6s) and 2, which start the buoyed channel through the Paglesham moorings. This fairway is used by many fishing vessels going to and from their moorings up the river and anchoring is prohibited. Boats wishing to anchor must do so either above or below the lines of moorings and set a riding light.

Immediately the Reach opens up, the old black, timber shed of Shuttlewood's yard (☎ 07546 828645) will be seen on the N side, together with a pontoon landing and hard. Landing on the pontoon is not encouraged, though it's unlikely you will face objections if going ashore by dinghy, but you may choose instead to use Shuttlewood's hard on the upstream side of the pontoon.

The Roach Sailing Association (contact details at start of this chapter) has a few buoys downstream from the hard that visitors may use with permission.

It is under the mud of the Paglesham foreshore that the remains of HMS *Beagle* are believed to have been found. Darwin's famous ship was pensioned off after her third voyage, a survey of Australia, and used for some years as a Customs watch vessel in the Roach. Then she was sold for scrap in 1870 and what are believed to be her remains have been discovered in the Paglesham mud, together with possible parts incorporated in the structure of Shuttlewood's old black shed.

Fairway PHB   Boatyard

Paglesham boatyard and its pontoon, with the hard just to the left

Roach buoy gate, nearing the end of the buoyed stretch before withies take over. Rochford in the distance

Paglesham to Rochford

A short way above the last of the Paglesham moorings, at fairway buoys Nos.3 (Fl.G.6s) and 6, N of Barling Ness, a creek forks off to the S while the main river runs on to the W. This creek, known as The Violet, runs a short way S and then divides with Barlinghall Creek to the W meandering narrowly and muddily up towards Little Wakering, and Potton Creek winding on S to Sutton's Boatyard near Great Wakering.

On the way S, Potton Creek crosses a ford, which is very hard and raised about 2ft above the river bed. It should be approached with caution, above half tide, by boats heading for the Potton swing bridge (VHF Ch 72 *Potton Bridge*, ☎ 01702 219491, HW±2hr). The channel to the bridge is narrow and winds a bit, but is marked with red and green topped withies. Be aware, however, that these are laid with the flood from seawards (Havengore Bridge) – i.e. red to port going N. Pass through the bridge close to the control tower on the Potton Island side for deepest water. Potton Creek can be used by boats with as much as 2m draught, but only near HW on a good tide.

Beyond Sutton's yard (for details see section on Yokesfleet Creek) the channel rejoins the Middleway, W of Rushley Island, and carries on towards the Havengore Bridge.

These are both creeks for exploration on the last of a rising tide with plenty of time to retreat before being stranded, but they do have an air of muddy secrecy that can be appealing.

The main channel of the Roach continues W above Barling Ness. There is good water with up to 1·5m at LW as far as the old Barling Quay on the S shore, but then it shallows considerably and, sensibly, can only be explored close to HW. That said, boats of up to 1·5m draught do make it up the next 1½M towards Stambridge Mills on the top of the tide. Pilotage in this section was made easier in 2014 with the laying of new lit buoyage for much of the route.

The buoys are brightly coloured plastic pillar buoys about a metre high, each lit Fl.6s in their respective colours. The first of these, Blackedge, is a SHB off Blackedge Point, just beyond the entrance to the Violet. The channel is wide and reasonably deep here and the second buoy, the Barling PHB, is ¾M further on, as the river bends to the SSW just before the old Barling Quay. The Bartonhall SHB is a further ¾M upstream, opposite Bartonhall Creek. The Mucking PHB closely follows, then a few hundred yards beyond and round the next river bend to W and then WNW, there are two 'gates' of new buoys, the Lower Rochford PHB and SHB, then Top Rochford PHB and SHB. Between the two gates, you may see 8kn speed limit reminder buoys with lollipop topmarks, and two gates formed by old faded small port and starboard hand buoys.

The channel swings to port after passing between the Top Rochford pair and passes another speed limit buoy or two, and another gate of old faded buoys. Now heading diagonally across the river, a pair of yellow buoys forms a safe passage gate across a charted power line.

Final approach to the head of the river is marked with withies, some coloured, some not – most are left to starboard as the channel gradually works its way past moorings and back to the northern edge of the river.

Where the river makes a final bend to starboard (towards the old Stambridge Mills) there is a SHB. Opposite, to port, you will see the Wakering YC pontoons (☎ 01702 542545
Email secretary@wakeringyachtclub.org.uk
Website www.wakeringyachtclub.org.uk).

Arriving at Rochford with Stambridge Mill to the right

Potton swing bridge and Suttons Boatyard with the Havengore Bridge in the distance

The final approach channel is marked with starboard hand withies, some of which have traffic cones balanced on top. There are 2 vert R lights on the end of the pontoons. The club has drying berths alongside the pontoons with water and electricity and space for visiting boats up to 1m draught. There are WCs in the clubhouse, which is open most days with meals available at weekends.

Following the river to starboard, round the SHB, you reach an active and expanding yard, Carter and Ward, at Sutton Wharf (☎ 01702 546147, ☎ 07850 767686), which appears to port after the bend. The yard has pontoon and quay berths with a 50 ton slipway and travel hoist facilities for boats up to 40ft. There's also a large area of hard standing with electricity and water points provided.

Yokesfleet Creek

Yokesfleet Creek branches S from the Roach in Devil's Reach at Potton Point between a long spit of mud extending from the Point and another broad flat area around the Foulness headland.

A good anchorage can be found close under Potton Point or further up the first reach with shelter from all but N or S winds.

Slightly under a mile into the Creek, two others branch off SE. The first is the narrow and drying Shelford Creek; the second is the dammed New England Creek. A distance of perhaps 2 cables further on along what is now called the Middleway, another creek branches off S called Narrow Cuts, which runs down the E side of Rushley Island and is the main route to and from the Havengore Bridge.

Continuing along the Middleway, down the W side of Rushley Island, the creek is narrow and tortuous but pleasingly full of muddy mystery. Potton Creek appears to starboard around the S tip of Potton Island and some drying pontoon moorings as well as the slipway and cranes of Sutton's Boatyard (☎ 01702 219422, ☎ 07763 062428 *Email* sales@suttonsboatyard.co.uk Website

www.suttonsboatyard.co.uk) come into view. Great Wakering village is a good mile's walk from the yard, but the yard has increasing facilities of its own with pontoon berths, diesel, water and WCs. There's a slipway with a 9 ton boat lift and cranes for craft up to 30 tons. A shipwright and engineer are also on site. There is good water up to the yard (over 3m at HWS) at HW±1hr.

From there, the creek, whether it is Potton or the Middleway is hard to tell, turns SE and then E to join the S end of Narrow Cuts at the Havengore Bridge. There are moorings in the first section of the creek giving some guidance as to where the channel is.

Narrow Cuts

Though drying, Narrow Cuts, as its name implies, is a narrow, dug channel that gives the best route between the Havengore Bridge and the Middleway. It is marked with poles, but do follow them carefully – and be aware that Narrow Cuts is marked from seaward, with the last of the flood tide, so the poles are green to starboard going N and the reverse heading S. Best water at the N end is close to the Havengore Island (E) shore.

SECTION 2

Approaches to the Roach across the Maplin Sands

The main barrier to entering via the Havengore Bridge is the depth on the Maplins, particularly over the Broomway, which is an ancient raised track that dries about 4m, so has only about 2m over it at HWS (on a big tide) and often as little as 0·5m at neaps. On an average spring tide boats with as little as 1–1·5m draught may still touch as they cross the Broomway and, sensibly, should only attempt it in smooth sea conditions. A local saying has it that when there's 5m at Southend, there's 5ft on the Broomway. It seems to be a reasonable equation, but monitor the PLA's broadcasts detailing actual tidal heights, which include Southend, on Ch 69 at H +15 and H+45, to discover any significant variation from the predicted height.

Approach to Havengore across Maplin Sands

The approach across the sands requires good weather and a suitably high tide, as discussed above, plus permission from the Shoeburyness Firing Range Officer (Ch 72 *Shoe Base* or ☏ 01702 383211) before setting off across the sands towards the Havengore Bridge. Maximum recommended draught for using this 'overland' approach (or exit) is 1·5m, even at HWS. The Shoebury ranges are used on most weekdays from 0600-1630 (1230 on Fridays), although permission to cross them may be granted with 24hr notice to the Range Officer. The bridge is manned every day HW±2hr (daylight hours only) and may be lifted on request. It has bars hanging beneath it and there is no room for any craft to pass without the bridge being lifted. Contact the Bridge Keeper (VHF Ch 72 *Shoe Bridge* or ☏ 01702 383436) to confirm opening – but be warned, it has been prone to breakdown in recent years. The *ECP* website usually carries news of any outages in its News section.

There are two suggested routes for the first part of the passage towards the bridge across the Maplin Sands shown on the chartlet on page 107. Start either route no earlier than HW-1½hr. Watch the depth constantly and keep your boat speed down, because uncharted obstructions do exist on the sands although these routes are used frequently by leisure craft. Contact the Bridge Keeper when about 1½M away.

The first route, for boats approaching from E, starts close to the Blacktail West beacon and requires a course made good of 308° for 2·8M to reach a large steel post that should be left close to starboard. This post is not usually charted – its approximate position is 51°32'·70N 000°52'·46E and is shown on the chartlet on page 107.

The second route begins close to the S Shoebury SHB (Fl.G.5s). If early, and the weather is quiet, the 'artificial island' close NW provides a waiting anchorage in a gully

on its W and N sides. Recent charts may show that this island (an experiment in land reclamation) does not cover, but it appears to be eroding quickly. From the island, a course of 006° made good for 1·7M will bring you to a charted wreck shown on the chart as an unlit IDM. Leaving this mark a good 25m to port, turn onto a course of about 065° for 0·45M to the steel post mentioned above at 51°32'·70N 000°52'·46E. This post is the first of four in a generally straight line leading 320° and the bridge will be seen some 1·6M distant, bearing 305°. The posts are dilapidated,

The first of the line of four posts encountered when heading towards the bridge, marked on our chartlet

some with reflectors and some with topmarks in varying states of disrepair. Leave each post close to starboard. The third and fourth posts are close to parts of the Broomway and are where the shallowest water may be expected.

After the fourth post, turn slightly to starboard and continue about 200m to a set of thin steel pipe 'withies', some painted green and one red, which also has a small traffic cone on top.

Pass these appropriately and turn onto about 285° to find the next SHM withy, then

The final run in to the bridge is marked with thin metal withies, some hard to see - this yacht is passing one with a red cone on top

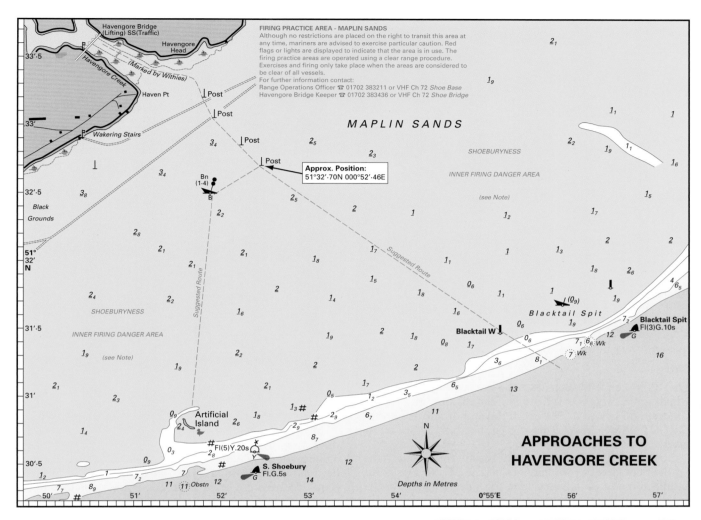

FIRING PRACTICE AREA - MAPLIN SANDS
Although no restrictions are placed on the right to transit this area at any time, mariners are advised to exercise particular caution. Red flags or lights are displayed to indicate that the area is in use. The firing practice areas are operated using a clear range procedure. Exercises and firing only take place when the areas are considered to be clear of all vessels.
For further information contact:
Range Operations Officer ☎ 01702 383211 or VHF Ch 72 *Shoe Base*
Havengore Bridge Keeper ☎ 01702 383436 or VHF Ch 72 *Shoe Bridge*

MAPLIN SANDS

Approx. Position:
51°32'·70N 000°52'·46E

APPROACHES TO
HAVENGORE CREEK

Depths in Metres

continue towards the bridge leaving a succession of pipe withies to starboard. They are all quite difficult to see from a distance, but binoculars help. It is important to follow the withies all the way to the bridge, because there are obstructions outside the marked route, which lies towards the N side of the channel between the sea walls. Ignore a group of similar steel pipes seen across the channel to port, on the S side near Haven Point.

Havengore Bridge

The bridge is much larger than might be expected and is heavily used by MoD traffic, but the Keeper will do his best to accommodate yachts wishing to pass through, after consultation with the Range Officer if the range is active. Traffic lights show clearly when to proceed through the open bridge. If the tide is still flooding, you may find it running hard beneath the bridge.

HAVENGORE

Havengore Bridge ✆ 01702 383436
Range Officer ✆ 01702 383211
VHF Ch 72 *Shoe Base* (Range Officer); Ch 72 *Shoe Bridge* (Havengore Bridge keeper)
Range activity information is often included in MSI broadcasts

Looking back through the bridge to the Maplins. Note the obstructions hanging below the bridge to prevent any craft passing when it is down

Close to local HW, the tide is still running hard to the N into the Roach

RIVER ROACH

14. Canvey and Leigh

Charts Imray 2100 Series, C1, C2
   Admiralty SC5606
Honorary Port Pilot Rob Scriven (☎ 07860 828048
   Email canvey@eastcoastpilot.com)

LEIGH, EAST CANVEY AND BENFLEET

⊕ **Landfall waypoint**
   51°31'·00N 000°42'·57E Close S of Leigh SHB
Tides HW Sheerness

Hazards

Apart from Ray Gut itself and parts of Hadleigh Ray, this entire area, including many moorings, dries soon after half ebb. Potentially extremely uncomfortable in strong E winds unless in the creeks. Only attempt entry on a rising tide and only in a shoal draught boat.

Entry

The unlit Leigh SHB marks the entrance to Ray Gut, which gives access to Benfleet, Smallgains and Leigh Creeks, and lies ½M 290° from the end of Southend Pier (2F.G.13m8M). Apart from the pierhead, there are no lit marks at all in this area.

Benfleet YC's members' rule of thumb for getting right up Benfleet Creek from here is that the Marsh End Sand should already be covered and the tide rising. There is excellent information available including a recent survey

and guidance notes on the Benfleet YC web site, www.benfleetyachtclub.org. Details particularly in Benfleet Creek itself can change from year to year.

Note that in recent years a distinct 'hook' has formed in the tip of the Marsh End Sand, curling round to the NW just inside the first PHB in the channel. From the Leigh buoy, head NW and pass through two pairs of R and G buoys during the first ½M. Then turn onto about 287°, heading for the large fishing boat moorings in Hadleigh Ray. About 0·9M further on, small buoys, some lit, leading off generally NW show the entrance to Leigh Creek.

LEIGH-ON-SEA

Leigh Creek is marked with lit buoys, the lights on some being unreliable, and has an exaggerated S-bend, first to right then left, as it passes outside the large cluster of yacht moorings. For a trip ashore to the interesting Old Leigh or beyond, you could consider staying afloat in Hadleigh Ray and taking the dinghy into the creek. There is a small and basic set of drying pontoon moorings with some facilities at the W end of the waterfront at Leigh Marina, reached by closing the waterfront and following the straight, narrow gutway past the town.

Instead of Leigh Marina, you may find room to dry out alongside Bell Wharf (W side has flat mud) or against the E side of Victoria Wharf, although both can be busy with fishing boat movements. Alternatively, request a spare mooring from one of the two clubs in the town. Leigh SC is based in the old railway station behind

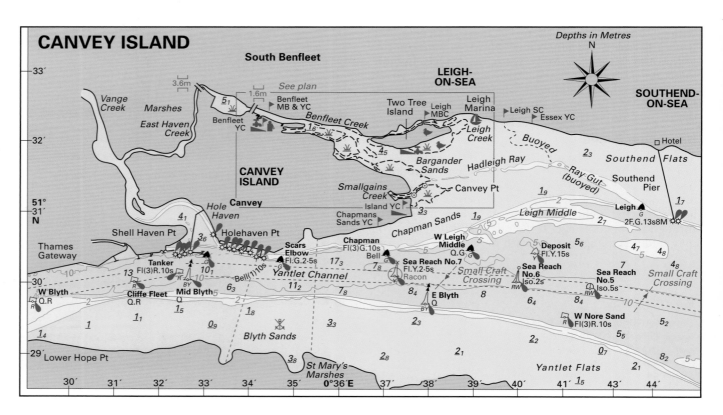

Leigh waterfront from the point where the creek turns west to run parallel to the shore.
Leigh Marina is near the shed with the white roof

LEIGH MARINA   SS9 2ES

Contact ☎ 01702 479009
    www.leighmarina.co.uk
Facilities WC, Showers
Electricity On pontoon
Water On pontoon
Boatyard Slipway, crane, 13-T travel hoist
Fuel Diesel from Mike's Boatyard ☎ 01702 713151
Clubs Leigh SC (☎ 01702 476788 www.leighsailingclub.org);
    Essex YC (☎ 01702 478404 www.essexyachtclub.co.uk);
    Leigh MBC (☎ 01702 714858 www.leighmotorboatclub.com)
Pub/Restaurant Several close by
Transport Bus station, trains to London
Taxi ☎ 01702 334455

The inlet beside Bell Wharf at LW

Bell Wharf, and the Essex YC is based in the old
minehunter *Wilton* 200 yards to the E where there is also
a drying pontoon with fresh water available. The two
clubs' moorings are mostly on firm flat mud where a
twin-keeler should stand upright, but do ask for local
advice as there are occasional holes and gullies,
especially if you choose to anchor instead. It is not
advisable to try to walk ashore at LW.

Leigh Creek meanders on behind Two Tree Island to
its road bridge, where you will find Leigh Motor Boat
Club based in an old barge.

Leigh Motor Boat Club

Smallgains Creek

The Island YC stands on the very E point of Canvey,
close by an old Roman dock and pottery on the S shore
of the drying Smallgains Creek, an inlet at the E end of
Canvey Island, and looks out SE across the Estuary. It
has a forest of wooden staging moorings along the S
shore of the creek with some more on the N side near the
entrance.

To reach the club, continue W past the entrance to
Leigh Creek, following the large fishing boat moorings
along the S side of the deeper water in Hadleigh Ray.
Monitor the depth constantly. Pass the club's yellow
waiting buoy (dries at LWS), then follow the channel
WSW between lit PHBs and SHBs to the entrance to
Smallgains and enter between the wooden piers, the
eastern ends of which are lit 2FR (vert) and 2FG (vert).

Smallgains Creek (foreground), Benfleet Creek and Two Tree
Island beyond

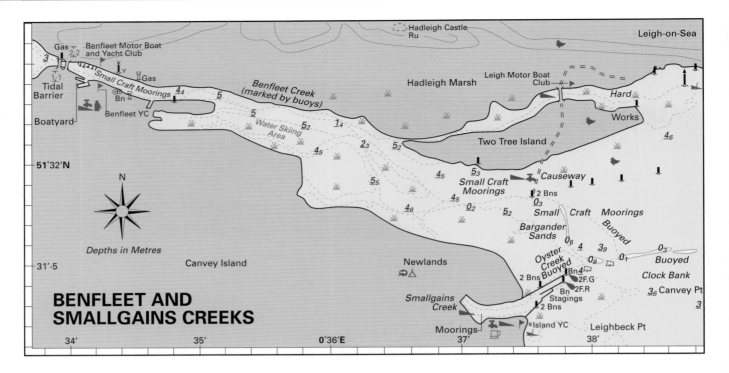

BENFLEET AND SMALLGAINS CREEKS

Just inside the entrance there is a short, steep slipway up onto the S staging, which is suitable for tenders.

The deeper water follows the N shore once inside, then crosses to the S after the creek bends to port – two green posts in the water and a pair of leading mark posts on the S bank show the crossover route. From there, follow the S shore one boat's length off the sterns of moored craft.

There's a broad club-owned slipway on the S shore and immediately before it is a visitors' pontoon, alongside Brinkman's Wharf, which is the quayside area where IYC stores boats and gear. Some visitors choose to pick up a mooring out in the Ray – anchoring there is not advised because of clutter on the bottom – and land by dinghy. However, the club says that visitors will always be found a space.

Passage from Hadleigh Ray to Smallgains Creek and Benfleet Creek shown clearly at LW

The entrance to Smallgains Creek, where a fishing boat is coming out between Island YC's stagings

The drying pontoon beside IYC's slipway, where visitors may be able to lie overnight

ISLAND YACHT CLUB
SS8 7TX

Contact ☎ 01268 510360
Email admin@islandyachtclub.org.uk
www.islandyachtclub.org.uk (includes sketch chartlet)
Access HW±1hr
Facilities WC, showers, visitors' pontoon, slipway
Taxi ☎ 01268 693355, 684433

AW MARINE 'The Marina'
SS8 7TJ

Contact ☎ 01268 680606
Harbourmaster ☎ 07900 517906
Email awmarine@btinternet.com
Access HW ±1hr
Facilities WC, Showers
Slipway 40-T cradle
Boat repairs Shipwright on site
Services Electrical, electronic, engineering, rigging services to order
Café On site
Taxi ☎ 01268 693355, 684433

Just up stream from the IYC slipway is the start of AW Marine's extensive staging and pontoon moorings, all drying, where you may be able to find a visitor berth on request. The business incorporates Mitchell Workboats and Cruisers, builders of fishing and workboats and bespoke motor cruisers. Half way along the S shore is the main slip, opposite which, on the N side, is another slip serving boats on that side of the creek.

Benfleet Creek

At the W end of Hadleigh Ray, a narrow buoyed channel heads off NW towards Two Tree Island and becomes Benfleet Creek. The Benfleet YC stands on the N shore of Canvey Island, E of the tidal barrier across Benfleet Creek, and has moorings in the creek. The creek and its approaches dry, so if you are unfamiliar with the creek

Yacht approaching the posts on the end of Two Tree Island causeway; she should then follow the line of moorings away to the left towards the distant moorings far left to find the beginning of Benfleet YC's buoyage

Start of Benfleet YC buoyage

Causeway posts

BENFLEET   SS8 0QT

Tides HW Sheerness +0010

Benfleet YC

Contact ① 01268 792278
   www.benfleetyachtclub.org
   Open every day with food available, hours
   vary

Facilities WC, showers, slipway

Fuel Diesel (cans)

Water From club

Chandlers (both close outside club gate):
   Dauntless Yacht Centre ① 07833 562536;
   Essex Marine (mainly engine spares) ① 01268 795554

Boatyard Dauntless Boatyard: Toilets, slipway, travel hoist
   20T/46ft, crane 18T, boat repairs and engines ① 01268
   793782

Gas Calor and Gaz from Camping & General (15 minute walk)
   ① 01268 692141

Pub/Restaurant Benfleet, 10 minute walk

Taxi ① 01268 556666

Approaching the Benfleet YC and tidal barrier

and are trying to reach the club, a rising tide is essential, as is shoal draught. You should phone ahead for advice about a mooring or a place on the slipway and refer to the guidance notes and diagrams on Benfleet YC's website.

There are two routes from the Hadleigh Ray roughly NW towards a pair of starboard hand posts with conical tops. Between them there are shallows and a sand horse. The N route was once buoyed, but is no longer. The S route, known locally as 'The Hole' is deeper and the preferred route, and can be found by following the line of moorings. When nearing the two green-topped poles, turn WNW to leave them close on your starboard side.

The two starboard hand posts mark the end of a wide concrete causeway/slipway extending S from Two Tree Island where there is water available. The island is a nature reserve and is 20 mins walk from Leigh Station.

Leaving the posts at the end of the causeway close to starboard, turn W and leave more moorings close to starboard, aiming for two large yellow/white moorings in the distance towards the S side of the creek, before reaching the first Benfleet YC large SHB. Then follow the R and G buoys (all these buoys are numbered and belong to the club, but be aware there are also a few yellow or white racing buoys, which do not mark the channel) as the channel meanders from one side of the creek to the other, eventually guiding you close to the N bank where you reach the start of the club's moorings. These consist of trots to starboard and bank-side staging berths to port. Just past the start of the stagings, take particular care to follow the buoyed dogleg from the N bank to the S bank – there is a submerged cliff of mud to catch you if you carry straight on. After crossing over, continue up stream along the S side until the clubhouse and slipway show on the port bow. Pontoon moorings lie parallel to the shore just beyond the slipway.

On the N shore, opposite BYC, are the moorings of Benfleet Motor Boat and YC (① 01268 753311), which may also be able to help out with a berth although in generally even shallower water.

Note that even the locals will not leave Benfleet Creek once the tide is ebbing – always leave with some flood left. The ebb is so fast that if you touch, you will almost certainly not get off.

Benfleet YC is in sight but here you must follow the buoys to cross from the N to the S side of the channel

HOLEHAVEN   SS8 0NR

⊕ **Landfall waypoint**
51°30′·50N 000°33′·19E (close S of creek entrance)
Tides HW Sheerness +0010
Haven Master ☎ 07834 824820
Fuel Petrol station 1M

HOLEHAVEN CREEK

Hazards and Approach
There is little depth in the entrance at LW. Heavy commercial traffic passes the entrance and has to be crossed on arrival and departure because all small craft in this part of the Thames must use the south side of the river, whether bound up or down stream.

Final approach to Holehaven Creek entrance will need to be made from a point on the opposite shore when traffic permits.

Entry
The entrance is not obvious until close to and the access channel is narrow with little water at LWS. There are three large yellow mooring buoys on the E side. Enter between the W and middle one of these buoys. Once over the bar and about 200m inside, it deepens to about 2·5m least depth. The line of moored fishing boats is in the best water. The gutway appears to be very narrow in places.

Anchor toward the S end (not amongst moorings) or you may be able to borrow a mooring – all are private, there are no visitors' moorings. Beware of stone groynes on the E side.

The Haven Master can give advice or, out of hours, ring the PLA Duty Officer ☎ 01474 562215.

Holehaven Creek

Holehaven Creek with its line of moorings, the NCI station on the pier in the foreground, and Chainrock Jetty in the distance

Two cables in, there is a slipway to starboard (with a starboard hand post at its outer end), which is steep at its inshore end where dinghies can land. Just beyond is the old HM's office on a pier, now occupied by the National Coastwatch Institution (☎ 01268 696971).

Behind the wall here is the Lobster Smack pub (☎ 01268 514297) with its popular restaurant; the pub is mentioned by Charles Dickens in *Great Expectations*.

The deep water runs on for another ½M before reaching the disused Chainrock Jetty, which has 11m air draught clearance. If access N is required by boats that can't pass beneath the jetty, follow the drying gutway that starts just W of the jetty to join the deeper water again behind Coryton.

The channel meanders on inland, marked by lit PHBs and used by barges, to a junction where the drying East Haven Creek wanders away NE towards Benfleet beneath a tidal barrier (2·8m) and a fixed road bridge (3·1m). Alternatively, the equally shallow Vange Creek can be followed NW beneath another tidal barrier (8·8m) then through small boat moorings to Wat Tyler Country Park.

Vange Creek · East Haven Creek · Chainrock jetty · NCI station · Alternative route to Vange Creek

15. River Thames

⊕ **Landfall Waypoint**
51°29'·56N 000°52'·61E Close N of Sea Reach No.1 North

Charts
Imray 2100 Series C1, C2
Admiralty SC5606 1185, 1186, 2151, 2484

Tides
HW Sheerness; HW London Bridge

Port of London Authority (PLA)
☏ 01474 562200; information available from
www.pla.co.uk and
www.boatingonthethames.co.uk

London VTS
VHF Ch 69 (PLA seaward limit to Sea Reach No.4)
Ch 68 (Sea Reach No.4 to Crayfordness)
Ch 14 above Crayfordness including the Thames Barrier
Control Zone **Call sign** *London VTS*

Coastguard
London Coastguard Ch 16 (Shell Haven to Teddington)
☏ 020 8312 7380

Thames Barrier Control
VHF Ch 14 **Call sign** *London VTS* ☏ 020 8855 0315

Main hazards

Large ships, floating debris, some shallows on the bends, fast river buses upstream from Woolwich. There are many very large mooring buoys, some now lit with a fixed blue light, but others unlit.

Approaches

The pair of Sea Reach No 1 buoys marks the seaward end of the dredged channel into the River Thames and is the gateway to the centre of the deep water shipping channel.

Small craft should stay outside this main channel and make their approach to the Thames following the edges of the drying shallows, staying well out of the way of commercial shipping to comply with the PLA's General Direction 39, which states: *'The Master of a sailing vessel or vessel less than 20m in Length Overall shall ensure that the vessel keeps out of the way and does not obstruct or impede the operation or safety of any vessel approaching, leaving or manoeuvring on or off any berth or ship facility on the Thames'.*

Sea Reach to Tower Bridge: General information

A first trip up the Thames from out in the Estuary may seem daunting, but should be an interesting experience to be enjoyed and remembered. The Port of London Authority (PLA) is responsible for navigational safety and related matters on the tidal Thames and publishes a useful *River Thames Recreational Users Guide*, available as a booklet or downloadable from its recreational website, www.boatingonthethames.co.uk/Cruising.

The river passage begins at the two Sea Reach No.1 buoys, but the PLA's Lower River Sector actually starts at the pair of Sea Reach No.4 buoys Fl(2)5s(sync) R and G respectively, N of the Medway entrance, and finishes at Tower Bridge. As on any river, floating debris can be encountered and a good lookout should be kept.

Southend Pier to East Blyth buoy

E Blyth (Q) BY
Cross Main Channel
0·97M 220°
W.Leigh Middle Q.G
Leigh
Southend Pier 2F.G
2·8M 262°
⊕ 51°30'·80N 000°43'·30E

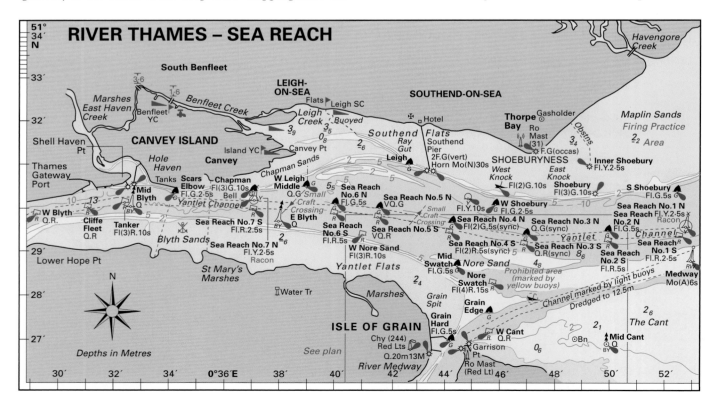

RIVER THAMES – SEA REACH

When planning your passage there are five particular areas of importance:

1. Will you have enough time?

The tides run strongly in the river, reaching 4kn in places at springs, and if you want to run the whole way to St Katharine's in one 'hit', the 40M can be readily achieved with a boat speed of 4-5kn – HW London Bridge is about 1hr later than at Sheerness.

Conversely, the trip down river gives only about 5hr of fair tide. However, the combination of the tide plus 5kn of boat speed should still see you off the Medway by LW if you set off down stream at HW-1 (London Bridge).

With the need to set off up stream at LW, the Queenborough moorings and Stangate Creek anchorage are ideal spots to wait for the tide. A good time to leave Queenborough is 1-1½hr before LW Sheerness.

A possible alternative point of departure is Holehaven (see Canvey chapter) on Canvey Island. It's 8M up river from the Nore Swatch and that allows a later start – check the charted depths at the creek entrance, though, to ensure you can leave when required.

You could also break the journey using moorings at several locations, described in this chapter.

2. Will the Thames Barrier be open?

The Thames Barrier is closed regularly for testing, as well as in times of flood risk, and the Barrier Duty Officer should be contacted when planning the river passage to ensure closure is not planned for the day of your trip. Test closure dates are published in advance by the PLA and can also be accessed via the 'Thames' page at www.eastcoastpilot.com. When the Barrier is closed, other flood gates are closed too, for instance sealing off Embankment Marina (Gravesend) and Gallions Point Marina.

3. Which side of the river should you use?

The first part of the up stream journey needs to be made along the S shore to stay clear of the commercial installations at Canvey, Coryton and the London Gateway Container Terminal, and well south of the buoyed Yantlet Channel and outbound Yantlet Secondary Channel. Note that you may encounter ships coming down stream in this Secondary Channel, which means they will be S of the buoyed main channel!

If leaving from Holehaven, cross *immediately* to the S side when safe to do so. If inbound from NE, cross to the S side of the estuary from W Leigh Middle SHB (Q.G) heading SW towards E Blyth NCB (Q). Note that this is a PLA requirement, although the authors have frequently seen skippers of leisure craft not complying with it. Skirt the shallows on the south side, stay out of trouble and stay safe.

Further up, in Lower Hope Reach, resume the starboard side of the river and stay to starboard for the rest of your journey up stream.

Outbound, it is again a PLA requirement to stay on the S shore throughout, crossing NE, if necessary, only between the pairs of Sea Reach Nos.4 and 5 buoys. These crossing points are clearly charted.

4. Have you got enough fuel?

It should be noted that there is only one location on the Thames between the Estuary and Tower Bridge where you can readily take on fuel alongside through a hose and that is at the fuel barge just down stream from St Katharine Docks. There is no fuel available at Queenborough. The nearest in the Medway is at Gillingham. There is fuel at Gravesend, at the Embankment Marina, but the pump is close to the marina gate and is only accessible near HW. Diesel is available at Gallions Point Marina, but behind the lock.

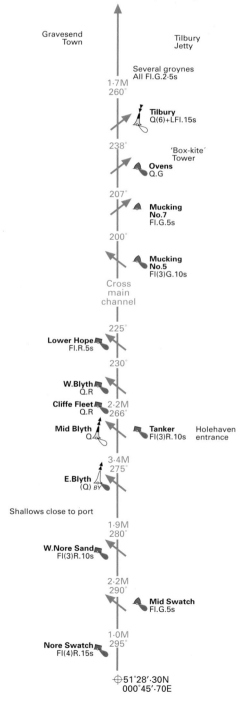

Coalhouse Point with its 'box-kite' tower, where you must take care to stay outside the line of groynes beyond it

5. Have you booked a berth?

Note that visitors are generally only accepted at the five London marinas – Gallions Point, West India, South Dock, Limehouse, and St Katharine's – if they have booked a berth in advance. The marinas are usually busy and often full, especially in high season. You may be asked to show proof of third party insurance on arrival. Incidentally, you may well be visited by the police making routine checks at any London marina, if not on the river itself.

VHF Communications

The river is heavily used by commercial traffic, large and small, and a constant radio watch on the appropriate 'London VTS' channel is sensible. Like any port controllers, the harbourmasters who man the VTS communications are primarily there for commercial shipping, but will always help leisure sailors with advice and guidance in a professional manner. If in doubt, ask, but remember that good and succinct radio procedure will smooth the way if you do talk to them.

Information is broadcast by 'London VTS' on Ch 14 and 69 at H+15 and H+45, and on Ch 68 at H and H+30.

Finally, a point about distress calls on the river – because virtually everyone is monitoring the correct 'London VTS' frequency, a distress call made on that frequency rather than the conventional Ch 16 would be instantly heard on many craft. The PLA Harbourmasters and London Coastguard, who sit in the same room at the Thames Barrier Control Centre, tell us that this is now common practice.

Medway to Gravesend

For the passage to London, leave Queenborough at LW-1hr or 1½hr and sail by way of Grain Hard SHB (Fl.G.5s) and Grain Edge SHB (unlit) to the Nore Swatch PHB (Fl(4)R.15s).

From Nore Swatch, make good about 295° through the Swatchway S of Nore Sand, past the Mid Swatch SHB (Fl.G.5s) and 290° to the W Nore Sand PHB (Fl(3)R.10s). Between these buoys, inshore, there is an arc of orange buoys marking a firing range off the shore of Grain. Just W is a wandering gutway marked with a conical beacon that leads into Yantlet Creek, a possible stopover for shoal draught boats able to take the ground.

Continuing past the Yantlet Flats, towards the E Blyth NCB (Q), the small town of Allhallows is prominent on Grain. From there the N and S shores close in and it feels more like a river than an estuary.

The entrance to Holehaven (see Canvey chapter) opens on the N shore just before Mid Blyth NCB (Q). It can be hard to make out from afar, but the entrance is just W of the four commercial jetties on Canvey. Take care with the depth along this stretch – the shallows on the S shore push further to the N. The developing Thames Gateway container port stretches along the N shore beyond Holehaven.

About 2M on, the river turns S into Lower Hope Reach (The Lower Hope). The shore to port is flatter and shallower around the bend, so do not cut the corner.

The deep water channel here is much narrower and it's time to change sides. Look for a gap in the traffic, watching astern for small, deep-laden coasters using the same inshore course and plan to reach the W side before Mucking No.7 SHB (Fl.G.5s).

The river now bends to starboard round Coalhouse Point, with its curious tower that looks exactly like a giant box-kite, into Gravesend Reach. Rounding the bend just inside the Ovens SHB (Q.G Bell), a line of yellow buoys stretches from the shore out to the S end of the first of six groynes, all marked with posts and lit Fl.G.2·5s. It is essential to leave them all to starboard. Pass close N of Tilbury SCB (Q(6)+LFl.15s) to keep clear.

Once in Gravesend Reach, Gravesend town is in sight ahead on the S shore. Large tugs moor along the shore off the Embankment Marina and the Gravesend SC, both of which can be hard to spot. The clubhouse is about 500 yards before the town proper and is a low building with a white flagpole. There is a long apartment block behind to the SW. The gated entrance to the marina faces NW and is immediately adjacent to the E side of the clubhouse and, like several locations on the tidal Thames, also has a floodgate.

The Embankment Marina is in the old basin of the Thames and Medway Canal, built early in the 19th century to carry munitions from the Thames to the naval dockyards at Chatham. The canal was never successful, was soon superseded by the railway, and much of it has been filled in. The marina, dredged to 1·5m over soft mud, is basic and in its early stages of development, but is a potentially useful stop, although limited by access – only the inner lock gate survives and so it is only opened near HW on free flow. It is possible to obtain diesel by arrangement near HW without going through the gate, berthing in the lock approach immediately outside the swing bridge. The approach to the entrance is along a gutway from the NW and through the bridge. Phone in advance to arrange a visit.

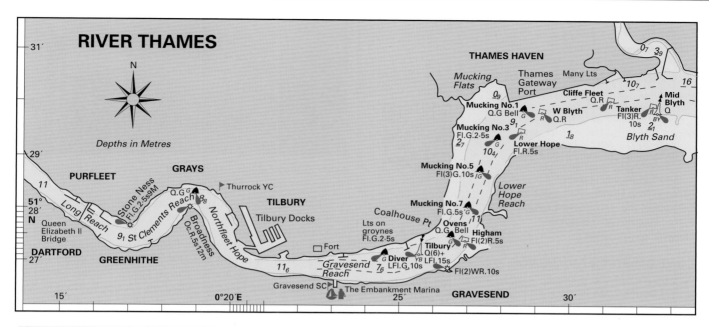

Embankment Marina

Departing through single pair of lock gates at Embankment Marina

The lock gate to Embankment Marina open at HW, next to Gravesend SC

RIVER THAMES

GRAVESEND

Tides HW Sheerness +0025

THE EMBANKMENT MARINA   DA12 2RN

Harbourmaster ☎ 01474 535700
    Email info@theembankmentmarina.net
    www.theembankmentmarina.net
Access HW-1hr to HW via lock gate,
    0800–2000 1 April–31 October;
    1000–1600 1 November–31 March
    All locking by prior arrangement
    Max length/beam 27m/6·4m
Facilities WC, Shower, Pump-out
Fuel Diesel (by arrangement during locking hours)
Water, Electricity On quayside
Slipway Inside marina

LONDON RIVER MOORINGS

Enquiries ☎ 01474 535700 (managed by
    Embankment Marina)
    Email enquiries@LondonRiverMoorings.com
    www.londonrivermoorings.com
Yacht Club Gravesend SC ☎ 07538 326623
    Email secretary@gravesendsc.org.uk
    www.gravesendsc.org.uk
Shore Access GSC pontoon approx HW±2hr; all-tide jetty just
    upriver by Rowing Club, end marked by red beacon; Town
    Pier all-tide pontoon (high sides).
Pub/Restaurant Many in town
Transport Trains to Medway Towns and London
Taxi ☎ 01474 369369, 353535, 535455

Gravesend SC has no visitor moorings, but will always try to allocate you a vacant club mooring if you ask. The club also has a useful pontoon attached to the frontage and parallel to the gutway, which affords brief access to dry land around HW without ladders.

S side of the pontoon on Gravesend Town Pier

There is also a sturdy wooden all-tide ramp at the W end of the promenade (300 yards W of GSC) where you can land from a dinghy.

The PLA has a number of local moorings. These are large yellow cans laid off and just up river from GSC, which may be available for a small charge. A PLA launch, call sign *Thames Patrol* on Ch 68, is often in the area (the PLA offices are just up river) and will collect fees and give advice.

It is also possible to moor on the inside of the large pontoon on the public Town Pier (this is the second pier you come to upstream from the marina and GSC). It is a very substantial metal-sided pontoon; its seaward side is used by the Tilbury ferry and it can be subject to wash from passing ships – be sure to arrange adequate fendering. A berth here is bookable with London River Moorings. They also advertise half-tide moorings against the wall immediately S of the Town Pier pontoon, and swinging moorings immediately downstream from the Town Pier. The wall and the buoys may be better suited to larger craft – call for advice.

Redevelopment of derelict industrial buildings immediately E of Embankment Marina was due to start late in 2014 and should transform the area. Gravesend itself is an interesting town steeped in history with pleasant riverside walks.

Gravesend waterfront – visitor moorings possibly available on
S side of pontoon at Town Pier

Embankment
Marina entrance

Royal
Terrace Pier

Town Pier

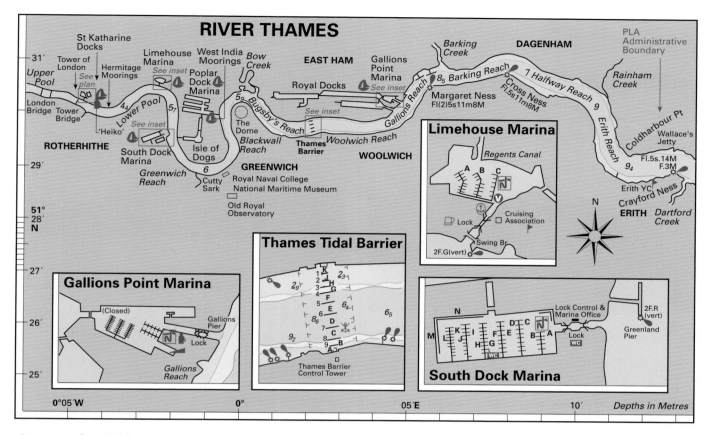

RIVER THAMES

Gravesend to Erith

As you continue westwards passing the town of Gravesend, the Tilbury cruise ship and ferry terminal are seen on the N side. A small ferry runs across the river here from the Town Pier, but is not so frequent as to be a problem.

The shipping activity continues, especially on the N shore, as you leave Gravesend Reach and turn gently to starboard into Northfleet Hope. (Incidentally, a 'fleet' is an area of shallow water and 'hope' means a small bay and the anchorage off it.) Round this corner, facing W, is the entrance to Tilbury Lock, used by merchant ships – your listening watch on Ch 68 will help with news of

movements and also a white light is shown on the cargo jetty just E of the bend if there are ships on the move in the area. There is a container ship terminal to starboard by the lock entrance, followed by a large grain terminal, which can be an unpleasant source of dust in a N wind.

Up ahead to starboard, as development thins out on both shores, is Thurrock YC, identifiable by three large grey and white tower blocks close by and yachts moored in the river near the end of the club's landing stage. Visitors' moorings may be available by arrangement and diesel may be available in cans from the Bosun on weekdays. The club is now in a building ashore, but was

Thurrock YC in front of the landmark white tower blocks

The shoreline at Greenhithe with its public slipway, and the QE2 bridge beyond

Greenhithe and public slipway

The Erith YC clubhouse and its drying pontoon

ERITH YC   DA8 2AD

Tides HW Sheerness +0030
Contact VHF Ch 37
Call sign *Erith Yacht Club*
    ☎ 0845 0942148, Hon Secretary ☎ 0845 0941328
    Email secretary@erithyachtclub.org.uk
    www.erithyachtclub.org.uk
    Open Sundays all year and some evenings
Facilities WCs, Showers
Max length on moorings 11m
Water On tidal pontoon
Fuel Diesel (cans) possible when club open. Otherwise, 1M
    away at garage

once in the ancient *Gull* light vessel, which lies nearby. Contact Thurrock YC RM17 6JF ☎ 01375 373720 www.thurrockyachtclub.org.uk. Open most weekdays until 1600, weekend lunchtimes, and Thursday evenings.

After Thurrock, the river turns SW for a mile or so in St Clement's or Fiddler's Reach and a modern housing development at Greenhithe covers the S bank with woods behind. Towards the W end of the modern housing there are a few PLA-owned moorings close inshore, some usually unoccupied, and a charted sturdy wooden slipway S of them where you can land by dinghy. The interesting historic part of Greenhithe is all close to the top of the ramp, fronted by the ancient Pier Hotel (no longer a hotel), which offers refreshments and food (DA9 9NN ☎ 01322 382291). There is a corner shop and a large superstore, both about a 10-minute walk, and a railway station very close to the river with trains to London and the Medway Towns.

The huge QEII road bridge (53m) dominates the view ahead as the river turns NW into Long Reach. Here the tide can run well in excess of 3kn under the bridge and you have 17M to go to Tower Bridge.

Watch for ships manoeuvring at berths on both shores just above the QEII bridge. There is an oil terminal to port and docks are strung along the starboard shore. In the far distance, large wind turbines can be seen at Dagenham and to port is the prominent concrete blockhouse of the Dartford Creek Tidal Barrier.

Rounding Crayford Ness to port (where you must switch your listening watch from Ch 68 to Ch 14), Erith YC, a large building with a sloping roof, is conspicuous ahead on the S shore with many yacht moorings close by.

The club welcomes visitors and offers a useful stop if you are running out of tide on passage between London and the Estuary – there may be a vacant mooring for monohulls up to 11m on request. Be aware that 2.1m below the surface there are bridles between adjacent moorings in each line. Larger boats can anchor just up stream, where holding is good in mud. You may be able to lie for a short time alongside the pontoon in front of the clubhouse – this has about 3·5m depth (max) and dries – but the club cannot accommodate overnight stays on it. Immediately upstream of the clubhouse is a long concrete jetty, its end marked by a red post, on which you can land from a dinghy at LW.

About ¾M further up stream (beyond the substantial commercial jetty) is the charted town causeway, where you can also land by dinghy, with a large supermarket close by.

Erith to Thames Barrier

Continuing up river, the environment once again becomes industrial with an enormous landfill site on the N shore at Rainham Marshes and the Ford motor works

Erith YC

Approaching Erith YC and its moorings from downstream

The entrance to Gallions Point Marina is beyond a single lattice tower on the N shore

Marina entrance

The lock gate, between two blue notice boards

Visitor moorings

Office

Gallions Point Marina

Alongside moorings in the old ship lock in Gallions Point Marina

GALLIONS POINT MARINA   E16 2QY

Pre-booking essential for visitors

Tides HW London Bridge -0015

Contact VHF Ch 80, 37

Call sign *Gallions Point Marina*

Harbourmaster ✆ 020 7476 7054

Locking hours 0800-1830H weekdays and weekends
   Email info@gallionspointmarina.co.uk
   www.gallionspointmarina.co.uk

Access HW±5hr

Max length/beam 22m/7·6m

Facilities WC, Showers, Pump-out

Slipway In marina

Fuel Diesel (cans)

Water On pontoons and quay

Electricity On pontoons

Gas Calor

Engineer On site

Sailmaker ✆ 020 8599 1413

Rigger ✆ 07828 388029

Provisions Retail Park to N; shops to W in N Woolwich; both 10 minute walk.

Transport Docklands Light Railway (Gallions Reach). Buses. London City Airport

at Dagenham beyond, around Jenningtree Point. On the S shore opposite Fords, a structure like a beached whale is actually a sewage works.

Rounding Cross Ness point into Barking Reach and passing the modern sprawl of Thamesmead to port, a huge illuminated sign board stands on the N shore. This is the downstream signal station for the Thames Barrier. It displays the London VTS VHF Channel and phone number, and the CEVNI symbol for 'Stop as required by regulations'.

The sign is 3M from the Barrier; call 'London VTS' at the Thames Barrier Navigation Centre on VHF Ch 14 after another ¾M as you round Margaret Ness, and announce your position and intentions. Keep it brief – for instance: *"London VTS, yacht 'XXXX', Margaret Ness, upstream, permission to pass through the Barrier please."* You will

The Thames Barrier downstream signal station, on the N shore at Barking

Approaching the Thames Barrier from E

usually be given the all clear and told which span to pass through. Small craft may sometimes be asked to call again when you have the Barrier in sight.

In Gallions Reach, you will find the gated entrance to Gallions Point Marina to starboard. The entrance is not immediately obvious, but is 400m upstream of a lattice radio mast. Note that if the Thames Barrier is closed, as a flood precaution or for testing, this marina will be inaccessible, because there is a floodgate outside the lock that is always operated at the same time.

There are shallows to be aware of on the N side of the final approach if near LW. There are no buoys or waiting pontoons. Advance booking is required.

The lock is a modern one built into the original huge lock that gave entry to the Royal Docks and takes a maximum length of 22m. The operator will be on your port side on entry and will usually pass down lines.

Being close to the end of the City Airport runway, the location is subject to aircraft noise, except at night and from 1230 Saturday to 1230 Sunday.

Two ferries operating at Woolwich on a weekday – they cross the river every 10-15 minutes

Thames Barrier Navigation Centre (TBNC)

VHF Ch 14
Call sign *London VTS*
☎ 020 8855 0315

Vessels on passage down stream from the non-tidal Thames often use Gallions Point Marina as a stopover to wait for the tide. It is also handy for visiting the ExCeL Exhibition Centre, close by. This part of the old docks is undeveloped and much of its hardware – huge capstans and bollards, for instance – remains and is kept smart, and there is much wildlife around too.

The river sweeps past Gallions Point with Woolwich to port, turning W into Woolwich Reach. Just ahead are the Woolwich Ferry terminals, large grey rectangular buildings standing on each shore. The two ferries (if both are operating) cross the river frequently, but they will use Ch 14 to give warning and will respond to a call on the radio if confirmation is needed.

The Thames Barrier

The Thames Barrier, less than a mile from Woolwich Ferry, displays clear lights on each bascule to indicate which span (gap) to use: the lights form a green arrow pointing in from each side of the span in use, and a red 'X' either side of spans that are closed.

Charts show the designation of the spans (B to G with C, D, E and F most frequently used), also see the diagram on page 113. When you are told which span to use, London VTS will use the letter, e.g *Span Foxtrot*. These letters are *not* marked on the barrier itself.

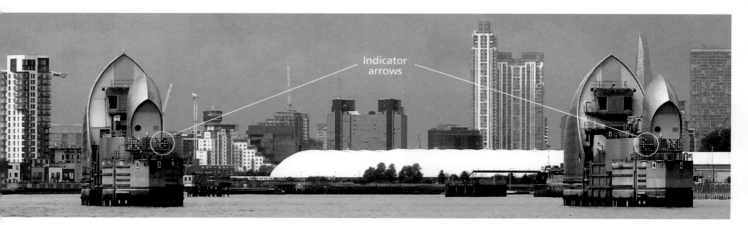

Be sure to pass through the correct span by obeying the red and green indicator arrows

Greenwich YC and its pontoon

GREENWICH YACHT CLUB
SE10 0BW

Tides HW London Bridge -0010
Enquiries ① 0844 736 5846 ext 0
Harbourmaster ① 0844 736 5846 ext 31
　Email
　harbourmaster@greenwichyachtclub.co.uk
Yardmaster ① 0844 736 5846 ext 41
　yardmaster@greenwichyachtclub.co.uk
　www.greenwichyachtclub.co.uk
Facilities (when club open) WC, Showers
Water On pontoon
Electricity On pontoon
Slipway Yes (public but a fee for parking at GYC)
Provisions Shops 20 minute walk
Transport Underground (N Greenwich) and Cable Car, 20mins

The ancient Trinity Buoy Wharf and its unique lighthouse

The huge blue bascule bridge leading into West India Docks

Provided you are on the starboard side of the river, the green arrows will be obvious – they have a narrow beam and would not be visible to anyone travelling up stream on the incorrect side of the river. Do not approach within ¼M of the Barrier unless you are on passage through it and, if you have a working engine, you are required to use it, not sail through. If in any doubt, do not hesitate to contact the TBNC, where your query will be handled with courtesy.

Less than 1M above the Barrier, the grey building of Greenwich YC stands on stilts against the S bank. The club welcomes visitors and is open on Tuesday evenings

O2 and cable car

and at weekends. A call to the Harbourmaster or the Yardmaster may result in permission for an overnight stop or short stay on a mooring or possibly against the all-tide pontoon in front of the clubhouse if you are less than 13m LOA. The pontoon has water and electricity and least depth about 1·7m. At night, the pontoon is lit 2F.R.(vert) and there is also a red light at each end of the club balcony.

Thames Barrier to Greenwich

Just beyond the elegant white towers that carry a cable car system across the river, the huge white dome of the O2 dominates the scene above the Barrier, virtually filling the Greenwich Peninsula at the end of Bugsby's Reach.

Beside the O2, on Blackwall Point, is the upstream-facing signal station for the Thames Barrier, identical to

RIVER THAMES

West India
Dock visitor
moorings

Blackwall
Basin

Poplar Dock
Marina

West India
Harbour Office

The 'Blue Bridge'

The Canary Wharf complex, looking west

the one down stream at Barking and serving the same function – from here you will call 'London VTS' again on your return journey.

A point of interest to starboard is London's only lighthouse, on Trinity Buoy Wharf, once used for testing and training at this former maintenance site for Trinity House.

Once past the Dome and into Blackwall Reach, the Greenwich Meridian is crossed and the massive office blocks of Canary Wharf stand out to starboard. Over on the W side of Blackwall Reach, through an impressive blue-painted lifting bridge, lies the West India and Millwall Docks complex; this includes marinas in Poplar Dock and Blackwall Basin, as well as extensive quayside moorings in West India Dock.

Access to Blackwall Basin and Poplar Dock involves an air draught limit of 5·2m, passage through a lock and five more bridges after the Blue Bridge and is not normally possible at all during business hours. Furthermore, neither generally offers visitor moorings.

Club fleets moored along the S side of West India Dock

WEST INDIA AND MILLWALL DOCKS

Tides HW London Bridge -0010

1. BLACKWALL BASIN
(Canal & River Trust)   E14 9SF

Visitor moorings not generally available
Contact for entrance See West India details below
www.canalrivertrust.org.uk

2. POPLAR DOCK MARINA
(British Waterways Marinas Ltd)   E14 8EG

Visitor moorings not generally available
Contact for entrance See West India details below
Contact for office See Limehouse Marina details p.128
www.bwml.co.uk

3. WEST INDIA VISITOR MOORINGS
(Canal & River Trust)   E14 9ST

Fleets of about six or more only; pre-booking essential
Contact VHF Ch 13
Call sign *West India Dock Control*
Marine Control (manned 24/7) ☎ 020 7987 7260
General Enquiries ☎ 0303 0404040
    www.canalrivertrust.org.uk
Access HW±4hr between 0700-1900 (but small craft schedule to arrive around HW)
Facilities WC, Showers, Launderette, Pump-out
Water Quayside
Electricity Quayside
Gas Calor or Gaz available nearby
Pub/restaurant Many in area
Provisions Shops at Canary Wharf
Transport South Quay (Docklands Light Railway), Canary Wharf (Tube), Buses

Greenwich Pier and the *Cutty Sark*

Greenwich to Tower Bridge

After Greenwich the river turns N into Limehouse Reach and, half way up on the W side, is London's largest marina, the 200-berth South Dock Marina at Rotherhithe.

Inbound, call the lock office when about 15 mins away. Advance booking is required. The entrance is just downstream from Greenland Pier, a large pontoon with a white painted and roofed ramp to the shore. This pier is a frequent stop for the fast river bus services and the area is often very choppy, especially in a breeze. In 2014 there was no dedicated waiting pontoon, nor any waiting buoys. It is possible to wait on the inside of the Greenland Pier pontoon – there's enough length for a 34-footer N or S of the ramp – but it can be very rough indeed there and boats must be well fendered and not left unattended. Alternatively, there are usually lighters moored downstream of the entrance and you may be able to hang off one of these. You may choose instead to wait on idling engine just downstream of the lock.

Traffic lights due to be installed by early 2015 will indicate when it is safe to enter. Beware of strong cross currents when entering the lock. Inside, there are permanent looped lines hanging down on each side of the lock and, if you can moor starboard side to, the lock keeper may also be able to pass lines.

This marina is unique amongst the London destinations in that it is on the S bank of the river; most Thames visitors seem to pass it by, but its public transport connections are very good indeed, it is

However, West India Dock, which covers a huge area behind the lock normally has visitor moorings available, but only for groups of six or more boats. It is popular for club visits and also regularly accommodates superyachts, Naval visits and tall ships. The lock is immense, hence the preference for fleets rather than single leisure boats. The dockside has water, power and toilets, but is in a public area without the security normally offered by a marina. Berthing is against the S wall, which has a low timber 'rubbing strake' that may be awkward for any less able crew members on boats under 30ft with low freeboard.

On approach to West India, having booked in advance, contact the dock office on Ch 13 when about 10mins away.

The nearby Museum of Docklands (E14 4AL, ☏ 020 7001 9844) is well worth a visit.

Beyond the entrance to West India, the river swings round Saunders Ness to reveal the glorious buildings of the Royal Naval College at Greenwich and the National Maritime Museum, together with the *Cutty Sark*.

Yacht entering the lock – note the strong cross-current in river

Greenland Pier – waiting on the inside not recommended

Approaching South Dock, its entrance just downstream of Greenland Pier

South Dock Marina and Greenland Dock

South Dock Marina

The huge expanse of Greenland Dock, looking E

Coots nesting on a handy transom step

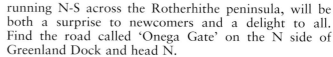

SOUTH DOCK MARINA

SE16 7SZ

Pre-booking essential for visitors

Tides HW London Bridge -0010

Contact VHF Ch 37, 80

Call sign *South Dock Marina*

Lock office ☎ 020 7252 2244
Email southdockmarina@southwark.gov.uk
www.southwark.gov.uk/southdockmarina

Access From 0700-1900 (0800-1700 Sundays and Bank Holidays) when tide allows: nominal 2m+ over the sill from HW-2½ to HW+1½hr

Max length/beam 27m/6·4m

Facilities WC, Showers, Pump-out. WiFi near office. Laundry on site.

Water On pontoons (use own hose)

Electricity On pontoons

Gas Available locally

Slipway At adjacent Surrey Docks Water Sports Centre ☎ 0844 893 3888

Crane 17·5T (20T without spreaders)

Boatyard For boat owners' use 0800–1800 weekdays, 0900–1400 weekends (but no noise on Sundays). Many boatyard trades available locally: ask at the office

Pub/restaurant Many close by

Provisions Small supermarket 150m from SW corner; many shops at Surrey Quays Retail Centre (10min walk)

Transport Buses; Rotherhithe, Surrey Quays and Canada Water Tube stations (15 minute walk). River bus

particularly close to the attractions of Greenwich and there is good local shopping. There is a sailing centre with a slipway in the adjacent huge Greenland Dock, once a centre for the whaling trade.

The area is very quiet, and wildlife abounds here. If you like country walks, then a visit to the park and Russia Dock Woodland created in the old Surrey Docks,

running N-S across the Rotherhithe peninsula, will be both a surprise to newcomers and a delight to all. Find the road called 'Onega Gate' on the N side of Greenland Dock and head N.

From South Dock Marina, the river runs ½M N before another turn to port. On the N side of the bend is one of the most popular destinations for cruising yachtsmen, Limehouse Marina.

The entrance actually faces SW and can be hard to identify from down stream. It comes after a tall apartment block that towers above others along this stretch and has a small painted turret on its roof. There is a white flagpole by the pub just W of the entrance. Strong cross tides at the entrance can make it very choppy in a breeze.

Conspicuous turret

Marina entrance

Approaching Limehouse from downstream – look out for the rooftop turret

Cruising Association

Marina office

Swing Bridge

Visitors' pontoon

DLR station

Limehouse Marina from the N

The road bridge is swinging open, the lock gate is beyond. Note the waiting pontoon

The waiting pontoons, one inside the road bridge, the other outside

Access is through a swinging road bridge and then a lock. Advance booking is required and insurance details may be requested.

There are two waiting pontoons accessible HW±1½hr, one before and one behind the road bridge, both with shore access. Particularly in a SW wind, waves can funnel into the entrance and cause the pontoons to heave around quite violently. Fenders must be set very low if using them. Once through the bridge and on the inner pontoon, a vessel is effectively trapped, so it may be better to jill about in the river while waiting to enter.

The lock has mooring lines hanging vertically against the walls and the office is in the building to port by the basin entrance. To starboard is the headquarters of the Cruising Association, where visitors, even if non-members, may use the bar and restaurant in the evenings. There are also several good restaurants close by in Narrow Street, including The Narrow (① 020 7592 7950), a pub owned by Gordon Ramsay, and plenty of other eating opportunities a few minutes' walk away in Commercial Road.

In the lock – the CA HQ is the building at the end of the lock, on the right

---

LIMEHOUSE MARINA   E14 8EG

Pre-booking essential for visitors

Tides HW London Bridge -0010

Contact VHF Ch 80

Call sign *Limehouse Marina*

Lock Office and bookings ① 020 7308 9930
   Email limehouse.marina@bwml.co.uk
   www.bwml.co.uk/limehouse-basin-marina

Access HW±3hr, 0800–1800 April–September, 0800–1600 October–March. Other times between 0500-2145 may be possible on request with 24hr advance notice

Max length/beam 28m/7·5m

Facilities WC, Showers, Launderette, WiFi, Pump-out

Water On pontoons, use own hose

Electricity On pontoons, uses prepaid cards from office

Gas Can be arranged through the office

Chandlery A few chandlery items in the office

Repairs Peter Lewis Marine – ask in lock office

Provisions Shops nearby and in Commercial Road, 5 mins walk

Pubs/restaurants In Narrow Street nearby and Commercial Road, 5 mins walk

Club Cruising Association ① 020 7537 2828
   www.cruising.org

Transport Docklands Light Railway from Limehouse Station, just NW of the marina; Buses on Commercial Road

Limehouse Marina

Limehouse Marina is another convenient and quiet base for visiting London with good facilities and supplies available nearby, plus good transport links. The Rotherhithe road tunnel entrance is close by.

When returning to the river from the marina, skippers are well advised to make a long sound signal, because approaching traffic heading upstream cannot be seen.

Beyond Cuckolds Point, opposite Limehouse, the river turns SW into the Lower Pool, passing the famous Prospect of Whitby pub to starboard. The next bend to starboard has the headquarters of the River Police on the N shore and brings Tower Bridge into sight ahead in the

The River Police headquarters at Shoreditch

Upper Pool with The Shard (1004ft high) dominating the scene beyond.

In this area, the river is usually made uncomfortably choppy by the wash from barges and coasters, as well as the many pleasure boats that ply the river. Great care should be taken when working on deck – prudent skippers should consider preparing fenders and shorelines when passing Greenwich.

Three cables W of the Police HQ, there is a substantial set of pontoon moorings joined to the N shore by a walkway. This is Hermitage Community Moorings, a not-for-profit location established mainly for large traditional river barges. There are two visitor berths on the downstream end of the outermost pontoon, one inside the pontoon, one on the outside. Minimum depth on the inside berth is approximately 1·0m LAT (beam and tide dependant, see details below) and the bottom is hard – there is more water on the outside berth, but it would be very uncomfortable in a small modern lightweight boat, even though the pontoons are very substantial and deaden some of the chop. The usual facilities are provided.

The moorings are a very short walk from St Katharine's and have the obvious benefit of being in the river itself and not behind a lock gate. Advance booking is advised. Initial contact is best made by phone. Special rates apply for historic vessels. There is paperwork available at the visitor berths in an 'honesty box' for weekend use when the place is unmanned, when members of the 'co-op' can help out if needed. If arriving at night, the visitor berths are either side of the post, which carries 2F.G lights.

Just upstream of Hermitage Moorings, also on the N side, is the large black fuel barge *Heiko*. Be aware that the advertised operating times (see the St Katharine Docks details) are approximate and the barge does not operate at all at weekends. If you require fuel, contact is preferred by phone (see St Katharine Docks details), or VHF Ch 14, and follow directions – you may be asked to moor on the N side of the barge to shelter from the chop.

The entrance to St Katharine Docks (widely known as St Kat's) is on the N shore just short of Tower Bridge.

This marina enjoys a splendid position, almost in Central London and within walking distance of many attractions, and its looks and ambience make it a tourist attraction in itself. Its prices do reflect this, although the period rates can be much better value than daily rates. It is very popular and often completely full, especially when one of the frequent large events is being hosted in

HERMITAGE COMMUNITY MOORINGS

E1W 1NG

Pre-booking advised for visitors

Tides HW London Bridge

Contact ☎ 020 7481 2122 (weekdays only 0930-1700)
www.hcmoorings.org
Email manager@hcmoorings.org

Access Outer berth: all-tide, least depth 2·1m. Inner berth: restricted near LW, least depth 1·0m at point 5m inshore from pontoon

Facilities WC, Showers, Pump-out

Water On pontoon

Electricity On pontoon

Fuel As St Kat's

Provisions As St Kat's

Pubs/Restaurants As St Kat's

Transport As St Kat's

Visitor berths each side of the downstream end of the outer pontoon at Hermitage Moorings

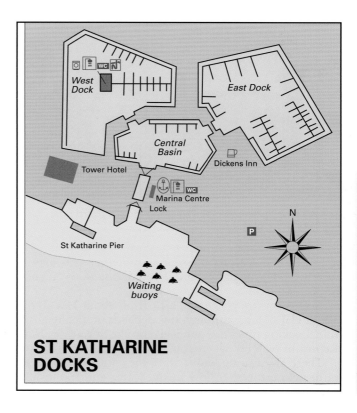

ST KATHARINE DOCKS

RIVER THAMES

Hermitage Moorings ahead, and beyond is Tower Bridge and The Shard.
The Thames barge *Will* is waiting on the outside visitor berth

Fuel barge between Hermitage Moorings and St Kat's entrance

Lock gate

The lock gate and waiting buoys

St Kat's lock – pontoon mooring along the starboard side,
wall along the port side

ST KATHARINE DOCKS   E1W 1LA

Pre-booking essential for visitors
Tides HW London Bridge
Contact VHF Ch 80 (during locking times)
Call sign *St Katharine's*
Office ☎ 020 7264 5312
  Email marina.reception@skdocks.co.uk
  www.skdocks.co.uk
Access Approx HW-2hr to HW+1½hr, Apr-Oct 0600-2030,
  Nov-Mar 0800-1800, but see marina website for
  exact daily times
Facilities WC, Showers, Launderette, Pump-out (mobile, also
  fixed in West Dock)
Water On pontoons
Electricity On pontoons, separate charge
Sailmaker ☎ 020 8599 1413
Gas Calor and Gaz from fuel barge in river
Fuel barge At barge *Heiko* in river ☎ 020 7481 1774 or
  07831 451260 VHF Ch 14, call sign *Heiko*.
  Opening times: Mon-Fri 0630-1430, closed at weekends
Pub/restaurant Several in marina, many nearby outside
Provisions Small supermarket outside to W, large one
  outside to E

the Central Basin. Advance booking (at least a week
ahead in mid-season) is essential; nonetheless it may be
worth calling the day before if you decide to try at short
notice.

Access is through a large lock from about HW-2hr to
about HW+1½hr, although this depends on the height of
tide. Locking times are published on the St Kat's website.
Report in by VHF when you are 5 minutes or so away.

There are waiting buoys SE of the entrance. These are
rather close together, low in the water and the inshore
row has only 1·2m least depth. The waiting pontoon
shown on older charts is no longer available, but shoal

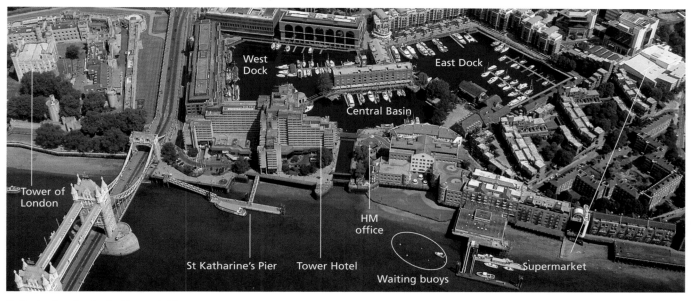

Labels on image: West Dock, East Dock, Central Basin, Tower of London, HM office, St Katharine's Pier, Tower Hotel, Waiting buoys, Supermarket

St Katharine Docks, by Tower Bridge

draught boats may wait on the inside of St Katharine's Pier just up stream of the entrance, although this again has perhaps 1·2m at LW. A better alternative if waiting overnight when the ferries and cruise boats are not running is to go on the outside of this Pier, at either end – do not use the middle.

At busy times, waiting outside for the lock can be hard work for helmsmen as they cope with stemming the strong current, avoiding other boats waiting to enter and frequent large and noisy river ferries using the neighbouring pier. You will normally be called in individually by VHF, but sometimes there can be an unseemly rush into the inviting lock by the waiting skippers as soon as the traffic lights on each pierhead change. Inside the lock, the starboard side is preferred, where there is a floating timber pontoon with cleats at deck height. To port is the old stone wall with bollards and hanging chains. There is often quite a surge felt in the lock until the outer gate closes.

From the lock, you pass through a lifting road bridge into the Central Basin where suddenly all is still. There are two more basins, East Dock and West Dock, leading off from it through lifting footbridges.

All berths are behind smart-card security gates. The whole area is usually beautifully kept and the marina is surrounded by trees, flower beds and hanging baskets. Although it's busy – there are many shops, cafes and restaurants and plenty of people walk through on their way to and from work – it can at times be uncannily quiet apart from constant daytime air traffic overhead. The East Dock is the quietest but has no washroom.

You may be asked to show proof of insurance. Locking out on departure must be booked in advance.

The West Dock in St Kat's (above)

A visiting club fleet berthed in the Central Basin (below)

16. River Medway

⊕ **Landfall waypoints**
From E 51°27'·20N 000°45'·60E
Close E of West Cant PHB (Q.R)
From W (Thames) *and N:*
51°28'·36N 000°45'·55E
Close N of Nore Swatch PHB (Fl(4)R.15s)

Charts
Admiralty SC5606, 1834
Imray 2100 Series, Y18

Tides
Entrance HW Sheerness
Chatham HW Sheerness +0009
Allington Lock HW Sheerness +0100

Harbour Authority (Medway Ports)

Contact VHF Ch 74 **Call sign** *Medway VTS*
Harbourmaster ☎ 01795 596596
Medway Navigation Service ☎ 01795 663025
For any additional leisure boating information, including a useful 'visitor chart', contact the Medway & Swale Boating Association, www.msba.org.uk

Main hazards

The lower part of the Medway is busy with commercial traffic, some of it large, and close attention should be paid to shipping movements. Listen to Medway VTS on Ch 74.

This traffic uses Sheerness Docks, close to the mouth of the river, Thamesport container terminal and a natural gas (LNG) terminal, both in Saltpan Reach, while other ships travel right up river almost to the fixed bridge at Rochester. The very large LNG tankers (often brightly coloured) have strict exclusion zone rules; again listen to Medway VTS.

THE MEDWAY

The tidal Medway stretches 25M from the sea inland to Allington Lock, although for most yachts the head of navigation will be the fixed bridge at Rochester, 13M up stream from Sheerness.

As a tourist destination the Medway Towns have much to offer with the Historic Dockyard Museum, Dickens World, modern shopping centres, Royal Engineers' Museum, Rochester Cathedral, castles and Dickensian festivals. Away from it all in the lower reaches of the river, there is fine sailing as well as interesting and peaceful creeks and inlets. The upper reaches beyond Rochester Bridge, also covered in this chapter, pass through an interesting mix of rural scenery, quiet villages and industrial history.

There is a dangerous wreck (the *Richard Montgomery*) immediately N of the approach channel, 2M NE of Sheerness, in a total exclusion zone marked by yellow light buoys.

There can be overfalls by Garrison Point on the first of the ebb and there are many drying areas on both shores along the river, with some shore features completely covered at HWS.

Approaches

A 244m chimney at Grain Power Station has stood on the W side of the river entrance for many years and is one of the most prominent landmarks in the Thames Estuary, being visible for tens of miles in clear weather. However, the power station is being demolished and the chimney is likely to disappear within a few years. Until then it remains a valuable landmark.

The Medway entrance from the N

Garrison Point   Grain Tower Fort

West Swale   *Stangate Creek*   Garrison Point   *River Medway*   Grain Power Station

LNG terminal   Container Port   Grain Tower Fort

Looking SW into the River Medway with Grain Power Station on the right and Sheerness on the left

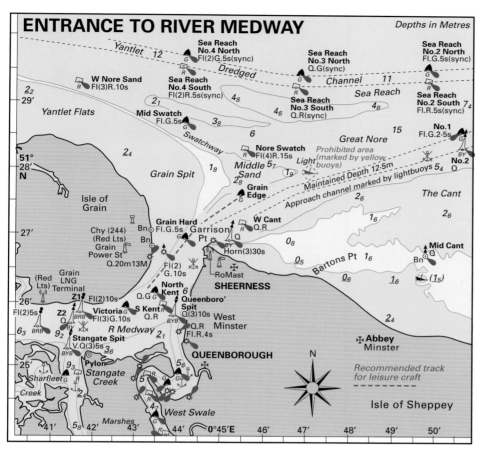

ENTRANCE TO RIVER MEDWAY — Depths in Metres

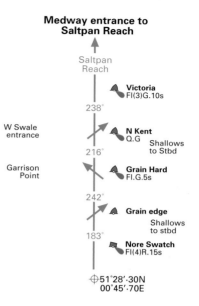

Medway entrance to Saltpan Reach

From E Approach across the Cant shallows from the Spile buoy or along the S edge of the main shipping channel. Note that there is a 'secondary' shipping channel along the S edge of the main channel, marked on its S edge by yellow buoys, all Fl(2)Y.5s. Stay S of both channels, but avoid the shallows S of the West Cant buoy (Q.R) and an outfall marked by a small NCB (V.Q).

From N, NE or the Thames The Nore Swatch (Fl(4)R.15s) marks a convenient point from which to head S to the unlit Grain Edge buoy on the N side of the main channel opposite the West Cant, avoiding the shallows of Grain Spit.

SHEERNESS

Contact VHF Ch 74
Call sign Medway VTS
Harbourmaster ☎ 01795 596596

Sheerness is a commercial port and does not accommodate leisure craft. However, one small part of the original Royal Naval Dockyard remains, a small dock called the Camber, just S of the old fort and Port Office at Garrison Point. This dock is used by fast pilot boats and Sheerness RNLI lifeboats, but could be a place of refuge in an emergency with the consent of the Harbourmaster.

Entry to River Medway

Beware a disused ferry terminal jetty protruding N from Garrison Point – the ebb sets quickly E beneath it.

The Port Control building stands on top of the large fort on Garrison Point and displays a bright light (Fl.7s)

warning of shipping movements. The light is directed up stream if traffic is inbound and to seaward if traffic is outbound.

Unless certain that there is no traffic, use the charted recommended leisure craft track on the W shore, from the No.11 SHB (Fl(3)G.10s) to Grain Hard SHB (Fl.G.5s). The ebb is also weaker on this side. Heading on towards the N Kent SHB (Q.G), take care not to stray onto the steeply shelving bank to starboard, especially W of Grain Hard buoy where there are charted obstructions.

Heavy shipping leaving the Medway is often escorted in this section of the river by large tugs, which can be unsympathetic to leisure craft close to the main channel.

Medway Entrance to Stangate

From the N Kent SHB, the entrance to the West Swale can be seen on the S side of the channel, marked by the Queenborough Spit ECB (Q(3)10s).

Once through the relative narrows of the entrance and into Saltpan Reach, which runs E-W, there is more scope for using the width of the river, shipping permitting. Off to starboard, on Horseshoe Point, the LNG terminal receives very large ships and further W stand the cranes at Thamesport container terminal. Stay well away from the LNG terminal, whether there is a ship berthed or not, and beware of very large ships being turned opposite either terminal.

Bearing about 240° from the Victoria SHB (Fl(3)G.10s), the Stangate Spit ECB (VQ(3)5s) marks the W side of the entrance to Stangate Creek, the first anchorage in the Medway. A line of electricity pylons from the SE, ending immediately E of the entrance, is prominent. There are heavy mooring buoys along the S side of the main channel, E of Stangate entrance, which can be almost invisible at night and are often occupied by huge barges. The buoys are unsuitable for use by small craft.

Stangate and Sharfleet Creeks

Stangate Creek runs due S from the Medway for 1·6M from the Spit buoy and is a very popular and peaceful anchorage, but be sure to display a riding light at night as boats are often on the move there after dark. The bottom is mud and holding is generally excellent. The marshes each side teem with birdlife.

The ruined building on Burntwick Island (to starboard at entrance) once housed a steam engine to pull a defensive boom across the Medway. Evidence of much older settlements includes fragments of Roman pottery still found there.

Half-a-mile into the creek, after passing an unlit SHB with a wreck very close W of it, Sharfleet Creek turns off to the W and then NW into a horseshoe curve. This creek too is popular, although you need to choose your spot so as not to take the ground at LW and to avoid

A typically peaceful evening in Stangate Creek

blocking the channel. There are no marks or withies. Parts of Sharfleet, once the best oyster grounds in the Medway, are very deep, and most of it has more than 2m at LWS. Many head for the deeper water on the W side of the 'horseshoe'. In a N'ly breeze, machinery noise can carry across from Thamesport, but otherwise this is a peaceful place. With shoal draught and a rising tide, the adventurous skipper can take a shortcut W across the Ham Ooze from Sharfleet to Half Acre Creek or to the Medway in Kethole Reach.

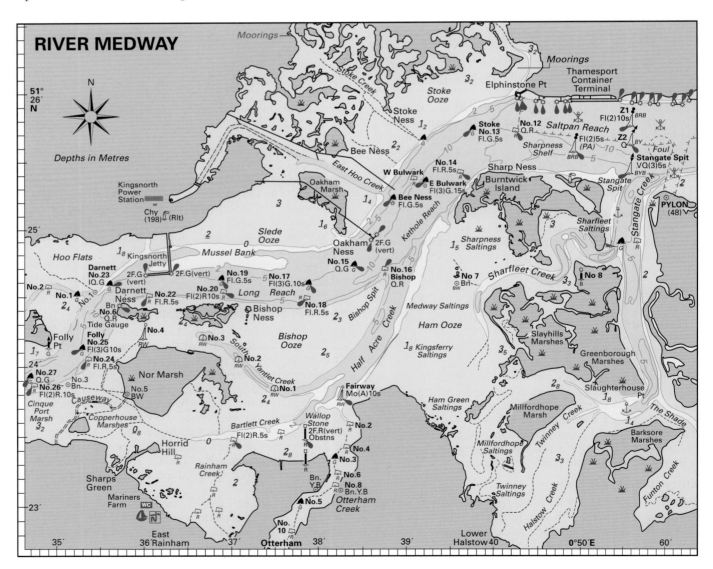

Lower Halstow YC and moorings

Stangate Creek continues S from its junction with Sharfleet Creek with good holding everywhere. Visitors generally bring up on the windward side of the creek, although the surrounding countryside is marsh and does not give much shelter from strong winds near HW. The creek divides at its S end with the Shade to port offering another possible anchorage. Beyond the Shade, Funton Reach soon peters out into the drying areas of Funton Creek and Bedlams Bottom, graveyard of the famous racing Thames barges *Sirdar* and *Veronica*.

To starboard at the S end of Stangate Creek, immediately S of Slaughterhouse Point, there is a pool affording better shelter in a N wind. Some charts show this pool, and an area near the N end of Stangate, as 'explosives anchorages', but there now seems to be no reason for these to be charted, a leftover perhaps from the Medway's naval dockyards.

SW from this pool, the drying Halstow Creek will take shoal draught boats right up to Lower Halstow on the tide, but the whole area dries.

LOWER HALSTOW

Lower Halstow is a peaceful village with an ancient church, a pub, a village shop and an old quay. The old Eastwood's Wharf, opposite the church and once used to load bricks onto barges, is a possible spot to visit if you draw little more than 1m, although you may find as much as 2m at springs. On entry, the best water is close to the W side until you reach the wall. There are no toilets and the usable section of wharf is sometimes largely occupied by the barge *Edith May*; rafting alongside her may be possible, but you may then not sit quite upright. If the wharf is empty, lie alongside it a few lengths in from the N end. The S section of wharf is

unusable, because there are barge blocks there, marked by a warning notice. Anchoring off and going ashore by dinghy over HW is an alternative.

In the SE corner of the inlet is Lower Halstow YC (www.lhyc.org.uk), access HW±1½hr, with its many drying moorings, a short jetty and a slipway. To reach the club from Stangate, head SW midway between the E shore and the small islet and aim for the middle of the club moorings seen ahead. The jetty displays a fixed red light at night. Ask in advance if you can use a club visitor buoy. The bottom is generally quite flat with 2m at HW.

Stangate Creek to Bishop Spit

N of the entrance to Stangate Creek, in Saltpan Reach, there is the Z2 NCB(Q) and, further N, the Z1 Isolated Danger mark (Fl(2)10s).

Pilotage W is straightforward, noting a second Isolated Danger (Fl(2)5s) on the S side of the main channel opposite Thamesport. Large ships turn in this area of Saltpan Reach.

Passing the No.12 PHB (Q.R), the river turns SW into Kethole Reach. Over to starboard, the drying Stoke Saltings was one of the areas in the Medway used by 19th century gangs of 'muddies', who, between two tides, could fully load a Thames barge with the blue clay used in cement making. An unlit SHB on the edge of the flats marks the start of Stoke Creek, another drying inlet with a small boatyard and moorings at its head.

Half way along Kethole Reach, the E Bulwark SHB (Fl(3)G.15s) and unlit W Bulwark PHB mark the extremities of the wreck of the 15,000T battleship HMS *Bulwark*, which exploded in November 1914 with the loss of over 700 lives. Here the Bee Ness disused jetty juts out from the NW shore and on its SW side is the

Notice indicates start of barge blocks

Eastwood's Wharf, Lower Halstow at HW

Lower Halstow YC behind trees

The wharf and, around the corner, Lower Halstow YC

Gillingham Marina   Folly Point   Tower blocks by Chatham Marina

The final SWB in S Yantlet Creek before rejoining the Medway in Pinup Reach

The *E* and *W Bulwark* buoys and, beyond, the ruined Bee Ness jetty

entrance to East Hoo Creek, a narrow anchorage running NW and carrying over 2·5m almost to its head in Damhead Creek.

If you venture into East Hoo Creek, another relic of WWI can be visited by dinghy near LW – the hulk of a German U-boat lies north of the jetty at about 51°25'·8N 000°37'·9E.

SW of the No.14 PHB (Fl.R.5s), a line of heavy mooring buoys stretches along the SE shore – these are virtually invisible at night. Just past the last buoy is the entrance to Half Acre Creek, marked on its W side by the No.16 Bishop PHB (Q.R), behind which lies the extensive and drying Bishop Spit.

Half Acre Creek

Running SW, Half Acre Creek provides a wide, deep water passage for a mile beyond the entrance. Keeping industrial buildings on Motney Hill on the bow, watch for cross-tides. The large tripod of the No.7 beacon is across the flats to port, in the area where a shortcut is possible to or from Sharfleet Creek near HW. Further on SW, some charts show a barge on the E side of the channel, but this has not been seen in modern times. At the Otterham Fairway SWB (Mo(A)10s), Half Acre Creek divides into three, as follows:

South Yantlet Creek runs off to starboard, curving NW following a string of unlit SWBs, numbered 1 to 3. Beyond the third of these is a drying area N of Nor Marsh island, which may be crossed with 2m above half tide towards the fourth and final red and white No.4 SWB pillar buoy. Best water is just S of this buoy. Continuing W for 2 more cables across mud that dries about 2·5m in places, the channel rejoins the Medway in Pinup Reach.

Medway, downstream from Upnor

Half Acre Creek   South Yantlet Creek   Nor Marsh   Middle Creek   Gillingham Marina   Port Werburgh   Medway YC   Chatham Marina   Upnor

OTTERHAM CREEK   ME8 7XE

Otterham Quay Boatyard ☎ 01634 260250
Boat repairs 9-T crane and dry docks (max. length 80ft)
Engineers On site
Access HW±1hr
Pub At Upchurch (1·5 miles)
Provisions Shops at Upchurch
Taxi ☎ 01634 233333

Otterham Creek runs S from the Otterham Fairway buoy for about 1·5M and is a buoyed but drying route to the boatyard at Otterham Quay, which is to port at the end, opposite a commercial wharf. Most tides will allow a 2m draught boat to reach the quay.

Bartlett Creek is the third, middle branch from the Otterham Fairway buoy and heads WSW past a prominent wreck to an unlit PHB, then W towards the Rainham Fairway PHB (Fl(2)R.5s) at the N end of the gutway of Rainham Creek.

Continue W from the Rainham Fairway PHB for a short distance with the distant Gillingham gas holder on the bow, then a gutway marked by occasional withies leads SW towards the unlit Mariners PHB off Horrid Hill.

MARINERS FARM BOATYARD   ME8 7TL

Contact ☎ 01634 233179
    www.marinersboatyard.co.uk
    Email enquiries@marinersboatyard.co.uk
Access HW ±2hr
Facilities WC, 8-T crane
Water At yard
Provisions Short walk to Sharps Green or
    Lower Rainham
Taxi ☎ 01634 233333

The Mariners buoy is laid by Mariners Farm Boatyard, a friendly DIY boat storage venue popular for winter lay-up, where a drying mooring may be available. Beyond the buoy, look SW for two posts close to the shore, topped with coloured cans – swing to port around the first, then sharply to starboard around the second and follow a short line of moorings that leads towards a wide slipway. On approach, do not worry that few masts are in evidence – the yard is hidden behind high trees.

With shoal draught and a rising tide, an alternative route from up river to Bartlett Creek runs SE from further up the River Medway opposite Folly Point, passing between a post and a red can to cross the causeway off the SW corner of Nor Marsh, then on SE past Horrid Hill to meet Bartlett Creek.

This remote and interesting area south of the main Medway channel is nationally and internationally important for many species of birds and is full of life in winter and summer.

The old fort on Darnet Ness where Long Reach
turns SW to join Pinup Reach

Bishop Spit to Darnet Ness

Continuing up stream on the Medway past the entrance to Half Acre Creek, the main river runs W in Long Reach. It is safe to stay out of the main channel by skirting along its N edge, past SHBs No.15 (Q.G), No.17 (Fl(3)G.10s) and No.19 (Fl.G.5s). Kingsnorth Power Station still dominated the view ahead to starboard in 2014 but, like Grain Power station at the Medway entrance, Kingsnorth has served its purpose and demolition has begun. It is unclear whether or not the long coal jetty will remain. The S shore along here shelves steeply and frequently catches out the unwary on a falling tide.

The final PHB in Long Reach, No.22 (Fl.R.5s), stands close to the steeply shelving N edge of Darnet Ness, a small island on the S side of the river where it turns SW into Pinup Reach with R beacon No.6 (Q.R) on its corner. A 'Palmerston Fort' stands on Darnet Ness, built in the 1860s and once housing heavy muzzle-loading rifled guns for defence of the Naval dockyards at Chatham.

Middle Creek

At this bend, the adventurous shoal draught skipper may choose to take the twisting Middle Creek that heads WNW by the No.1 Beacon, either to visit the boatyard at Whitton Marine or to circumnavigate Hoo Island, at suitable states of the tide. The channel is buoyed, but the buoys are not shown on all charts. Starting with a SHB No.1, follow WNW to a PHB marked No.2, rounding this and turning SW, using the gas holder at Gillingham as a transit to find No.3 SHB. The channel then roughly follows the shape of Hoo Island about 50m off, turning NW towards No.4, an SCB in line with a distant church steeple.

The No.1 Bn, nearby the first SHB in Middle Creek near LW

Middle Creek entrance

At this point, with enough tide, you could carry on NW past No.5 PHB towards the Hundred of Hoo SC and Whitton Marine (ME3 9LB ☎ 01634 250593) www.whittonmarine.co.uk, which offers services including marine engineering.

Otherwise, continue W through some moorings towards the R and G posts close to the Hoo Island shore, which indicate a gap in the causeway between Hoo Island and the mainland.

From the R and G markers, head SW (initially staying close to Hoo Island shore – this stretch is the shallowest of the route) and join the Orinoco Channel, which leads either NNW to Port Werburgh, or SSE back to Short Reach in the Medway beside an unlit WCB.

Darnet Ness to Gillingham Marina

If not entering Middle Creek, head SW through Pinup Reach, where the shortcut through to South Yantlet Creek (see above) may be seen to port, before passing the No.25 Folly SHB (Fl(3)G.10s) and No.24 PHB (Fl.R.5s) off Folly Point. The channel is narrow here so take particular care with large traffic. An unlit G post stands on the SE corner of Folly Point to starboard and the shallows extend a long way S of Hoo Island – this island houses a fort matching that on Darnet Ness. Gillingham is now in clear view ahead with a prominent gas holder standing close S of Gillingham Marina.

Note The speed limit upstream from here reduces to 6kn.

At SHB No.27 (Q.G) and PHB No.26 (Fl(2)R.10s), the channel turns just N of W into Gillingham Reach and yacht moorings line both shores. Those on the N shore are close to shallows. Medway Cruising Club (ME7 2SE ☎ 01634 856489 www.medwaycruisingclub.org.uk) and Segas SC (ME7 1TT ☎ 01634 855365 www.segassailingclub.co.uk) are on the south bank, just beyond the next PHB, No.28 (Fl.R.5s). Both clubs are

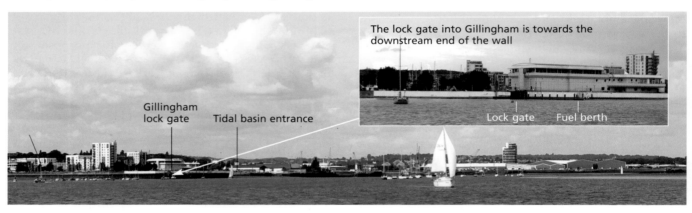

The lock gate into Gillingham is towards the downstream end of the wall

Gillingham lock gate   Tidal basin entrance

Lock gate   Fuel berth

Looking west in Gillingham Reach, the walls of the marina left of picture

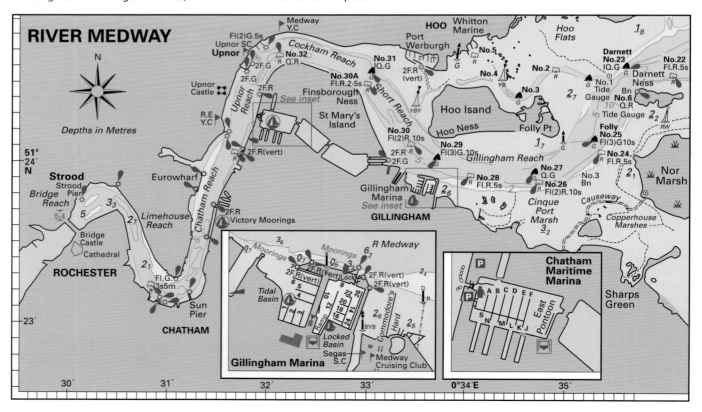

usually open at weekends. The Commodore's Hard public slipway stretches into the river between these two clubs and can be used to launch or recover dinghies and small craft.

Immediately next to Segas SC is the high E wall of Gillingham Marina, which has two basins, one behind a lock, the other tidal. Viewed from the river, the lock gate is towards the downstream end of the N wall, to the left of the large pale-coloured building (a leisure centre) and the tidal basin is round behind the wall at the right hand end. The tidal basin dries to soft mud.

Berths should be booked in advance if possible. All berths in the locked basin are either alongside finger pontoons or stern to (preferably) against pontoons with the boat's bow secured between piles (like the Dutch 'box' system). Boats wishing to depart outside lock operating hours can be offered berths in the tidal basin. The marina office is in the large building at the S end of the wall between the two basins.

Locking is not 24hr (see marina details) but there is a row of waiting buoys in deep water in front of the marina wall. The lock has traffic lights. Vertical cables are set in the lock walls to put lines around, if you cannot reach the bollards at the top, and there are floating fenders on each side. Free flow is sometimes used near to HWS.

There is a refuelling pontoon on the river just up stream of the lock gate. It is angled out into the stream, which can make it a little awkward to leave on the ebb.

The locked basin is commendably quiet; the once derelict dockyard area behind and W of the tidal basin is quickly being redeveloped with many flats and houses.

Immediately up stream from Gillingham Marina is a rectangular inlet known as Gillingham Pier, where there is a high wharf, plus a wide Victorian stone slipway and

GILLINGHAM MARINA   ME7 1UB

Contact ☎ 01634 280022
   www.gillingham-marina.co.uk
   Email berthing@gillingham-marina.co.uk
VHF Ch 80
Call sign *Gillingham Marina*
Access Locked basin HW ±4½hr approx,
   0600–2200 (summer) and daylight hours
   (winter)
Tidal basin HW ±2½hr approx
Max length/beam 16m/5·5m
Facilities WC, showers, launderette, pump-out, WiFi
Water On pontoons
Electricity On pontoons
Fuel Diesel and petrol from pontoon outside lock
Gas Calor and Gaz from office
Boat repairs 65-T and 25-T boat hoists
Engineer On site
Rigger Pier Rigging ☎ 01634 893303
Sailmaker Dolphin Sails agent on site
Chandler Outside marina gate ☎ 01634 283008
   Email chandlery@gillingham-marina.co.uk
Provisions Supermarket, turn right outside marina, 2 min walk
Pub/restaurant On site The Quarterdeck marina bar/restaurant, Spinnakers bar/restaurant in Leisure Centre. Hours vary. Pubs The Ship, The Barge, both 10 mins walk – directions from office.
Taxi ☎ 01634 222222, 582582
Transport Buses outside. Trains to London, Ramsgate and Dover

Gillingham from the west

Gillingham Marina lock - note floating fenders

Gillingham Marina, locked basin - note pile moorings

The curiously-named Gillingham Pier is an inlet with a slipway

some pontoon moorings. The area is operated by Medway Council and anyone wishing to use the slipway or moorings should call them first, on ☎ 01634 331153. A lightship and a replica of the paddle steamer *Medway Queen* (a new hull, but many original components within) are moored there permanently against the western wharf.

GILLINGHAM AND HOO TO ROCHESTER BRIDGE

At No.29 SHB (Fl(3)G.10s), which stands opposite Gillingham Marina, the river turns sharply NW round Hoo Ness into Short Reach. Watch out for shipping entering and leaving Chatham Docks through the locks on the W side of this bend.

Halfway along Short Reach, there is a small unlit WCB on the edge of the shallows to starboard. This marks the W end of the route behind Hoo Island (see section on Middle Creek above); the Orinoco Channel leads NNE from the WCB, branching to port to the Port Werburgh entrance, and starboard to join Middle Creek. Port Werburgh, the collection of residential barges and lightships seen on the N shore, has absorbed the old Hoo Marina, and does not accept any visiting craft. However, Hoo Ness YC (☎ ME3 9LE 01634 250052 www.hooness.org.uk) remains on the shore there, with its drying jetty and slipway accessed through Port Werburgh's entrance, and can accommodate club visits by prior arrangement. The club also has swinging moorings in the river. The Orinoco is withied (although beware some are metal and may be covered near HW) and has about 1·5m from HW-2 to HW+2, while the surrounding area has perhaps 2m at HW.

Continuing NW along Short Reach, Cockham Woods are ahead on the N bank and, to port, lies St Mary's Island. St Mary's was once part of the Chatham Naval Dockyard and is now a major waterside housing development, the shore lined with modern houses.

MEDWAY YACHT CLUB   ME2 4XB

Contact ☎ 01634 718399, 0900–1630 Monday–Saturday (office); ☎ 01634 718169 (clubhouse)
www.medwayyachtclub.com
Email medwayyc@aol.com

Trot Boat 0900–2000 (Saturday and Sunday), 0930-1630H weekdays, call sign *Invicta* on VHF Ch 37

Restaurant Wednesday, Friday, Saturday and Sunday evenings also lunch Saturday and Sunday

Numerous yacht club moorings line the S side of the channel, spreading to the N shore once past the No.30A (Fl.R.2·5s) and No.31 (IQ.G) buoys. Beyond No.31, the dinghy sailors' Wilsonian SC stands on the shore, followed, as Cockham Reach bends to port, by Medway YC's headquarters beneath the woods on the N bank at the apex of the bend.

Medway YC can often provide a mooring for visitors on request, at a small fee. Visitors are welcomed and may use the clubhouse and facilities, including the bar and restaurant. There is an all-tide floating jetty for landing by dinghy, also a trot boat service, although you may be allowed to moor on the jetty overnight during midweek.

Up stream from Medway YC is the all-tide landing for Upnor SC (ME2 4UY ☎ 01634 718043, www.upnorsailingclub.co.uk) where, as at Medway YC, it may be possible to borrow a mooring on request. Its clubhouse is set in a row of cottages behind the sea wall and close by are two large pub/restaurants, the Pier (☎ 01634 717317) and the Ship (☎ 01634 290553), both popular with yachtsmen.

The river continues SW in Upnor Reach, where Upnor Castle sits on the W bank. Cannon fire from here failed

NW along Cockham Reach, Upnor in the distance

Medway YC and its all-tide pontoon

Upnor YC's jetty and moorings

Upnor Castle, on the W bank opposite Chatham Marina

Approaching the lock entrance to Chatham Maritime Marina

Entrance to the Chatham lock is quite narrow, with cross-tides.
Note high pontoon moorings on both sides

A view east across the marina, the fuel berth in the foreground

Lock

Chatham Maritime Marina from the west

to stop the Dutch raiders under Admiral de Ruyter in 1667, who sank 16 ships of the Royal Navy.

On your port side, across the river from Upnor Castle, you will find the lock gate entrance to Chatham Maritime Marina, built in the old No.1 Basin of the Naval Dockyard.

The tide runs hard directly across the entrance, which is fairly narrow – the lock widens in the centre part. Always seek permission before entering. Care needs to be taken not to end up going sideways into the lock. Check the tidal flow and apparent strength before entering and leaving. Inside the lock there are floating pontoons on each side with cleats at deck level. There are traffic light controls and sometimes the lock runs free-flow near to HW with the inner road bridge raised.

This 360-berth marina is relatively new and has the usual facilities – it is popular and often full at peak times. The lock can be very busy indeed during summer weekends. Its surroundings have undergone major regeneration from dockyard days with housing and businesses springing up. There is one pub/restaurant and a small supermarket nearby, plus an 'outlet shopping mall' (which includes eating places, but closes quite early), a multi-screen cinema, the Dickens World tourist attraction (☎ 01634 890421, www.dickensworld.co.uk) and several other family restaurants.

The town is several miles away, but there are bus stops on the marina side of the cinema with regular services until late evening.

Historic Dockyard | Victory Moorings at Thunderbolt Pier | Sun Pier | Upnor Castle

Looking S along Chatham Reach

CHATHAM MARITIME MARINA ME4 4LP

Contact VHF Ch 80
Call sign *Chatham Marina*
☎ 01634 899200
www.chathammaritimemarina.co.uk
Email chatham@mdlmarinas.co.uk

Access 24hr (1·5m over cill at LWS). Possible limited access at top of HWS

Facilities WC, showers, launderette, WiFi

Water On pontoons

Electricity On pontoons

Fuel Diesel and petrol inside immediately to starboard beyond lock

Gas Calor and Gaz

Boat repairs 16-T crane in yard

Sailmaker, electronics, maintenance, rigger Duncan Ross ☎ 07767 425101 www.rossyachtservices.co.uk (Agent for OneSails)

Chandler Pirate's Cave ☎ 01634 295233 (across river at Frindsbury, requires transport; Volvo Penta agent)

Pub/Restaurant Several nearby – marina office may have discount arrangements with some of them

Provisions Supermarket nearby

Trains Chatham or Rochester stations, services to London, Ramsgate and Dover

Taxi ☎ 01634 222222

Just up river from the marina, enormous sheds stand on the E shore. These are relics of the old naval dockyard, covered slipways where ships were once built and maintained, but now part of a vast museum, the magnificent Historic Dockyard (☎ 01634 823800 www.chdt.org.uk for opening times), which is rated as one of Britain's major tourist attractions. If you are visiting Chatham Marina, ask in the office for details of

any special offers on entrance to the museum, which is a 15-minute walk away. Rope making is one of the many fascinating items to be seen, still being done in the traditional way on a 'rope walk'. Naval ships were built here from the late 1500s (including HMS *Victory*) and continued right up to the days of modern submarines, the last of which, HMS *Ocelot*, is one of the ships on display.

Towards the top of Chatham Reach, on the E shore, is a very long floating pontoon, Thunderbolt Pier, running parallel to the stream and connected to the shore at its N end. There, Victory Moorings (☎ 07785 971797 *Email* asm-victory@hotmail.co.uk) runs as a berth holders' facility, which may have room for visitors, but only if pre-booked.

Sun Pier

The all-tide pontoon at Sun Pier provides a short stop for supplies or crew changes

Victory Moorings at Thunderbolt Pier

The rusting remains of the huge Russian submarine

Continuing along Chatham Reach beyond Victory Moorings, you will see in the distance the blue-painted Sun Pier on the S side as the river turns sharply round to NNW at Chatham Ness. Brief landings for shopping or crew changes should be possible, if there is space on its 70ft steel landing pontoon, which has electricity and water and at least 2·5m on its outside at LWS (queries to Medway Council on ☎ 01634 338122). Set your fenders high if you stop here. In late 2014 it was expected that a token system for access to and from the shore would be installed.

About a cable further upstream is the privately owned Ship Pier, a substantial pontoon between piling and connected to a jetty by a gangway. Once available for brief stops, it's now only available for commercial craft.

Unless you have sufficiently low air draught to pass beneath Rochester Bridge, the final stretches before you reach it have little to offer the visitor other than perhaps an interesting sail or motor.

Note The shallows of the Chatham Ness Shoal – the deeper water in Limehouse Reach is towards the W side for the first half of its length. Much of the W bank of this reach has new walls, the old industries above having been cleared away in preparation for the new builds of the extensive Medway Towns regeneration scheme.

The fixed bridge at Rochester, head of navigation for most yachts

Nearly a mile further on, having run up Limehouse Reach and turned SW again into Bridge Reach, Strood Pier on the NW shore is also unfortunately not available to visitors. A very large Russian-built Foxtrot-class submarine has lain rusting on the river here for some years – quite a sight.

Just upstream, the fixed Rochester Bridge carries road and railway across the river with an air draught of 5·4m at HWS. Best water is on the starboard side, but there is negligible water under the bridge at LW and easy passage is only feasible for motor cruisers or shoal draught yachts with easily lowered rigs. You are unlikely to meet any large commercial craft under the bridge, but monitor Medway VTS on Ch 74 to be sure.

Looking downstream from the Medway Crossing

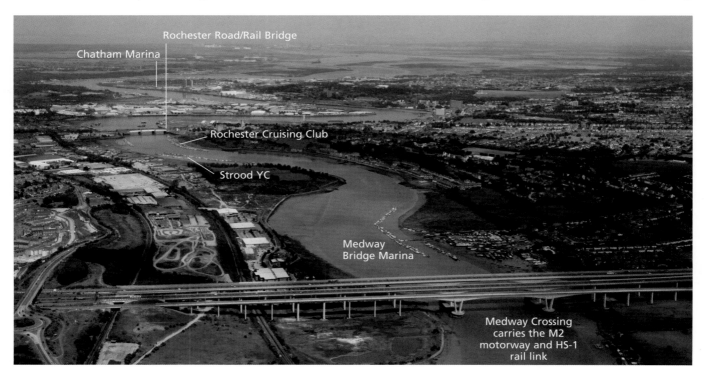

ROCHESTER TO ALLINGTON

General notes

Navigation beyond Rochester Bridge is best done on the flood from about half tide onwards and is very largely confined to motorboats with only a handful of small yachts to be seen. A journey along the full 12M to Allington Lock needs careful timing in relation to your boat's draught and overall height, not only to ensure adequate depth as you progress, but also to arrive at Aylesford Bridge while there is still enough air draught to pass beneath it and then to arrive at the lock during operating hours. Departure from Rochester at about HW-3½hr (Allington) can work well. As a double check on the HW time at Allington Lock, it is about one hour after HW Sheerness.

Although the river banks have a busy industrial past – and there is certainly clutter on the bottom in some stretches – you are very unlikely to encounter any small cargo ships of the type that once ran up to the paper mill wharves.

The lock keeper at Allington (*see details below*) will be happy to help with advice on request.

Rochester to the M2 Bridge

Immediately above the bridge there are jetties and pontoons on both sides of the river. The first jetty to starboard belongs to Strood Pelican Cruising Club, which doesn't normally accept casual visitors, and beyond is Strood YC (ME2 2AH ☏ 01634 718261 www.stroodyachtclub.btck.co.uk), some of whose moorings are on an all-tide pontoon and some beyond on the drying saltings. Visiting boats can be accommodated here, up to 40ft LOA.

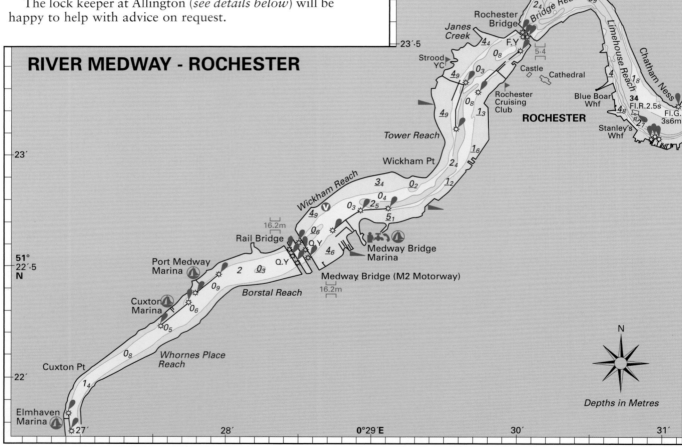

Strood YC

Strood YC Clubhouse

The council-run public pier at Rochester lies to port immediately after passing beneath the bridge

The river curves to the S and, ahead on the port side, in front of a mass of modern housing, are the remains of the slipways of the old Short Bros seaplane factory dating back to 1917 and now used as the base for the local rowing club.

Past Wickham Point, the river again turns SW towards the huge bridges of the Medway Crossing.

Just short of the Crossing, on the S shore, is the large Medway Bridge Marina where advance booking is requested. There is a mix of all-tide, half-tide and mud berths, engineers, a chandler and, in a 1930s Rhine

Over on the port side beneath the towering ruin of Rochester Castle is Rochester Pier, a public pontoon that may be used for short daytime stops (requires a token, bought on the jetty, to return from shoreside – queries ☎ 01634 338122). Access is locked overnight from sunset to 0700H. Next, also on the Rochester shore, are the extensive pontoon moorings of Rochester Cruising Club (ME1 1QN ☎ 01634 841350 www.rochestercc.co.uk). This club welcomes booked club visits and can also take individual visitors. It has diesel available for members and visitors too. The ancient keep of Rochester Castle looms behind the club, which is in a great location as a base for local sightseeing.

MEDWAY BRIDGE MARINA ME1 3HS

Contact ☎ 01634 843576
www.medwaybridgemarina.co.uk
Email info@medwaybridgemarina.co.uk
Fuel Diesel and petrol
Gas Calor and Gaz
Facilities WC, showers, WiFi, slipway
Water On pontoons
Electricity On pontoons
Chandler On site
Shipwrights and Engineers At marina with 25-T hoist. KMS Medway Engineers ☎ 01634 845380 within marina
Boatyard Full boatyard services at Beacon Boatyard (outside marina gate). 7-T crane. ☎ 01634 841320 www.beaconboatyard.co.uk
Provisions Shops in nearby Borstal village
Café/Restaurant The Sovereign B&B and Café ☎ 01634 400474) in the marina, also separate café/bar on site
Taxi ☎ 01634 818777, 848848

Rochester CC's clubhouse (by the flagpole) and its moorings, in the shadow of Rochester Castle

Looking downstream to the large Medway Bridge Marina on the E side of the river

Water ski club jetty   Caxton Marina   Port Medway Marina

Looking downstream to Cuxton Marina, and Port Medway Marina beyond it, both on the W bank

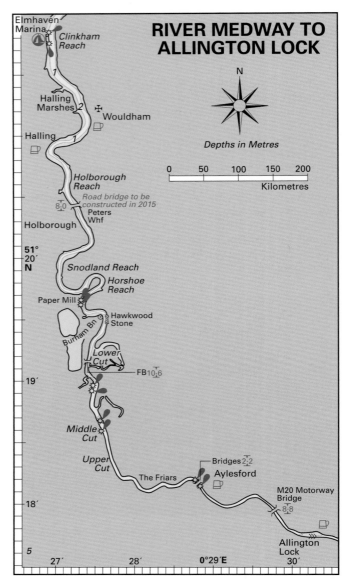

RIVER MEDWAY TO ALLINGTON LOCK

N

Depths in Metres

Kilometres
0   50   100   150   200

Elmhaven Marina
Clinkham Reach
Halling Marshes
Wouldham
Halling
Holborough Reach
Road bridge to be constructed in 2015
Peters Whf
Holborough
51° 20′ N
Snodland Reach
Horshoe Reach
Paper Mill
Hawkwood Stone
Burham Bn
Lower Cut
FB10.6
19′
Middle Cut
Upper Cut
The Friars
Bridges
Aylesford
M20 Motorway Bridge
18′
Allington Lock
5
27′   28′   0°29′E   30′

cruising ship, a café that also offers bed and breakfast. Fuel here is the last on the river before Allington Marina, beyond Allington Lock. Beacon Boatyard is a separate moorings, dry dock and full-service boatyard business at the downstream edge of the marina.

Beyond the marina, the river runs beneath the Medway Crossing, which carries the M2 motorway and the Channel Tunnel Rail Link. If moving near LW, beware unmarked shallows on the W side once through the bridge.

M2 Bridge to Aylesford

Still heading generally SW, two more marinas swiftly come up on the starboard side, the first of which is Port Medway with moorings, engineering and electrical facilities, plus two dry docks. There is a train station just outside the gate.

Immediately upstream from Port Medway, with the same road access, is Cuxton Marina, with full- and half-tide moorings, a slipway and hoist.

Above Cuxton there is a de-restricted stretch of the river used for waterskiing by the local club, whose clubhouse and short jetty are a few yards beyond the marina's pontoon.

PORT MEDWAY MARINA   ME2 1AB

Contact ☎ 01634 720033
    www.portmedwaymarina.co.uk
    Email enquiries@portmedwaymarina.co.uk
Access 24hr on outside pontoons
Facilities WC, showers, launderette
Water On pontoons
Electricity On pontoons
Boat repairs 20-T and 65-T hoist, dry docks (one roofed), slipway
Provisions In Cuxton, 10 minutes walk
Pub/Restaurant In Cuxton
Trains To Maidstone and Strood
Taxi ☎ 01634 515253

CUXTON MARINA   ME2 1AB

Contact ☎ 01634 721941
    www.cuxtonmarina.co.uk
    Email enquiries@cuxtonmarina.co.uk
Facilities WC, shower, slipway, 12-T hoist
Provisions Restaurant, transport: as above

ELMHAVEN MARINA   ME2 1AQ

Contact ☎ 01634 240489
    www.elmhaven-marina.co.uk
    Email elmhaven@btconnect.com
Facilities WC, showers, slipway
Provisions Shops at Halling, 10 minutes
Taxi ☎ 01634 420134

Elmhaven Marina on the W bank

The river runs on through open country with a chalk escarpment rising to starboard and, at Cuxton Point, the river bends left. Here to starboard is the peaceful and small Elmhaven Marina, close to the village of Halling, set at the foot of a chalk cliff. Visitors are advised to phone at least 24hr in advance.

Beyond Elmhaven, the village of Wouldham with its prominent church tower sits on the left bank; buried here is Walter Burke, who was purser on board HMS *Victory* at the Battle of Trafalgar and in whose arms Lord Nelson died. The river curves round sharply to starboard and modern housing in Halling stands on the river bank ahead with a short, modern promenade on the river's edge. In the centre of the wall beneath this promenade there is a small modern pontoon landing stage at the foot of a ladder set in the high walls and there are also stone

Wouldham Church, resting-place of Nelson's purser

The landing pontoon at Halling, agility required to get ashore!

steps at the upstream end of the wall. A short shopping stop in Halling village is therefore possible, although the promenade railing's low gates accessing the ladder and the steps are both usually kept locked.

The river runs on through a contrast of rural scenery and the remains of the industries that once lined the banks. There are numerous old wharves, many rotting and overgrown, and although there are one or two more modern-looking docksides by the paper mills there is currently no traffic using them. Many of the reed covered bends have beacons on them, needed because in flood the edges of the main channel may be covered. Some charts may still show lights on wharves along sections of the river, but it seems these have now all gone.

In between the dereliction there are delightful stretches where one could be miles from anywhere, each bend bringing a surprise. Sometimes the banks are lined with very tall reeds and many wild birds are to be seen, especially grey herons.

Beyond Halling, a new road bridge is being constructed across Holborough Reach in 2015, air draught 8m, in connection with a large housing development called Peters Village on the E bank.

The depth steadily reduces and we stress the need to continue to match boat speed with the flood tide to ensure adequate depth and sufficient clearance to get under the bridge at Aylesford and to reach the lock at Allington within locking hours.

A result of the reed beds is that there can be a fair amount of floating dead reed debris at some times of the year, which can wrap around and disguise more significant floating hazards.

Once past Snodland, the river snakes round a tight S-bend past Burham Marshes, reaching the Hawkwood Stone on your port side where the chart warns mariners to stay clear of the banks from here to Allington, because of piles and other obstructions. The Hawkwood Stone marks the southern limit of the Rochester Oyster Fishery, founded in 1728 and still ruling over fishing rights in the Medway between here and Garrison Point, Sheerness.

An inlet opens up to port a little further upstream, which the chart suggests was once the original course of the river, now drying up as an 'oxbow lake'. The shallowest patch you are likely to encounter on the passage is opposite this inlet.

Passing under a high (10·6m) disused footbridge, the river runs past New Hythe alongside a long wharf from more modern times. Beyond some untidy scrapyards, there is a recent housing development to starboard above

Aylesford Priory

a high stone wall, then the river swings to port and passes the beautiful Aylesford Priory, now known as 'The Friars', an ancient religious house of the Order of Carmelites and founded in 1242.

Around two more bends where great trees lean down to touch the water, the village of Aylesford comes into view on the left bank, a visual treat topped by its Norman church tower. Near here in 455AD, Hengist and Horsa fought Vortigern in a defining battle between the Britons and the Saxon invaders, said to be centred around a ford where now stands an ancient stone road bridge with only 2·2m clearance at HWS. A gauge on the port side about 50 yards below the bridge shows the air draught. There is a wharf on the starboard side just before you reach Aylesford where, if bound upstream on a falling tide, you could wait for sufficient clearance beneath the bridge. Do not dry out here, though, as the bottom is an unknown quantity.

The village is a delight to visit, but sadly (and very surprisingly) there is nowhere provided to stop by boat.

Aylesford to Allington Lock

A more modern road bridge follows soon after the old bridge at Aylesford. After two more tree-lined bends, the M20 motorway bridge is seen ahead. Take special care along here to stay in the middle of the stream as collapsed wharves jut out a long way beneath the surface.

Stretches of the river above Aylesford are wooded

Aylesford and its bridge, looking upstream; air draught gauge on wall at left

Air draught gauge

Allington Lock, on the right bank

Beyond the bridge and soon after passing a boatyard on the starboard bank, you will reach Allington Lock, the head of the tidal navigation.

The lock is on the starboard side of the river with a large weir beyond to port. Subject to space, short-term or overnight mooring may be possible within the lock cut – phone ahead to check with the helpful lock keeper. There is also a camping area and some heated cabins for hire next to the lock keeper's cottage.

The lock is managed by the Environment Agency (EA), which requires any boat using the river beyond the lock to be registered. Registration can be on a daily or long-term basis.

Half a mile upstream from the lock is Allington Marina, the first on the non-tidal navigation. A river bus runs between Allington and Maidstone.

ALLINGTON LOCK   ME16 0LU

Contact ℡ 01622 752864
  Email allington.lock@environment-agency.gov.uk
Tides HW Sheerness +0100
Operating hours 0700–sunset (March–October) or 0800–1600 (November–February) and HW -3hr to HW +2hr. Locking may be available outside these hours on enquiry and with 24hr notice.
Max beam 6m
Facilities WC, showers, pump-out, electricity (limited), water, chemical toilet disposal
Slipway Above lock
Additional useful info www.allingtonlock.co.uk (website not run by the EA)
River Licence See www.gov.uk/register-a-boat/who-to-contact; ℡ 03708 506506; *Email* boatreg@environment-agency.gov.uk
Pub/restaurant Malta Inn (just above lock on port side of river, at ME14 3AS) ℡ 01622 717251

ALLINGTON MARINA   ME16 0NH

Contact ℡ 01622 752057
  www.allingtonmarina.com
Facilities
  WC, showers
Chandler On site
Water On pontoons
Electricity On pontoons
Fuel Diesel
Gas Calor, Gaz
Taxi ℡ 01622 750000

Allington Marina

17. The Swale

⊕ **Landfall waypoint**
51°24'·10N 001°01'·73E Immediately E of line between
Whitstable Street PHB and Columbine SHB

Charts
Imray 2100 series
Admiralty SC5606; 2571, 2572

Tides
Tides HW Sheerness

Harbour Authority
Medway Ports VHF Ch 74 Call sign *Medway VTS*

Honorary Port Pilots
Conyer and The Swale
Simon Smedley ℡ 01795 521562 *Email* conyer@eastcoastpilot.com

Faversham moorings information
Mike Canty (℡ 01795 591140 or 07831 589794)
For any additional leisure boating information, contact the
Medway & Swale Boating Association, www.msba.org.uk

Main hazards

Tides The Swale is not a river but a tidal waterway
between the Isle of Sheppey and the mainland and the
tide floods and ebbs at both ends but not in a logical
fashion. The stream runs E for much longer than it runs
W, which can be put to good use on a passage E.

At HW Sheerness, the whole Swale is slack. The ebb
then begins to run E throughout the Swale for the first
hour or so. After that it splits between Queenborough
and Kingsferry Bridge with the W Swale ebbing into the
Medway and the E Swale into the Thames Estuary. The
separation point gradually moves E towards Elmley and
all flows stop at LW with the exception of a back eddy
along the W shore opposite Queenborough.

The East Swale,
looking eastwards

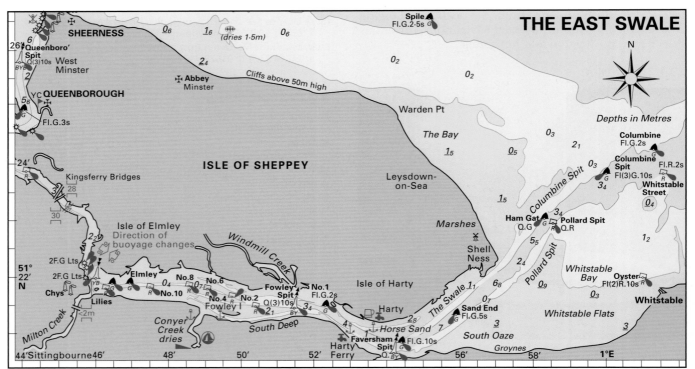

THE SWALE

When it was wider and had greater depth, the Swale was a main route from the English Channel to London, but the channel has narrowed and become shallower by silting and land reclamation to the point where the central section is barely navigable at LWS Sheerness.

With saltmarshes and mudflats on both sides, the Swale forms an area of international importance for breeding and wintering birds. Brent geese, widgeon and avocet are frequently seen, taking little heed of the hundreds of boats kept in the three main creeks – Faversham, Oare and Conyer – as well as at Queenborough.

At low water, the bones of many ships can be seen along the shores of these creeks and in the Swale itself, many of them relics of the hundreds of Thames barges that served the thriving local industries of brick, cement and gunpowder manufacturing, which are all now gone.

If you love the East Coast and the solitude it can offer, the Swale has considerable charm. It brings its own pilotage challenges, especially if you are on the move around low water, but if you run out of luck, the bottom is forgiving and there is plenty to look at while you wait for the water to return.

When the flood starts, it comes in from both ends, the streams meeting at about Elmley. Later, the meeting point often moves E towards Fowley.

Although every day follows this general pattern, detailed tide timing and heights can be greatly affected by wind, weather and barometric pressure, especially in the E Swale.

Wind over tide in the popular anchorage at Harty, especially strong easterlies against the ebb, can raise a very steep chop.

Shipping Commercial shipping uses the W Swale, almost always entering and leaving via the Medway, to reach docks just E of the Kingsferry Bridge. On rare occasions, small coasters may use the E Swale as a short cut on a good tide.

Approaches to East Swale

From the E, make along the coast to the Whitstable Street PHB (Fl.R.2s) as described in the North Kent Coast chapter.

From the W, take the Four Fathoms Channel from the Spile SHB (Fl.G.2·5s), making good about 105° to avoid isolated shoals to the S. If draught allows, and on a rising tide, alter course at the 001°E meridian to make 180° and join the E Swale approach at the Columbine Spit SHB Fl(3)G.10s. With deeper draught (or less water) continue E to Columbine SHB (Fl.G.2s) for more depth.

Note The lights on these buoys and those further into the Swale are sometimes used by Trinity House in experiments with sequencing. Watch www.eastcoastpilot.com for any changes.

From the N, again if draught permits, follow the 001°E meridian past the Red Sand Tower and the Middle Sand SWM. For more water, once S of the Middle Sand, turn

Pollard Spit buoy

Ham Gat buoy

Passing the Ham Gat buoy inbound

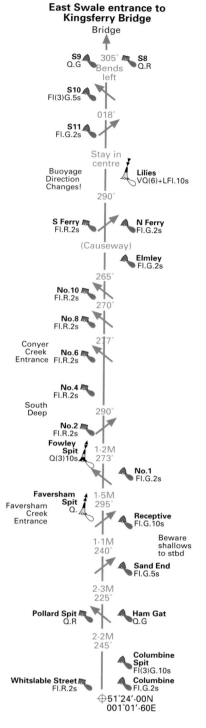

East Swale entrance to Kingsferry Bridge

Bridge

S9 Q.G — 305° Bends left — S8 Q.R

S10 Fl(3)G.5s

018°

S11 Fl.G.2s

Stay in centre

Buoyage Direction Changes! — Lilies VQ(6)+LFl.10s

290°

S Ferry Fl.R.2s — N Ferry Fl.G.2s

(Causeway)

Elmley Fl.G.2s

265°

No.10 Fl.R.2s

270°

No.8 Fl.R.2s

217°

Conyer Creek Entrance — No.6 Fl.R.2s

No.4 Fl.R.2s

South Deep

290°

No.2 Fl.R.2s

Fowley Spit Q(3)10s — 1·2M 273° — No.1 Fl.G.2s

Faversham Spit Q. — Faversham Creek Entrance — 1·5M 295° — Receptive Fl.G.10s

Beware shallows to stbd

1·1M 240°

Sand End Fl.G.5s

2·3M 225°

Pollard Spit Q.R — Ham Gat Q.G

2·2M 245°

Columbine Spit Fl(3)G.10s

Whitslable Street Fl.R.2s — Columbine Fl.G.2s

⊕51°24'·00N 001°01'·60E

Approaching the East Swale from the E off Whitstable

Shell Ness | Conspicuous trees (*see text*) | Leysdown

THE SWALE

Inbound off Shellness

SE to enter the Swale at the Columbine buoy. If your draught makes it impractical to cross any of these flats, from the Princes Channel a SE course alongside the W edge of the Kentish Flats wind farm will keep you in more water, until close by the SW corner of the wind farm, then 225° to the vicinity of the Columbine SHB (Fl.G.2s). However, in 2014 there were plans to extend the wind farm W and S, with construction due to start in 2015, so this route would then require passage through the turbines. Skippers of deeper draught craft may prefer to approach the East Swale from the NE, passing S of the wind farm.

Enter the channel by passing between the Whitstable Street PHB (Fl.R.2s) and the Columbine SHB (Fl.G.2s).

East Swale

With a strong SW'ly blowing against the flood tide there is often a nasty chop in this area, only smoothing out at the Ham Gat SHB (Q.G) and the Pollard Spit PHB (Q.R). Indeed, any kind of W'ly seems to funnel straight out of the East Swale.

In daylight, from out by the 'Street' (Whitstable Street), the small Pollard Spit and Ham Gat buoys are difficult to locate against the bright sand of Shell Ness, but their bearing is about 240°, range 2·1M from midway between the Street PHB and Columbine SHB. Making good that course just scrapes the S side of the deep water in the channel. In some conditions a clump of trees around a farmhouse on Sheppey appears as a single prominent feature on the approximate bearing, as shown in the photo on p151.

With the Pollard Spit PHB close to port, a course made good of 225° will take you on another 2·3M to the Sand End SHB (Fl.G.5s), which is again hard to see against the background clutter. In daylight, a good indication that you are heading in the right general direction is the pair of unusually tall electricity pylons that cross Faversham Creek, 4M from the Pollard.

From Shell Ness westwards, most of the Swale has an 8kn speed limit enforced by the Port Authority.

Passing the prominent Shell Ness, its bright beach (often covered by thousands of oystercatchers) and collection of remote houses, the W bank of the deep water channel is very steep to, while the E side remains a fairly gentle shelf. Avoid grounding on the charted shellfish beds in the area and, if tacking in, note there is a substantial mound on the E side of the channel, SSE of the Sand End SHB.

From the Sand End SHB there is a shallow route WSW passing N of the Horse Sand, but it is advisable to follow the main channel SW to the Receptive SHB (Fl.G.10s), which also marks a wreck. Follow a slight curve to port of the rhumb line from the Sand End to the Receptive, to avoid the edge of the Horse Sand, where seals are often hauled out. On the S side of the channel is the Faversham Spit NCB (Q), at the entrance to Faversham Creek.

HARTY FERRY

From the Receptive SHB, the Swale turns NW, passing through the anchorage known as Harty or Harty Ferry. The Isle of Harty, no longer an island but part of the Isle of Sheppey, stands on the N side of the anchorage with an ancient Saxon church on the skyline and the white Ferry House Inn (ME12 4BQ ☎ 01795 510214 www.theferryhouseinn.co.uk) nestling on the S side of the hill.

The pub is named for the ferry that once ran between here and the mainland. A public causeway provides landing for visitors to the pub, which has toilets,

A quiet morning on the moorings at Harty

Ferry House Inn

The Ferry House Inn on the N shore at Harty

showers, accommodation and a restaurant. The landing is a little muddy, but the causeway is hard. It does not extend as far as LWS, but the mud beyond is quite firm. The pub runs clay pigeon shooting several times a month, which can be quite a disturbance on an otherwise peaceful day.

The S shore, also known as Harty Ferry, has a hard causeway, marked by substantial posts, which extends right across the mudflats.

The village of Oare is a pleasant walk away, just over a mile along the lane from the mainland causeway, with two pubs but no shop. Or a dinghy trip can take you to the Shipwright's Arms at the junction of Faversham and Oare Creeks (see details for Oare Creek).

A dark-roofed building owned by the Kent Wildlife Trust peers over the S sea wall and just across the road from it is a useful fresh water spring, unusual on marshland and once a supply for the long gone munitions factories on the marsh.

There are a few moorings on the N shore and many more to the S of the channel. These are a mixture of club and private moorings, where the usual rule applies that they may be used unless the owner returns; the private ones occasionally attract a charge levied by the local moorings manager. The club moorings are marked 'HCC', 'CCC' or 'WCC' (all W of the causeway) and, if free, may be used for one night only at no charge. Anchoring clear of the moorings either side of the main channel generally finds good holding in soft mud.

The Harty anchorage is exposed to strong E winds, when it should be avoided if possible. With some N in the wind, you may find shelter under the N shore about a ½M W of the causeway, although it is much shallower and you must avoid charted wrecks on the mudflats.

Harty is a classic East Coast anchorage, but the tide can run hard here and this must be considered when going ashore by dinghy, especially with wind over tide. The area teems with bird life that may wake you early on a peaceful summer morning.

The hard causeway on the S shore at Harty

FAVERSHAM CREEK

Faversham Creek initially runs SW from the Swale at the Faversham Spit NCB (Q). Speed limit in the creek is 6kn and careful progress on a rising tide is advisable. Iron Wharf, the first berthing point in the creek is about 2¼M away. There is no commercial traffic but quite large leisure vessels including Thames barges use Faversham Creek. If you are hoping for a berth at Faversham at Iron Wharf, Front Brents or Town Quay, it would be best to phone ahead.

Entry

Leave the NCB to starboard and follow the line of unlit PHBs, and a single SHB, until the creek bends to port opposite an SHM post marking a wreck. Give the PHBs room; in some wind and tide conditions they lie over the shallows. (The wreck is a useful tide gauge – if its ribs are completely covered then there is sufficient depth in Oare Creek for a 1·5m draught boat to reach the head of the creek.)

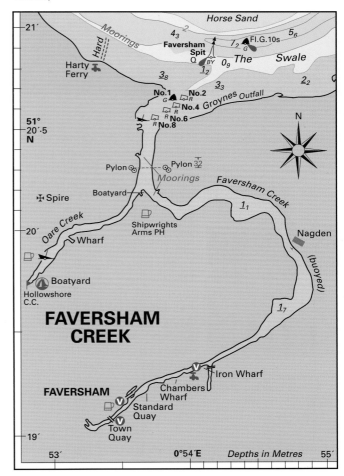

Faversham area from Harty Ferry near LW

Once past the final PHB, follow the centre of the channel S towards the buildings ahead at Hollowshore. Leave moored boats to starboard and be aware that sometimes there are ropes trailing in the water from laid-up derelict fishing boats. Overhead is a high tension electricity line with a charted safe air draught of 32m.

Wreck marker just inside Faversham Creek, a useful tide gauge (see text)

The larger of the buildings at Hollowshore is a boatyard shed and the smaller white building is the Shipwright's Arms pub. These are at the junction of Faversham and Oare Creeks where Oare Creek splits off to starboard (*see below*).

Hollowshore to Iron Wharf

The general rule for going up Faversham Creek, unless you know it well, is to start at half flood or soon after, before the saltings are covered. The notes that follow are detailed, but in general the channel follows the outside of bends – quite extremely, in some cases, so don't be afraid to get close in to the bank. Don't just buoy hop – weave gently to stay with the best depth on your echosounder. The upper stretches of the creek have about 2·5m in the gutway at HW.

Enter Faversham Creek proper with the pub to starboard and, passing PHBs 10 and 12, follow the line of the starboard bank until abeam the section of stone sea wall. Turn to port to bring the nearby pylon fine on the port bow to pass PHB 12A, getting close to the left bank N of SHB 3, before turning SE towards SHBs 5 and 5A. Stay roughly mid-channel from here to pass SHB 7, then 7A, before crossing to starboard to pass PHB 14. From here, aim for a pontoon mooring attached to two large posts beyond some houses on the left bank (a boat may be moored there), opposite SHB 9, and then generally follow the outside of the right hand bend. SHB

Entering Faversham Creek, initially SW then swinging S towards Hollowshore at the No.8 buoy

Faversham Creek swings SE off Hollowshore

Approaching Iron Wharf from downstream

The wall at Iron Wharf – visitors may be accommodated against the wall or rafted out. The area dries

flat soft mud by half ebb (although boats rafted out may lean outwards) and is advertised as suitable for boats up to 8m LOA. Provided there is room, however, it may be able to accommodate shoal draught boats longer than that. There is a tide gauge at the downstream end, showing the depth in feet, and the tidal height above LAT in metres. There are no toilets nearby other than those for customers of the Albion pub/restaurant beside the jetty.

Slightly further up the creek, on the port side just before the fixed road bridge, is the small Town Quay, a length of wall that usually has room alongside for two 10m boats, plus perhaps one more rafted alongside. Fender boards are recommended. A drawback if boats are moored end to end is that the only ladder is at the centre of the wall. Depth is similar to that at Front Brents, perhaps 1·75m at HW, and also dries to soft mud and is quite flat. A very high HWS can reach the top of the wall. There is no security, nor any facilities, so visiting boats will need to be self-sufficient. Town Quay is run by the borough council, which sets a maximum stay of two nights, and fees may be paid by phone to ☎ 01795 417850. Customers having work done by Wilkinson Sails may be able to moor against the wall outside their building just downstream of Town Quay, by prior arrangement only.

There has been talk of the road bridge being rebuilt one day to once more become a swing or lifting bridge to enable access to the basin beyond, but at the time of writing there were no plans in place.

11 follows, then a left hand bend around PHB 16. Keep in the middle of the stream until you reach PHB 18, when you'll see Iron Wharf ahead to port.

Iron Wharf is a large DIY boatyard with a well stocked chandler. There are no pontoons, and any spare drying berths for visitors (on previous enquiry) will be in perhaps 2m (at HW) against a wall or possibly rafted out from it.

Iron Wharf to Town Quay

Immediately above Iron Wharf and also to port are Chambers Wharf and Alan Staley's wooden boatbuilding and restoration yard. Then you will see a tall brick building with an ancient sign saying 'United Fertiliser' followed by Standard Quay opposite the start of some modern housing. The best water tends to be along the starboard side of the creek in front of the housing, and ahead are some private pontoon moorings in a small inlet. Rounding a slight left-hand bend and resuming your passage in the centre of the creek, the Front Brents Jetty lies parallel to the shore on the starboard side, a few hundred yards ahead, with a fixed road bridge beyond it.

Front Brents is owned by the town council (*Email* faversham.towncouncil@virgin.net) and has security, power and water. For berths, phone the moorings manager ☎ 01795 591140 or 07831 589794. It dries to

The drying Front Brents' Jetty and tide gauge

The drying Faversham Town Quay at HWS

FAVERSHAM

Tides Sheerness
Access HW-2hrs to HW+1½hr
Boatyard Iron Wharf Boatyard ME13 7BY
   ① 01795 536296 www.ironwharf.co.uk
Boat repairs 16-T crane, dry dock
Fuel Garage in town, ¾M
Gas Calor and Gaz from chandler
Facilities WC, showers, launderette
Chandler (at Iron Wharf) Faversham Chandlery ① 01795 531777
   www.favershamchandlery.co.uk
Shipwright Alan Staley ① 01795 530668
Sailmaker Wilkinsons ① 01795 521503 www.wilkinsonsails.co.uk
Rigger Rigtek ① 07867 790685 www.rigtek.co.uk
Other Moorings Front Brents Jetty, Town Quay – see text for contact
Provisions, Pub/Restaurant Many in the town
Town information www.faversham.org
Taxi ① 01795 538887, 535555
Transport Trains to London Victoria or Ramsgate and Dover via Canterbury

Faversham, looking downstream at LW from the road bridge

Faversham is an interesting historic town to visit with more than 475 listed buildings and what is said to be the country's best preserved mediaeval street, Abbey Street. Front Brents Jetty and the Town Quay are very close to the centre with its good mix of shops, pubs and facilities including restaurants. Shepherd Neame, the country's oldest and largest independent brewery, is across the road from the Town Quay.

HOLLOWSHORE

Hollowshore is the old name given to the small area at the junction of Faversham and Oare Creeks. It has one ancient pub (the Shipwright's Arms ME13 7TU ① 01795 590088 www.theshipwrightsathollowshore.co.uk), a boatyard and one private house. Only recently has this area had mains electricity. It is remote and there is no public transport.

The boatyard, Hollowshore Services ① 01795 532317, where the Tester family restores and repairs traditional wooden working boats, is one of the many sites where Thames barges were built. With permission, a spare mud berth near the yard may be available, otherwise anchor off to the N and dinghy ashore.

The Shipwright's Arms has its own ghost, reputed to be a barge skipper shipwrecked one stormy night out in the Swale, who managed to get ashore and stagger to the pub door, but who could make nobody hear and was found dead there next morning.

OARE CREEK

If going far up Oare Creek, start at about HWN - 1½hr or HWS -2hr – at springs the creek floods earlier. The tide ebbs from the creek faster than it floods and it dries entirely after about half ebb. Watch the depth constantly as the gutway described below wanders from time to time.

Once past the craft moored in the first part of Faversham Creek, keep heading straight towards the pub (white building to left of large boatshed) and look for the end of a low fence that comes down to the shore from the sea wall to port. Look also for a very small R buoy in the entrance to Oare Creek, N of the boatshed. When you judge you are between the fence and the buoy, turn towards the R buoy and pass close N of it. About 20m further on, leave a larger orange buoy close to port. It marks the end of a slipway from the boatshed.

For its first ½M, the port shore is lined with boats moored on wooden jetties and some pontoons, all

Entering Oare Creek, pass close to two small buoys off Hollowshore

privately owned. The channel is unmarked. Stand about 10m off the sterns of the moored boats, keeping to the port side of the channel around the right hand bend where you may find a large floating dry dock and moored barges. Pass as close to these as you dare for the best water, then resume a distance of about 10m off the moored boats until about 200m before a left hand bend whose right bank has an ancient wooden wharf. Reach mid-channel opposite the beginning of the wharf and continue mid-channel around the bend.

Around the left hand bend there's an old gunpowder dock to port and the channel moves across close to the pontoon moorings by the old red-roofed shed (known locally as the Cylinder House, once a saltpetre store). These moorings are owned by Youngboats where a spare berth may be available if requested in advance. Power and water is available here, but toilets are at the head of

The lower stretch of Oare Creek where the best water is towards the E side

the creek. Boats of up to 1·3m draught should reach these berths on most tides and should sit reasonably upright on soft mud.

From the Cylinder House onwards, the channel meanders, gets shallower and is marked by pairs of withies although these are not constantly maintained. Halfway along this final stretch the channel veers all the way to the S shore then back to the middle. There are many more pontoon moorings at the head of the creek at Youngboats' main base. Boats much over 10m LOA will be tricky to turn at the head of the creek. If in doubt, phone Youngboats for advice.

Also in Youngboats' yard is the HQ of Hollowshore Cruising Club, a small, welcoming club for the many boat owners in these creeks. It's open on Sundays at lunchtime, usually with snacks available.

Oare village at the head of the creek has two pubs, both of which serve food. Basic provisions are a 15 min walk from the head of the creek, in Davington, along the road into Faversham. There is an occasional bus service from Oare; the bus stop is by The Castle pub. Faversham itself is perhaps a 30-minute walk away.

OARE CREEK   ME13 7TX

Access HW±1½hr

Boatyard Youngboats (Terry Young) ☎ 01795 536176
(Closed Mondays)
www.youngboats.co.uk
Email info@youngboats.co.uk

Boat repairs 8-T crane

Water On pontoons

Electricity On pontoons (tokens from yard)

Scrubbing berth Max length 9m

Chandler Basic, on site

Facilities WC, shower

Gas Calor and Gaz from chandler

Club Hollowshore CC
www.hollowshorecc.co.uk

Pubs/restaurants The Castle ☎ 01795 533674
The Three Mariners ☎ 01795 533633
www.thethreemarinersoare.co.uk

Transport Buses

Taxi ☎ 01795 538887, 535555

Approaching Youngboats moorings from the Cylinder House; the dinghy is following the channel, which is marked with withies beyond

The head of Oare Creek lies beyond the withied stretch

THE SWALE – HARTY TO CONYER

Continuing NW from Harty, the deep water channel runs close to the Swale No.1 SHB (Fl.G.2s), past remnants of the local disused gunpowder industry on the S bank. Also to the S and opposite the No.1 SHB are some scrubbing posts, although these have not been seen in use for a while.

The Swale now opens up into a much broader stretch of water, a row of narrow chimneys at a paper mill prominent 4M W, but at LW much of the water disappears.

On the N shore, beyond the No.1 buoy, is Windmill Creek, which generally dries although a very shallow draught boat might stay afloat in a hole near the junction with Bells Creek.

The Fowley Spit ECB (Q(3)10s) marks the entrance to South Deep, with Conyer Creek beyond.

South Deep

South Deep, particularly towards its W end inside Fowley Island, is a delightfully quiet and sheltered spot for an overnight stop and is also the main route to the entrance to Conyer Creek.

Start close to port of the Fowley Spit ECB and aim for an unlit SHB off the E end of Fowley Island. Keep an eye on the depth, because the channel moves from time to time. Two cables beyond the SHB there are four large white waiting buoys laid by moorings operators at Conyer. Carry on past the charted sluice (R.Bn) on the S shore and after about 100m you should find a hole with 1·5m at LWS. Fowley Island is low lying, little more than saltings that virtually cover at HWS, and is a wildlife reserve where landing is prohibited. Beyond this secluded anchorage, the route W leads to an unlit PHB, then SW

via a channel marked with small red and green buoys to an equally small ECB just inside the mouth of Conyer Creek.

Fowley Spit Westwards

After Fowley Spit ECB the channel W narrows considerably and is marked with PHBs as far as Elmley. All of these, Nos.2, 4, 6, 8 and 10, are lit Fl.R.2s.

Boats drawing up to 1m can pass through this shallowest section of the Swale after LWS+1hr, provided the PHBs are followed meticulously. The No.8 PHB marks the last chance to turn S into Conyer or South Deep. At night, constantly check that you are heading for the next PHB in the sequence – with their identical light characteristics, it is possible to be misled.

CONYER CREEK

Conyer, which dries from half tide, can be approached from the W from the Swale No.8 PHB, but the approach via South Deep (see above) has consistently more depth. Look for the charted islet of Little Fowley N of the creek entrance. Little Fowley is marked with a small black buoy and has eroded away in recent years, so that it's still fully covered long after HW. Near HW you should find 2m all the way from No.8 to a point S of the islet, although depths change suddenly as you cross the gutways that meander across the flats.

There are two well marked routes for the final approach to the creek entrance. Either continue SE to the start of the E channel (the unlit PHB in South Deep), following between the red and green (same shape) buoys, or use a deeper W channel called the Butterfly.

If using the Butterfly Channel, find the first pair of marker posts for this about 300m NNW of the creek

Conyer Creek and approaches at LW

The Fowley Spit buoy looking W, the flood running hard

Blackden Moorings

Swale Marina

Conyer Marina

Buoyed channel

East Cardinal buoy

Buoyed channel from South Deep

Butterfly Channel marked by posts

The entry into Conyer Creek from the two channels

entrance, then follow between the posts, heading directly SW towards the sea wall, turning abruptly to port very close to the wall before meeting the E channel at the small ECB.

From the ECB, the channel is marked by more small buoys leading first of all close to two wrecks on the E shore, then gradually moving out between a mix of buoys and posts to the W side of the creek approaching a sharp left hand bend. Around the bend, where buoyage ends but posts continue at intervals, the channel is nearer to the centre and the village of Conyer comes into view.

The small Conyer Creek Marina is reached first, on the E bank, and is also the base of builders and repairers North Quay Marine. There may be drying berths available for visitors (see Conyer details). Use the port side of the right-hand bend as you approach.

Once past the housing on the port bank, Blackden Moorings' drying pontoon berths lie directly ahead of you to port in Conyer Dock. They can only occasionally accommodate visitors, so phone ahead to check availability ☎ 01795 522833.

Turn to starboard opposite Blackden Moorings into the large Swale Marina, providing 200 drying mud berths alongside pontoons extending all the way to the

head of the creek. Access all the way to the marina is about HW±2hr – phone the harbourmaster for advice. The well kept marina has a splendid clubhouse which is also the base for Conyer Cruising Club.

Ship Inn

Swale Marina dried out at LW

CONYER

Tides Sheerness
Access HW±2hr

SWALE MARINA

Contact office ☎ 01795 521562
    Email enquiries@swalemarina.co.uk
    www.swalemarina.co.uk
Facilities WC, showers
Water and Electricity On pontoons
Fuel Diesel
Gas Calor and Gaz
Boat repairs 30-T travel hoist, 30-T slipway
Rigger Rigtek ☎ 07867 790685 www.rigtek.co.uk
Club Conyer CC www.conyercc.org.uk

CONYER CREEK MARINA

Contact ☎ 01795 521711 ☎ 07971 641129
    Email marina@conyercreekmarina.co.uk
    www.conyercreekmarina.co.uk
Facilities WC, showers
Water and Electricity On pontoons
Boat repairs North Quay Marine on site
    ☎ 01795 521711 www.northquaymarine.net
    10-T crane, engineer, shipwrights on site

Pub/Restaurant Ship Inn/Smugglers Restaurant on Conyer Quay (including breakfasts at weekends) ☎ 01795 520881
Provisions Teynham village (bus or taxi)
Transport Buses (infrequent) to Teynham and trains from there to Ramsgate and Dover or London
Taxi ☎ 01795 430400, 444444

Conyer Creek Marina, next to North Shore Marine

Head of Conyer Creek – Blackden Moorings to port, Swale Marina to starboard

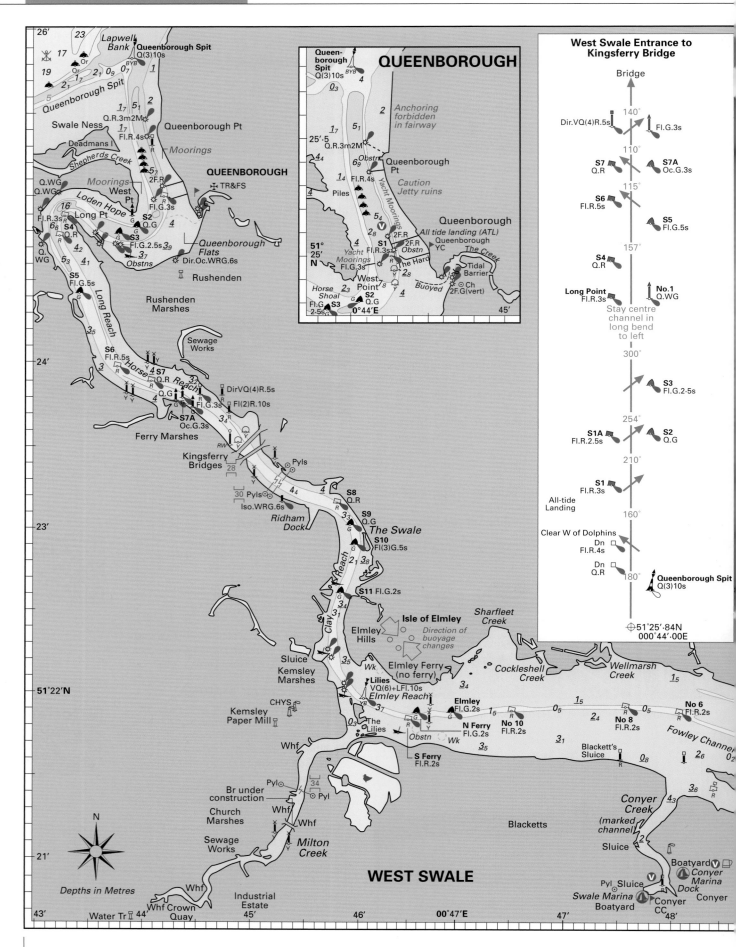

THE SWALE – CONYER CREEK TO KINGSFERRY

Heading W from the Swale No.8 PHB (Fl.R.2s), past No.10 PHB (Fl.R.2s) and the Elmley SHB (Fl.G.2s) near LW, the next obstruction is the disused ferry causeway at Elmley. (King James II is said to have fled the country from around here, hence the local name, Kingsferry.) The deepest water can be found slightly N of centre in the gap between two pairs of posts on the causeway. A buried gas pipe runs N-S just E of the causeway, so care should be taken not to anchor in the vicinity.

The No.8 buoy, N of Conyer, is typical of the PHBs used in the central Swale

From the causeway, steer between the North Ferry PHB (Fl.G.2s) and the South Ferry SHB (Fl.R.2s). Depth will increase as you head for the Lilies SCB (VQ(6)+LFl.10s).

Milton Creek branches away S here. Once a busy trading waterway, it leads to Sittingbourne town centre, but a low level road bridge (air draught 4·2m) bars access in the lower reach. Sadly the creek has little to offer anyway since the closure of the Dolphin Sailing Barge Museum at its head.

Note At this point in the Swale, the direction of lateral buoyage reverses.

Beyond the Lilies, on the W side of the channel, is the Grovehurst Jetty used by ships delivering china clay to the nearby paper mill. N of this jetty the channel is marked by lit SHBs (to be left to port when heading N), S11 (Fl.G.2s) then S10 (Fl.3.G.5s) in Clay Reach. At S9

Heading W, approaching the causeway at Elmley

The Lilies buoy, where the Swale curves northwards into Clay Reach

Turning NW into Ferry Reach at the No.9 buoy, Kinsgsferry Bridge coming into view

(Q.G) it turns NW past S8 (Q.R) and widens into Ferry Reach with the Kingsferry lifting bridge in view less than a mile away. From here to Long Point, beyond the bridge, the speed limit does not apply and the stretch is used by fast powerboats.

In Ferry Reach there is a busy dock on the S shore, Ridham Dock, which takes frequent coaster traffic – you should learn of any imminent traffic by monitoring the channel for Kingsferry Bridge, VHF Ch 10.

Kingsferry Bridge

Kingsferry Bridge carries rail traffic and some local road traffic; the high level road bridge just W carries the bulk of road traffic between Sheppey and the mainland. It is best to call on VHF Ch 10 when you are an hour away, to ensure that the bridge keeper knows well in advance that a lift is required, and monitor Ch 10 thereafter.

The lifting bridge, operated by Network Rail, does not open to a timetable, but it is required to lift on request if circumstances allow. In practice, although the bridge is manned continuously, the duty bridge keeper cannot open the bridge without permission from the railway signalman at Sittingbourne.

The train timetable allows for two lifts per hour, Monday to Saturday. On Sundays there is a lift just once per hour, usually on the hour. The bridge is, however, said to be restricted to three lifts in two hours to allow the machinery to cool. Normal courtesy and reasonableness when requesting a lift will probably ease your way through. Commercial shipping takes priority, but you will usually be allowed through immediately before or after a ship, as advised on Ch 10. In this situation do not assume anything – ensure that the bridge

Heading NW with the bridge lifting and our boat waiting for the green light on the S pier

THE SWALE

keeper tells the ship's pilot that you are waiting and that agreement is reached as to whether you lead or follow the ship through.

If the lift is just for you and perhaps other leisure craft, help the bridge keeper reduce delays by keeping station close to the bridge at the time advised to you. The lift sequence starts with flashing R/G lights. Wait until a fixed G light is displayed before passing through. A loud horn is sometimes sounded with the G light.

When planning a passage through the bridge, bear in mind that there can be circumstances when the bridge cannot be lifted. In very hot weather it is sometimes not lifted at all for fear of unequal expansion jamming the mechanism. Such failures, or scheduled maintenance, are usually advised in the MSI broadcasts by HMCG.

Kingsferry Bridge

VHF Ch 10
Call sign *Kingsferry Bridge* ☎ 01795 423627
Lights Alt Q R/G – bridge lifting
F.G – bridge open (29m MHWS)
Q.R – bridge lowering, keep clear
Q.Y – bridge out of action
No lights – bridge down (3·35m MHWS)

WEST SWALE

⊕**Entry waypoint**
51°25'·84N 000°44'·00E Immediately NE of Queenborough Spit ECB (Q(3)10s)
Tides Sheerness

Main Hazards

Ruins on E shore marked by dolphins. Some commercial traffic.

Approaches

Approaches to the W Swale will be from seaward or down river from the Medway.

From seaward, follow directions for entering the Medway (see chapter 15) then, watching for commercial traffic, make for the W Swale entrance marked by the Queenborough Spit ECB (Q(3)10s).

Heading E down the Medway, the Queenborough Spit ECB can be hard to locate against the Sheerness shore and can be obscured by large tugs on moorings W of it. These tugs are active during shipping movements.

Heading S in the Swale, leave the Queenborough Spit ECB to starboard and pass two large lit dolphins on the E shore (Q.R and Fl.R.4s) guarding dangerous remains of an old pier.

The Queenborough Spit buoy and, beyond, the moorings at Queenborough

QUEENBOROUGH   ME11 5AA

Tides Sheerness
Contact Harbour Office ☎ 01795 662051 or 07456 459754
Email info@queenborough-harbour.co.uk
www.queenborough-harbour.co.uk
VHF Ch 08
Call sign *Sheppey One*
Access 24hr all tide landing (pontoons) and Town Hard
Facilities Trot-boat, WC, Showers in club, if open, or public facilities nearby, key from harbour staff
Water On all-tide landing and planned for pontoon
Electricity None, but in long-term plan for pontoon
Fuel From petrol station ½M in Queenborough Rd, also in long-term plan for pontoon
Repairs Jim Brett's yard in Queenborough Creek, with 8-T crane ☎ 01795 668263
Gas Calor and Gaz from petrol station
Provisions In town, also large supermarket 20 mins walk
Pub/Restaurant Queenborough YC (see below)
Flying Dutchman ☎ 01795 667189
Old House at Home ☎ 01795 662463
Others in town
Club Queenborough YC ☎ 01795 663955
Transport Taxi ☎ 01795 665555; Buses; Trains to Sittingbourne for connections to London, Dover and Ramsgate

Queenborough

Queenborough town is on the Isle of Sheppey at the entrance to the West Swale, a little under 2M S of Garrison Point at the mouth of the Medway. Except in strong N through NW'lies, it offers a safe and sheltered anchorage and almost always has visitor moorings available. The harbour is run by the Queenborough Harbour Trust.

Immediately S of the second dolphin, lines of moorings begin on the E shore, closely followed by more on the W side. In general you will find the E buoys are yellow visitors' moorings, which are for single boats only.

Beyond the moorings on the E side, a long pontoon (2F.R) lies parallel to the shore, connected at its S end by a bridge to the hammerhead (2F.R) of the all-tide landing (ATL) floating jetty, which stretches across the mudflats from the E shore. Overnight berthing is on the pontoon and not on the hammerhead.

Amongst the single-boat visitor moorings there are usually four large visitors' buoys on the E shore, two yellow and two grey. Up to four boats may raft together on each of the large yellow buoys and up to six on the grey ones. They are very wide and only have a ring in the

The 'concrete lighter' at Queenborough is popular for club visits

Queenborough at LW, looking N

Image labels: Garrison Point, Commercial Docks, Sheerness, Harbour office on pontoon, Town Hard, Queenborough, Visitor moorings, ATL, HW route to Queenborough Creek

centre, so a 'mooring gadget' may be helpful in getting a line onto the buoy if you are the first to arrive.

SW of the ATL on the W side of the channel, a large concrete lighter is also available as a mooring and is popular for groups of boats cruising together. Rafting is allowed on its W side. It can be booked for groups in advance with the Harbour Office. (There is a board on it which tells potential visitors whether or not it is already booked).

Do not anchor in the fairway, because commercial traffic operates 24hr through the Kingsferry Bridge, but you may find a place to bring up under the N shore of Loden Hope.

The Harbour Trust runs a trot-boat service for those who are on buoyed moorings, trot-boat hours varying with season. If using your own dinghy to get ashore, be aware that the tides run strongly here.

The ATL has a turnstile at its shore end, which lets you ashore, but requires a purchased token to pass seawards again. Tokens are available from the harbour staff, Queenborough YC (QYC), the two nearby pubs, and from the Queenborough Stores in the High Street.

The QYC welcomes visitors who may use its facilities when it's open. If the club is closed, there is a public toilet/shower block on the small green just behind the sea wall (see info panel).

To the S of the ATL is the long, sloping concrete Town Hard, usable by dinghy, which allows free access to and from the shore but is not clean.

Queenborough Creek

Along the south side of the town is the drying Queenborough Creek. Access is across the mudflats closely following the small markers from the S1 PHB (Fl.R.3s) off the end of the concrete hard, then through the floodgate (usually open). The Town Quay can be crowded, but the bottom is flat and free from obstructions, so rafting out is possible, but ask the Harbour Office first. Also ask about use (at a small charge) of the scrubbing berth in the Creek where the bottom is a large concrete slab.

Flood gate activity is indicated by Control Lights as follows: 3F.R(vert) barrier closed; 3Fl.R(vert) closure imminent.

QUEENBOROUGH TO KINGSFERRY BRIDGE

The passage from Queenborough to the bridge is straightforward with good depth in the channel, plenty of lights at night and no unmarked obstructions. To help ships navigate at night, the channel is covered by sectored lights and leading lights.

Call the bridge keeper (Ch 10) before leaving the moorings at Queenborough to find out when the next lift will be.

The channel runs round a right hand bend into Loden Hope, past S2 (Q.G) and S3 (Fl.G.2·5s) SHBs. To port is an old wharf with cranes.

At the end of Loden Hope is a hairpin bend to port with best water midway between the banks all the way round. Do not cut this corner. There is a PHB (Fl.R.3s) off Long Point and two sectored lights (Q.WG) on the outside of the bend.

Once round Long Pt, Long Reach runs past S4 (Q.R) PHB and S5 (Fl.G.5s) SHB to S6 (Fl.R.5s) PHB where the channel bends to port past S7 (Q.R) PHB. Do not cut this corner.

From S7, Horse Reach leads past S7A (Oc.G) SHB and lit beacons on either hand before the final stretch to the bridge on about 140°. There is a WRG sectored light located E of the bridge to guide shipping through and the port authority specifically warns against looking directly at this bright light.

The waters each side of the bridge are the only areas in the Swale without an 8kn speed limit and powerboats and PWCs are active there, especially at weekends. This stretch can be crowded in summer with yachts waiting for a bridge lift and sharing a fairly small area with much faster boats. Skippers may find it easier to wait NW of the fixed road bridge rather than between the two bridges, especially when the stream is running SE.

18. The North Kent Coast

Ramsgate to North Foreland

On passage from Ramsgate N towards the Foreland, you can safely keep as close as ½M from the shore unless you have exceptional draught and it's LWS. Beware pot markers in the whole area. Apart from the very obvious steel dolphin (Fl.R.2·5s) ½M N of Ramsgate harbour, there are no charted individual hazards and you can enjoy the scenery of Thanet's chalk cliffs, soon giving way to the tiny haven of Broadstairs.

Broadstairs is a pretty little place and a bustling seaside resort in summer. The harbour, formed by a short stone arm at the N end of the bay, provides little shelter and dries completely to hard sand, but is not a serious proposition for a prolonged visit unless you have a sense of adventure, a suitable craft and the weather is settled. A lunchtime anchorage stop for a swim a few hundred yards off or a row ashore for an ice cream is something you might consider. Like Ramsgate, the harbour is managed by Thanet Council and, if needed, a local official can be contacted on ☎ 01843 577274. Broadstairs SC runs dinghy races just offshore and occasionally hosts large events, which are best avoided by heading a little further out round them.

North of Broadstairs, the cliffs quickly rise again, surmounted by houses most of the way to the N Foreland lighthouse (Fl(5)WR.20s57m19-15M), which was notable for being the last in the country to be manned before it, too, became fully automated.

The cliffs reduce in height as you round the N Foreland and are punctuated by sandy bays. Off the Foreland itself, strong winds can produce very rough conditions – it's the meeting place of two tidal streams, where the waters of the Estuary meet the English Channel. In a strong SW'ly, however, it's usually sheltered inshore, but be aware of the charted chalk ledges.

Broadstairs from the ESE at LW. Note: The beacons mark rocky shallows

Broadstairs Harbour at half-tide; note the beacons each side of the entrance

Botany Bay below the North Foreland lighthouse; note the chalk ledges stretching out to sea

Heading E from the Foreland, stay outside the outfall dolphin

North Foreland Westwards

Boats heading W have a choice here: to keep along the coast inshore of the mass of sandbanks that fills the Estuary (the 'overland' route) or to make N, turning NNW in the vicinity of the East Margate buoy (Fl.R.2·5s) and heading for the Queens Channel or Princes Channel. Without local knowledge the inshore route should be treated with great caution in strong onshore winds and especially around LW, particularly through the shallows off Reculver.

The Princes Channel is a main shipping route and should be treated accordingly. Skippers of leisure craft should generally follow its S side taking care to avoid the significant shallows of the Ridge and the Pan Sand.

The Queens Channel, too, avoids the Reculver area if the shallows there are a concern in your passage plan.

When following the inshore route along the Kent shore, head NW from the Foreland, rounding Foreness Point between the large steel dolphin marking an outfall (lit FL.R) and the unlit Longnose PHB three cables to the NE, and then on W through the South Channel.

A little less than two miles W of the Longnose is the small drying harbour of Margate. If planning to take a closer look at it, be sure to avoid the hidden remains of the pier just E, which was destroyed in a storm and is marked by a very large NCM (Q.3M). The harbour itself, with its single stone arm and stone lighthouse (F.R.4M) on its outer end, has limited attraction to a visiting yachtsman, being totally open to the W and drying at least 2m. From a distance, the harbour location is obvious from the N, but less so from the NW. HW is at about Sheerness -0035.

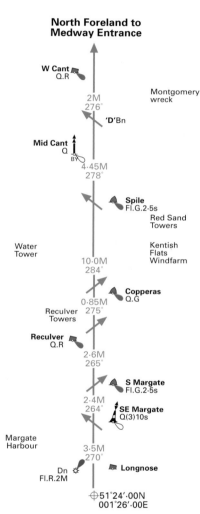

North Foreland to Medway Entrance

W Cant Q.R

Montgomery wreck

2M
276°

'D' Bn

Mid Cant Q
BY

4·45M
278°

Spile Fl.G.2·5s

Red Sand Towers

Water Tower

Kentish Flats Windfarm

10·0M
284°

Copperas Q.G

Reculver Towers

0·85M
275°

Reculver Q.R

2·6M
265°

S Margate Fl.G.2·5s

2·4M
264°

SE Margate Q(3)10s

Margate Harbour

3·5M
270°

Longnose

Dn Fl.R.2M

51°24'·00N
001°26'·00E

Margate at LW from NW

Tower block

End of harbour arm

NCM

Approaching Margate Harbour from the NE, it is essential to stay outside the nearby N Cardinal post

The Turner Contemporary gallery is close E of the harbour and a trip ashore to visit it, or perhaps the seafront delights of Margate, may be the only reasons to enter, although a suitable craft could certainly take shelter from winds in the sector from NE to S. There is a broad slipway in the SE corner of the harbour and another narrower one outside, close E – do not obstruct these as they may be needed by the Margate lifeboat. Fender boards are advisable against the wall – the best stretch of wall is perhaps between the first and second bends in, having more timber to lean on. This harbour is also managed by Thanet Council and a local official can be contacted on ① 01843 577274 if needed. Margate YC, mainly a dinghy sailing club, is just across the road at the foot of the hill.

Heading on W, the shore beyond Margate rises again as a low chalk cliff, which finally peters out again at Minnis Bay. The N side of the route on through the Gore Channel is marked by the SE Margate ECB (Q(3)10s), then S Margate SHB (Fl.G.2·5s); along here the deep channel is sheltered from the N by the Margate Hook Sand. Keep well S of the area around the S Margate buoy near LW as it's quite shallow in the vicinity. Beyond Minnis, the coastline sinks to barely more than a sea wall, blocking off the sea from what was once the Wantsum Channel, which separated the Isle of Thanet from the mainland.

Reculver Towers are seen ahead. These two rectangular towers, linked together, are part of an ancient ruined church that stands inside the Roman 'Saxon Shore' fort of Regulbium, whose garrison guarded the N end of the Wantsum.

The old church at Reculver was built using materials from the Roman fort, but was largely demolished and moved a mile inland in the 19th century when it became clear that the sea would take it if unchecked. That the original Towers still stand today, on a low promontory, protected just yards from the waves by a sea wall, is due in part to their importance as a landmark for mariners. From time to time the towers are floodlit until midnight.

Steering about 265° from the S Margate SHB, the Reculver PHB (Q.R) marking the start of the Copperas Channel is some 2·4M distant. The Margate Hook beacon is a prominent, unlit SCM on the sandbank to starboard and once housed a refuge for shipwrecked sailors.

Leave the Reculver buoy at least 50yd to port, then turn onto 275° for the Copperas SHB (Q.G). When about 250yd past the Copperas, turn NW for the best water, watching the depth closely as you cross the tail of the Last Sand, and continue for at least ½M before resuming a W'ly heading across the Kentish Flats. Be aware that near LW the Copperas Channel is suitable only for shoal draught boats. Note particularly the unmarked Black Rock, SW of the Copperas buoy, which dries at LWS.

Best wall for mooring / Turner Contemporary Gallery / Margate YC / Public Slipway

Inside Margate Harbour

Incidentally, copperas, or iron pyrites, used in dyeing and tanning, was the basis of a major industry in the area.

Conspicuous to the NW are the turbines of the Kentish Flats wind farm, 5M off the Kent shore at its nearest point and being extended further S and W in 2015.

Reculver Westwards

Having skirted the shallows W of the Copperas SHB, Herne Bay lies WSW, across a generally flat area of further shallows.

If going to Whitstable or the Swale, make for the Whitstable Street PHB (Fl.R.2s), about 6M W. If you plan to go to the Medway instead, the Spile buoy will be your target, just over 10M away bearing about 280° via the Overland Passage.

Approaches to Herne Bay from E

About ½M N of Herne Bay SC (the dinghy club at the eastern end of the town) there's a substantial steel dolphin, lit Fl.Y 5s. On high ground inland, due S of the club, there is a prominent water tower in the shape of a cocktail glass. Out at sea NNW of the town is the massive abandoned timber pierhead.

Herne Bay pierhead

Reculver Towers and the 'Reculver' buoy, left to port when heading westwards

Herne Bay Harbour, looking east

HERNE BAY · CT6 5JG

⊕ **Landfall waypoint**
51°22'·70N 001°07'·20E

Charts
Imray 2100 Series, C1
Admiralty SC5606, 1607

Tides
HW Sheerness -0025

Contact Foreshore Manager ☎ 01227 266719 (out of hours ☎ 01227 862000)
Email foreshore.services@canterbury.gov.uk

Access HW±2hr

Approach to Herne Bay Harbour from the N; enter between the stone pierhead to port and the raised jetty to starboard

Herne Bay harbour. Deepest water inside is close to the arm

Main hazards

Entire approach is across flat shoals.
Disused pierhead (Q.18m4M) 0·6M NNW.
Steel dolphin (Fl.Y 5s) 0·95M ENE.
Area used by fast powerboats and PWCs.
Very soft mud in harbour.

This Council-owned harbour dries completely and is open to the W. It is formed by a rough stone arm (its root at the E end) that acts as a sea defence for the town. The harbour has no provision for visitors at all, but does represent a possible emergency haven or an adventurous short visit for shoal draught craft that can take the ground. In strong N'lies at spring tides, waves can overtop the harbour arm at HW and the place should be avoided if at all possible.

Approach to the harbour is from the N. The bottom is hard flat sand from some distance out and the harbour entrance is close to a conspicuous block of flats. Yellow buoys in the area define an 8kn inshore speed limit. The entrance is about 50m wide, the W side being a flat platform on piles carrying fairground items (like a helter-skelter) from time to time, which is the remains of the shore end of an old pier, lit 2FG(vert). The W end of the arm, on your port side, is also lit, 2FR(vert). Turn E as soon as you pass the end of this arm to find the deepest water, which follows close to the arm.

The harbour dries completely to very soft mud over clay, which is fine for bilge keelers or centreboarders, but possibly not deep enough for a deep fin keel. A number of local fishing boats and other craft are moored here and it would be wise to buoy your anchor. Note there are no moorings provided, although you might find a spare one. If anchoring, it could be best to choose a spot at the W end.

Use the contact number when you arrive if you have not already got in touch.

Around HW you could lie briefly in at least 2m alongside the S edge of the broad public slipway inside the E end of the harbour which, in season, can be busy with powerboat launching and recovery. Until perhaps HW+3 you can land by dinghy on this slipway or on the beach, but do not even think of trying to wade ashore through the mud. Its treacherous nature is such that HM Coastguard uses the harbour for national training in mud rescue!

Approaches to Whitstable from E

Between the old Herne Bay pierhead and Whitstable is a popular area for pots, not all of which are properly marked.

The Whitstable Street shingle bank bars the way W and dries for 1M from shore at LWS. The Whitstable Street PHB (Fl.R.2s) at its N end, 2M from the shore, is the normal turning point for craft approaching the town.

WHITSTABLE

Main hazards

Shallows in approach.
'The Street' shingle bank to E.
Some commercial traffic.

Whitstable is the third refuge harbour along this stretch of coast, but is again not commonly visited. It's very much a working port, home to the local fishing fleet and service craft for the wind farm; coasters carrying aggregates or timber frequently call. It dries to soft mud at LWS and is not a yacht-friendly place. In an emergency it would be available, but try to contact the HM before attempting to enter. The walls are high and unforgiving and fender boards are needed, unless you can raft alongside. In onshore winds there can be a considerable swell in all parts of the harbour.

The harbour entrance is difficult to make out even in clear weather. It is lit, but in daylight the town behind is fairly featureless. Look for a long low roof (visible well out to sea) and a tall silo, both just E of the harbour.

Whitstable Harbour from the W

Approaching Whitstable Harbour from the N; a separate dolphin stands NW of the starboard pierhead

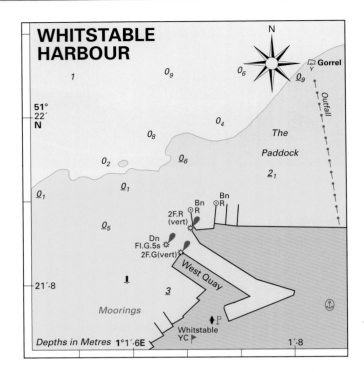

Whitstable from the Street buoy – white roofs are close to the harbour

The harbour approach is across shallows. At night, locate the lit Oyster PHB (Fl(2)R.10s) and a SHM dolphin (Fl.G·5s) close to the West Quay head. The two pierheads display 2F.R(vert) and 2F.G(vert) respectively.

The town is very much an East Coast place, much more like the coastal towns of Essex and Suffolk than its neighbours in Kent and can be worth a visit if you are prepared to anchor or moor offshore and use the dinghy. It has become fashionable in recent years and local prices can reflect this. There are many small specialist shops and art galleries and a number of good restaurants. There is also a fish market on the S quay of the harbour.

The yacht club is just W of the harbour and, although predominantly a dinghy club, it has a small cruising section and may have a spare mooring on enquiry from the secretary. The beach in front of the club and for 150m W is firm, flat shingle compacted on mud (it was a Thames barge hard) and is an ideal spot for a scrub or

Warning light   Garrison Point   Grain Power station

Approaching the Medway entrance from the West Cant buoy

WHITSTABLE   CT5 1AB

⊕ **Landfall waypoint**
51°22'·70N 001°01'·20E

Charts
Imray 2100 series, C1
Admiralty SC5606, 1607

Tides
HW Sheerness -0010

Harbourmaster Whitstable Harbour Office ☏ 01227 274086
(out of hours, ☏ 01227 862000)

VHF Ch 09 (monitored only during shipping movements)

Call sign *Whitstable Harbour Radio*

Access HW±3hr

Slipway Timber ramp between YC and W arm of harbour

Club Whitstable YC ☏ 01227 272942 www.wyc.org.uk

Chandler and engineer ☏ 01227 274168
www.whitstablemarine.co.uk

Rigger At chandler above; Rigtek ☏ 07867 790685
www.rigtek.co.uk

below waterline maintenance in quiet weather – as a guideline, a boat with 1·2m draught will ground at about half tide. There is a public slipway and close by there is a chandler where help may be available for rigging or engineering problems. A few hundred yards further west you may find an area of flags, posts and/or buoys marking shellfish beds, just off one of the restaurants.

Southwest in Whitstable Bay are charted oyster beds; the local oysters are called Whitstable Natives and sold in the town in season.

There is no shelter on the shore of Whitstable Bay in strong SW through N winds, when a far better option is to make for the Swale. A NW'ly in particular can make life very uncomfortable with a vicious, steep chop quickly building up.

RECULVER TO THE MEDWAY

On passage from the Copperas Channel to the Medway, passing outside the Isle of Sheppey, shape a course of about 280° to the Spile SHB (Fl.G.2·5s) at the W end of the Four Fathoms Channel, just over 10M distant.

This takes you along the Overland Passage, an ancient name still shown on charts and referring to the shallow water where least charted depth is around 2·5m. Just N of the rhumb line from the Copperas SHB to the Spile SHB, note the charted buoyed exclusion area marking shallows (0·9m at LAT) where wind farm export cables cross each other on the sea bed and are protected by piles of rock armour. Three of the four buoys are lit Fl.(4)Y.10s, while the fourth and southernmost is a SCB lit Q(6)+LFl.15s. It is possible that this area will grow in future years as more cables are added.

Off Whitstable, another old name takes over, the Four Fathoms Channel, which on some charts has the legend 'at HWS' wisely added after it. If passing through at less than half tide, avoid going too close inshore off NE Sheppey where there are several shallow patches only highlighted on large scale charts. In particular, there is a tricky patch about 1·5M SE of the Spile Buoy.

W of the Spile, the route crosses an area of continuing shallows called the Cant. The chart warns of *'numerous pieces of wreckage, some of which dry at LWS'* across the Cant, but despite this there is much fishing and trawling activity and the area is heavily used by small craft.

The Cant has various substantial charted posts dotted across it, but these do not mark hazards. Obstructions stretch N from the shore towards the Mid Cant NCM (Q), but these stop three cables short of the post itself.

If depth is not an issue, head 278° from the Spile to the Mid Cant NCM and then 275° towards the West Cant PHB (Q.R) on the SE side of the Medway approach channel. Otherwise stay further out to round the Cheyney Spit, which extends to the N of the unlit 'D' beacon, which is topped with an orange diamond.

The infamous wreck of the *Richard Montgomery* lies on the Sheerness Middle Sand, NW of the approach channel, with her masts still visible. A Liberty Ship on her maiden voyage in 1944 with a cargo of munitions bound for Normandy, she was at anchor when she swung onto the sands and broke her back; she was partly unloaded soon afterwards, but a huge quantity of bombs and other munitions still lie there. The wreck is regularly surveyed, but the cargo has always been considered too dangerous to touch and the wreck is surrounded by an exclusion zone defined by lit yellow buoys.

The wreck of the *Richard Montgomery* from the south

When approaching the Medway, listen on Ch 74 to Medway VTS for shipping movements and maintain a good lookout astern. Note that smaller ships do use the buoyed secondary channel that runs along the S edge of the main Medway Channel. A flashing light on the buildings at Garrison Point and visible out to sea indicates any outbound shipping movements. There is a charted Recommended Yacht Track for those entering or leaving the Medway, which runs along the western edge of the entrance.

19. Ramsgate

⊕ **Landfall Waypoint**
   51°19'·53N 001°30'·27E (Immediately S of 'RA' SCB)
Charts
Imray 2100 series, C1, C8
Admiralty SC5606, 5605; 323, 1828, 1827
Tides
HW Dover +0030
Contact Ramsgate Port Control VHF Ch 14
Call sign *Ramsgate Port Control*
☎ 01843 572112
www.portoframsgate.co.uk

Main hazards

The N section of the Goodwin Sands lies only 4M from the harbour entrance and any passage N of this area, heading E or W, must be undertaken with extreme caution, particularly on the flood tide, which sweeps SW onto the sands.

Shallows lie S of the harbour entrance, the Quern Bank being closest, and the Cross Ledge further S. To the N, the shallows shelve gently with no uncharted hazards, but stand well off the North Foreland in strong E winds, because confused seas build up inshore.

Ramsgate has become a busy base for wind farm construction and maintenance, which has added to existing fishing boat and fast pilot boat traffic. At the time of writing, cross-Channel ferry traffic had ceased with no sign of starting up again.

There is a dredged approach channel running E-W (least depth 7·5m), but small craft should use the Recommended Yacht Track that lies parallel to the S side of the channel.

Ramsgate's outer breakwaters are low lying, built of rubble and can be difficult to make out from the E. The N pier head has a G beacon (Q.G 5M); the S has a R beacon (VQ.R 5M).

The tide sweeps across the entrance at up to 2kn, roughly NE-SW, between local HW-1¼ and HW+4hr.

A long-standing local byelaw, which prohibited animals on board or anywhere in the harbour, is being rescinded and pets are currently allowed, provided they have arrived directly from a UK location.

Approaches

From N Follow the coast S from North Foreland keeping ½-1M offshore. There is a Small Craft Holding Area a short distance N of the approach channel No.3 SHB (Fl.G.2·5s) and a track S from there crosses the channel just W of No.3 SHB and No.4 PHB (Q.R) to join the E-W Recommended Yacht Track.

Exercise great care crossing the approach channel and if in doubt, check with Port Control before doing so.

From E In daylight, first sighting will be the chalk cliffs of the Foreland, N of the harbour. By night, North Foreland light (W sector) should be identified. Approach the 'RA' SCB (Q(6)+LFl.15s) then join the Yacht Track on the S side of the channel. Keep a sharp lookout for commercial traffic.

From SE Approach outside the Goodwins, keeping clear of the Goodwin Knoll, to arrive at the 'RA' buoy. Do not risk turning NW across the N end of the Knoll, especially when the flood tide is setting hard onto the bank. Every year, unwary skippers are caught out here.

Ramsgate's twin pierheads from the North. Port Control is in the top of the building on the right, above a restaurant

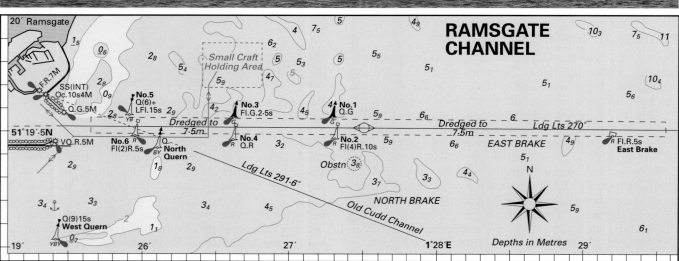

Above and below Ramsgate Harbour

From S From the S, either follow the Gull Stream NE from Deal Pier, turning N towards the No.4 approach channel buoy once past the Brake PHB (Fl(4)R.15s) or stay close inshore through Ramsgate Channel to W of the Brake and Cross Ledge banks.

Entering Ramsgate's outer harbour. The Royal Harbour entrance and marina are to starboard, behind the lighter coloured wall

The inshore route requires extreme caution, especially close to the B2 SHB (Fl(2)G.5s), which is small and difficult to locate. It guards the Cross Ledge bank, which shifts frequently and must be left well to starboard. Once past, continue in a wide arc W to pass well W of the West Quern WCB (Q(9)15s) to arrive close S of the harbour entrance. This route is not advised at night.

There is a small craft holding area immediately off the S breakwater.

Entry

From the No.4 channel PHB, follow the charted Recommended Yacht Track. Pass close N of the North Quern NCB (Q) to clear shallows.

It is essential that skippers call Ramsgate Port Control on Ch 14 and ask for permission to enter the harbour. Control lights are displayed (3.vert.G clear to enter; 3.vert.R no entry) on the cream painted Port Control building at the root of the N breakwater. They can be difficult to identify against town lights at night. When a light (Fl.Or) is displayed there, it means a ship is manoeuvring and you must not enter or leave harbour.

On receiving permission to enter, proceed under power through the outer entrance. If required to wait, use one of the charted holding areas.

Royal Harbour entrance and 'Harbour' buoy. Deeper water is to port in the entrance. Once inside, turn to port to find the West Marina

Ramsgate Entrance to Ramsgate Marina

Maintain a listening watch on Ch 14. From the outer harbour, the marina lies to the N in the Royal Harbour behind high stone walls. Leave the Harbour SHB (Q.G) to starboard and light (F.R) on end of W Pier close to port. There may be a seasonal PHB (Fl.R.2s) paired with the Harbour buoy. Beware the drying bank on starboard (E) side and watch out for boats leaving. They may appear suddenly round the pierhead. Once round the pierhead, call Ramsgate Marina on Ch 80 to request a berth (0600-2200H in summer). Outside hours, Port Control may advise.

Ramsgate Marina

There are actually three parts to the marina – West, East and Inner. Leisure craft use the West Marina, immediately to port inside the Royal Harbour entrance. The older part, the East Marina, lies N from the entrance and is entered between two lit dolphins at its W end. Beware the drying East Bank to starboard guarded by a SHB (Fl.G.5s), which is moored actually over the bank. The East Marina is mainly used by commercial craft.

Visitors' berths in the West Marina are usually plentiful, except during large events, like Ramsgate Week. By day in summer, you may be allocated a specific

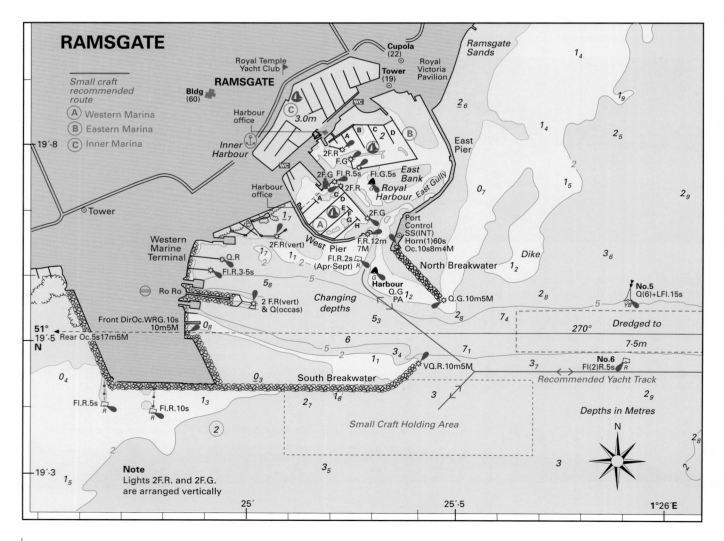

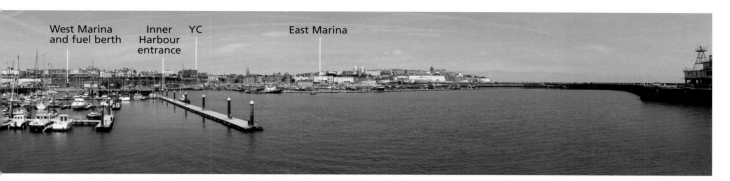

West Marina and fuel berth Inner Harbour entrance YC East Marina

Ramsgate's Royal Harbour, from the West Pierhead

berth, but generally you will be advised to find an empty one, on a choice of pontoons, where no 'Reserved' notice is displayed. In 2014 the W Marina was dredged to about 2·5m.

In strong winds from N through E and S or even SW, the harbour can be affected by swell, the E Marina more so than the W, but you will normally be allocated a berth in the W Marina anyway.

For long term stays only, and only by previous arrangement, you may be able to berth in the Inner Harbour. This is entered through a lifting bridge and gate, NW beyond the W Marina, and open free-flow approx HW±2hr. A red and yellow flag by day and a single green light by night indicate if the gate is open, but always call Dock Office on Ch 14 for clearance to proceed.

The Marina Office is a wooden building immediately W of the lifting bridge, and there is a secondary office at the top of the NW ramp out of the W Marina. Access to the pontoons and toilet buildings is protected by key codes issued on payment of berthing fees. There is also a small unsecured toilet block on the W Marina pontoons.

Remember to call Port Control on Ch 14 for permission before leaving your berth.

The Royal Temple YC overlooks the harbour with fine views and is friendly and welcoming to visiting yachtsmen. Ramsgate is not only a busy stopover for leisure craft, it has excellent eating, shopping and provisioning, an interesting maritime museum, and is a short bus ride away from historic Canterbury, Sandwich, and Broadstairs. Aircraft enthusiasts will enjoy the famous Spitfire Museum at Manston (✆ 01843 821940 www.spitfiremuseum.org.uk).

The friendly Royal Temple YC enjoys a fine position overlooking the harbour

RAMSGATE MARINA   CT11 9LQ

Contact VHF Ch 80
Call sign *Ramsgate Marina*
Marina Berthing Office ✆ 01843 572110
Harbourmaster ✆ 01843 572100
Email portoframsgate@thanet.gov.uk
www.portoframsgate.co.uk

Access 24hr

Fuel Diesel and petrol from fuel barge by Commercial Jetty pierhead at N side of W Marina

Facilities WC, showers, launderette, WiFi, pump-out (inner harbour), 40-T boat hoist

Water On pontoons

Electricity On pontoons

Gas Calor and Gaz at Bosun's Locker chandler and Marlec Marine (see below)

Chandler Bosun's Locker ✆ 01843 597158

Engines and spares Marlec Marine ✆ 01843 852452 www.marlecmarine.com (open from 0800)

Rigger Bosun's Locker (above); Rigtek *Mobile* 07867 790685 www.rigtek.co.uk

Sailmakers Northrop Sails ✆ 01843 851665 www.northropsails.com (also distributor for Hyde Sails)

Paint and materials Bowman ✆ 07900 562111

Electronics Positive Marine Electronics ✆ 01843 499429 or 07770 382920

Boat repairs Steve Parish ✆ 07973 469211; Ron Cannon ✆ 01843 587780

(All above businesses are in the 'arches' behind the inner harbour)

Slipways Two – one in inner harbour near chandler, the other by the E Marina. Both 5T limit. Use by prior arrangement only – contact marina berthing office (see above). Larger slipways, repairs and maintenance behind E Marina – Ramsgate Harbour Slipways ✆ 01843 593140 www.ramsgateslipways.co.uk

Provisions In town

Post Office, Banks In town

Pubs/Restaurants Royal Temple YC (lunchtime bar food). Many others in town

Yacht Club Royal Temple YC ✆ 01843 591766 *Email* info@rtyc.com www.rtyc.com

Transport Trains – mainline station with frequent services to London (Victoria) and Dover

Buses Stop opposite Inner Marina

Taxis ✆ 01843 888888, 333333

RAMSGATE

20. Thames Estuary Passages

Introduction

In this chapter we suggest routes for some typical passages around and across the Thames Estuary, and discuss the factors that can affect them.

HAZARDS

Tides

Tides can run hard in the estuary, approaching 3kn in some areas during springs – see tidal stream diagrams on pages 5-7. There's also a kind of 'roundabout' effect in the area of the Shingles banks, SW of the Long Sand.

The Estuary is, in effect, a bottleneck and this topography, combined with wind speed and direction and barometric pressure, can significantly affect predicted tidal times and heights. These factors must be taken into account when planning a passage, especially if short cuts across some of the banks are to be used.

Timings for passages will often have to be a compromise. For example, a bank may need to be crossed on the flood near local HW, which may mean having to fight the ebb on the final leg up river to a planned destination.

Charted buoys and sand banks

Although the shores of the Estuary are mostly soft mud, the offshore banks are certainly not. They tend to be extremely hard sand and grounding a small craft here on the ebb in rough seas can be very dangerous. Even being stranded on a rising tide in deteriorating weather can be an alarming situation.

Despite their hard nature, however, the sands are also constantly shifting and the UK Hydrographic Office publishes frequent corrections to the charts of the Estuary. Indeed, many of the charts are re-published as often as every two years to take account of all the changes. Note, however, that new surveys almost certainly do not look at areas that leisure sailors are most interested in, such as swatchways across sandbanks. These may not have been surveyed for many years.

Our advice is to keep up to date with corrections and buy the new chart versions when they are published. Chart suppliers Imray can supply corrections by post or from their own website, www.imray.com, while corrections to Admiralty charts can be obtained from Notices to Mariners on the website www.nmwebsearch.com.

In the same vein, published lists of the positions of navigation marks should be treated with caution. Buoys are frequently moved and occasionally removed altogether or relocated and given new names. A chart corrected up to date should be the primary source of waypoints. The positions published in the nautical almanacs each year are probably the most regularly updated, but these books are printed well in advance of publication and, unless thoroughly corrected as well, should only be used as a 'reality check' for your own waypoints derived from the chart.

Altered or updated waypoints must also be corrected in the ship's GPS set and on any electronic plotters.

Wind and weather

The NE-SW tidal streams, coupled with prevailing SW winds and frequent NE winds over the area, mean that rough seas and wind against tide conditions will often be met in the Estuary. The 'Thames Estuary chop' can be as unpleasant a sea as you can find anywhere, even in as little breeze as a F4. Many yachtsmen have a rule of not setting off if there's a '6' in the forecast and that is probably an excellent general rule to follow in the Estuary, especially for windward passages across very shallow areas, such as the Kentish Flats, and in fast-running channels like the Swin and the Wallet.

Traffic

The whole Estuary is busy with commercial shipping, some of it very large and fast moving and almost invariably 'Constrained by Draught'. A good lookout is essential, as is a listening watch on VHF Ch 16 and 69 (the Port of London Authority (PLA) channel for the outer Thames). Be aware of the charted 'Precautionary Areas'. The Oaze area in particular can be tricky to cross N/S because it contains the junction of several channels – ships approaching in the distance do not follow a fixed course, so beware of making assumptions based on radar or AIS-derived information.

Tidal heights

When navigating the Thames Estuary it's worth remembering that current tidal heights at gauges at Walton, Margate, Shivering Sands and Southend are broadcast every half hour (H+15 and H+45) by London VTS on VHF Ch 69. This information can help you make routing decisions if you are considering taking a

Heading N past the Red Sand Tower, a ship is passing in the Oaze Deep and more ships are anchored beyond

Towering turbines on the Kentish Flats dwarf the ruin of the South Girdler Beacon

shortcut. Tidal heights and timings can be dramatically affected by the weather.

Wind farms

The Scroby Sands, Gunfleet, Kentish Flats, Thanet, and London Array wind farms are now operational. The Kentish Flats farm will be expanded S and W in 2015, and it is entirely possible that others will be expanded and new ones constructed. Further development will have an increasing effect on passagemaking across the Estuary, as is discussed on page 3. Cable laying during construction, in some cases across long distances, is another typical modern hazard we have to contend with.

Before planning a passage across the area, it would be wise to get the most up-to-date information about the wind farms and to plan accordingly.

General advice

Work up a comprehensive passage plan before you start, including detailed tidal information for points on your journey. The *Admiralty Tidal Atlas* can be a great help in doing this.

Do not attempt shortcuts in bad weather. Shortcuts across sandbanks will, by their nature, offer little water under the keel and in rough seas there will be increased danger of grounding in the troughs. Unless certain of adequate depth, the prudent navigator will take the long way round and have contingency plans for using an alternative route or even abandoning the passage.

The estuary is littered with old beacons – the Cant, the Whitaker and the Blacktail to name just three – that are useful reference points, but are reaching the end of their lives. Most were erected long ago by an Admiralty Hydrographic Training Unit, possibly to aid surveys of the estuary, but they are not maintained and they are not being marked when they collapse. There are other marks

Seen here from the E at 10 miles range, the 244m chimney at Grain is a prominent landmark across the Estuary, but is scheduled for demolition

usually visible in good weather, such as the WWII forts at Red Sand, Shivering Sand, Knock John and Roughs, all of which can be useful position fixing aids. The towering chimney on the Isle of Grain, on the W side of the Medway entrance, has long been visible at quite extraordinary distances, but will eventually be demolished.

Use every opportunity and device to maintain an up-to-date position on the chart. During a passage across the Estuary, decisions and course changes will come up very frequently and each will demand precise knowledge of the vessel's position. Such position fixing has been made considerably easier for most navigators with the widespread use of GPS, but nevertheless maintain the log, as often as every 15 minutes in poor visibility, recording each buoy or beacon identified and passed. Do not ignore the chance to confirm a GPS position by visual identification or hand-bearing fixes. Everything will be of use should the electronics fail.

ROUTES

Along the coast

Passages between the area of the Medway and Swale in the S and the Essex and Suffolk rivers in the N will follow the 'coastal' route and be able to take advantage of the tide.

A passage from the E Swale to the Blackwater or beyond, for example, might start from Harty just before local HW, push the last of the flood down to the Columbine or Columbine Spit buoys, then head N (with an appropriate W component to allow for tide) to pass the Middle Sand SWM and the Red Sand Towers and across shipping lanes before entering the SW entrance to the W Swin at the SW Barrow WCB as the ebb gathers pace.

From the Medway the passage to this point is straightforward, albeit needing similar close attention when crossing shipping channels to reach the Essex shore.

The route would then pass the Maplin SHB, cross into the E Swin by the Maplin Edge SHB and head on via the NE Maplin SHB to the S Whitaker SHB. This buoy is some 18M from the Columbine and the passage will have used at least 3hr, perhaps 4hr, of ebb out of a total of little more than 5hr of ebb tide available on this down tide route.

From the S Whitaker, if the Crouch is your destination, head NW towards the Inner Whitaker SCB (being careful of the depth over the Whitaker Spit), then SW into the Crouch. Otherwise, the route heads NNW to the Swin Spitway SWB, crossing the Buxey Sand to the Wallet Spitway SWB before heading NW for the Blackwater. If your destination is the Orwell area or beyond, then the Wallet is the best route, even if you have to cross the Spitway near local LW, because the early flood runs hard SW on the S side of the Gunfleet, while the streams in the Wallet are weaker.

This inner northern Estuary route is readily reversible, timing a departure S from the Whitaker area to ensure enough depth at the planned destination. Due care must be taken with timing at the Spitway, because this route will usually cross the shallows on a falling tide.

E. Swale to Wallet

Wallet Spitway
LFl.10s
1·2M
325°

Swin Spitway
Iso.10s
1·9M
345°

S.Whitaker
Fl(2)G.10s
3·8M
045°

NE Maplin
Fl.G.5s
2·3M
020°

Maplin Edge
Fl.G.2.5s
3·6M
032°

Maplin
Q.G
Bell

SW Barrow
Q(9)15s

Red
Sand
Tower

8·4M
000°

Middle
Sand Bn

Columbine Spit
Fl(3)G.10s

⊕51°23'·8N
001°00'·00E

North Foreland to W Swin

SW Barrow
Q(9)15s

Shivering
Sand
Towers
5·0M
303°

Princes No.7
Q(9)15s
Cross shipping lane

Princes No.2
Fl(2)R.5s
7·0M
275°
But staying out
of shipping lane

Princes S
Q.R
5·4M
290°

E. Margate
Fl.R.2·5s
4·5M
350°

N. Foreland
Light

⊕51°22'·60N
001°28'·00E

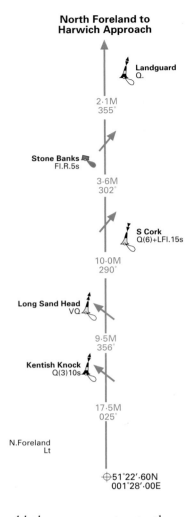

The Swin Spitway buoy marks the southern end of the route across the Buxey Sand to the Wallet

Round the Outside

Between N Foreland and Harwich, given a favourable wind, the simplest route is one that goes around the outside of most of the banks.

Leave N Foreland at around HW Dover -1hr and head for the Long Sand Head. You can sail down the Knock Deep, passing through the London Array wind farm, or go outside the Kentish Knock Sand. On this outside route, note that the 'Long Sand Head Two-Way Route' runs E of a line joining the Kentish Knock ECB and the Long Sand Head NCB. Stay W of this line, turning just inside the Long Sand Head buoy to track NW across the SW portion of the Sunk Inner, making either for the Medusa Channel or the Roughs Tower and the Cork Sand Yacht Bn, and then on into Harwich. You should be able to carry a favourable tidal component until about HW Dover -6hr which should then mean entry to the Orwell in the first hours of the flood.

In reverse, a departure from the Orwell on the last of the ebb would give about 6hr of SW-going stream, but the ebb from the English Channel starts heading N off the Foreland at about HW Dover -1hr.

Across the Middle

Between the N Foreland and the Crouch or the Blackwater, typical routing has in the past used the N Edinburgh Channel or Fisherman's Gat to cross the Long Sand, and shortcuts across the Sunk Sand. However, shipping route changes and the demise of beacons on the Sunk Sands have altered some of the options. Note also that craft of less than 6m draught are now discouraged by the PLA from using the Knock John Channel and Black Deep.

The Naze Tower on its headland, and the cranes of Felixstowe beyond

North Foreland to Harwich Approach

Landguard
Q.
2·1M
355°

Stone Banks
Fl.R.5s
3·6M
302°

S Cork
Q(6)+LFl.15s
10·0M
290°

Long Sand Head
VQ
9·5M
356°

Kentish Knock
Q(3)10s
17·5M
025°

N.Foreland
Lt

⊕51°22'·60N
001°28'·00E

Skippers on passage SW on this inner route from the Ore, Deben or Orwell areas are recommended to time their departure to reach the Whitaker as suggested above. They will be at sea during most of one ebb and one flood tide and it is preferable to fight the ebb in the Wallet and carry the flood in the Swin. If bound for the N Foreland via this inshore route, perhaps because of poor weather, time your departure to arrive at the SW end of the Swin near HW Sheerness, then cross to the Kent coast and carry the ebb down towards Margate – the Kent sector being described in Chapter 18.

North Foreland to Crouch

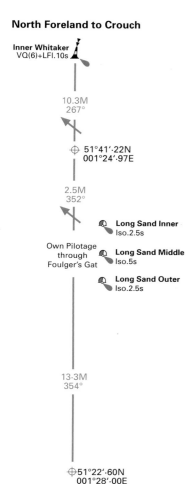

Inner Whitaker
VQ(6)+LFl.10s

10.3M
267°

⊕ 51°41'·22N
001°24'·97E

2.5M
352°

Long Sand Inner
Iso.2.5s

Own Pilotage
through
Foulger's Gat

Long Sand Middle
Iso.5s

Long Sand Outer
Iso.2.5s

13.3M
354°

⊕ 51°22'·60N
001°28'·00E

The N Edinburgh Channel across the Long Sand is no longer buoyed and has been replaced as a shipping route by Fisherman's Gat, to the NE. Fisherman's Gat was once the preferred route for small craft, but in recent years yachts have also used Foulger's Gat, even further to the NE.

Despite the availability of Foulger's Gat, consider use of the unbuoyed N Edinburgh Channel, although this requires careful navigation. Better still is Fisherman's Gat, which offers an easier passage, but keep outside the buoyed shipping channel – although it's not busy, remember it is a confined space where ships will be constrained by their draught. There is plenty of room for leisure craft outside the buoyed channel, especially on its N side, and passage through it is generally less stressful, and barely further, than using Foulger's.

Although Foulger's Gat is now enclosed within the boundaries of the London Array wind farm, the developers left a route open through it marked by the Long Sand Inner, Middle and Outer SWBs. However, there may be occasional short-term closures during maintenance and wide exclusion zones are enforced around towers. Refer to www.eastcoastpilot.com for the latest information. Beware of strong cross-tides at each end of the Gat, be aware that the SWBs can be hard to make out from a distance, and because the route is a dogleg, you may not be able to see the next buoy hidden behind turbines. It is possible, too, to become disorientated with so many identical turbines around you, unless you pay special attention to maintaining your heading. We do think that Fisherman's Gat is worth considering instead.

There are now no helpful marks for crossing the Sunk Sand between the Black Deep and Barrow Deep channels. Crossing in the right conditions of weather and tide is still possible, but the navigator must be particularly careful. One possible crossing point from the Black Deep is roughly due N from No.8 ECB (at the NW end of Fisherman's Gat), taking care to keep clear of the unmarked sunken wreckage of the Sunk Bn. A second lies SW of Black Deep No.3 SHB, on a heading WNW towards the Barrow No.2 PHB, and a third uses a route not far from the submerged ruin of the SW Sunk beacon.

Looking N through Foulgers Gat by the Long Sand Middle buoy

Thames barges seen across the Foulness Sand from the Crouch

If using the first of these, note that special care is needed over the extending NE end of the E Barrow Sand.

Again, the navigator must exercise due caution if using any of these crossing points and especially see our comments about the book *Crossing the Thames Estuary* below.

To avoid navigating across the Sunk Sand, you may choose to make NE to the Sunk Head Tower NCB and from there NW to pick up the Medusa Channel towards Harwich and the rivers further N.

On a passage from the N Foreland towards Essex, the timing is difficult overall, because the need for sufficient water at the Sunk may require fighting the start of the ebb in the Crouch or Blackwater on arrival. Equally, when departing from either of these rivers you may again be faced with arriving at the Sunk on a falling tide. Shallow draught certainly increases your options and with good weather the trip from the Foreland to the Crouch may be better accomplished by starting at around HW Dover +2½hr, reaching the Barrow Deep at LW Dover, nicely positioned to carry the new flood to your destination.

An alternative is not to take the shortcuts at all, but to use the E and W Swin and the Princes Channel, cutting across the shipping lanes between the SW Barrow WCB and the Princes No.7 ECB. This route is longer (but not that much longer if going from or to the Crouch or the Blackwater) and carries its own tidal considerations, but in poor conditions it would probably be the best option.

Crossing the Thames Estuary

The Imray publication *Crossing the Thames Estuary* by Roger Gaspar is designed to help with all of these tidal and passage planning decisions in much greater detail than we can cover here and is thoroughly recommended as a companion to *ECP* at your chart table. Its very useful supporting website: www.crossingthethamesestuary.com often has current information about using uncharted routes across the banks.

Index